Directing
Television

A Professional Survival Guide

B L O O M S

Bloomsbury Publishing Plc

1 3 5 7 9 10 8 6 4 2

First published in 2012

Bloomsbury Publishing Plc
50 Bedford Square
London WC1B 3DP
www.bloomsbury.com

Available in the USA from Bloomsbury Academic & Professional,
175 Fifth Avenue/3rd Floor, New York, NY 10010.
www.BloomsburyAcademicUSA.com

A CIP catalogue record for this book is available from the British Library

ISBN: 978 1 408 13981 3

Typeset by Margaret Brain
Printed in the UK by MPG Books Ltd, Bodmin, Cornwall

Directing
Television
A Professional Survival Guide

Nick Bamford

B L O O M S B U R Y

Contents

Preface

This book has been informed not only by my 30 years' experience directing television and theatre, but also by what I have learned from teaching TV Production students at Bournemouth University.

Whilst I hope it will be an engaging read straight through from beginning to end, I also wanted to make it usable as a reference book to dip into as required. Few Directors will be embarking on studio and location, drama and factual entertainment all at the same time and perhaps it might be something to pick up for some tips, or as a refresher when booked for the first time to make a property show, a drama or an ob.doc., looking just at the relevant chapter. But if that chapter doesn't contain all the relevant information then the book cannot be used in that way.

When dividing it into three parts – Pre-production, the Shoot and Post-production – it occurred to me that it is difficult to plan your shoot properly until you know how you're going to approach the filming. The shooting technique must inform the planning. How can you plan your mountain climb until you know how a mountain is climbed? But it would seem perverse to put the Shoot section before the Pre-production section!

For both the above reasons there is repetition in the book. I'm also aware that my colleagues who have contributed material sometimes say the same as I have said. I assure you they weren't prompted by me! So if I've said something twice, or two of us have said the same thing, then maybe it's important, so please bear with me on that.

When referring generically to colleagues I've tended to use the pronoun 'he'. For this please read 'he or she'. Television is probably one of the most gender-blind industries there is, and though there are certain roles which tend to attract one or other sex, most are regularly undertaken by both men and women. It's just cumbersome constantly to write 'he/she'!

I hope TV Directors of all genders will find something useful in the following pages.

Nick Bamford

2012

PART 1

Pre-production

1 Introduction

I have been involved in making TV programmes for more than thirty years now, during which time the way in which they are made, the equipment used and the way they look on the screen have changed almost out of recognition.

When I started, programmes were either shot in the studio on large, heavy cameras mounted on massive cast-iron pedestals and recorded on tape two inches wide running on machines the size of two dishwashers—you needed to be a strong man to carry two 90-minute tapes!—or they were filmed on location using stock which was so expensive to buy as well as to process that saying 'Turn over' was a serious commitment only made when you were more or less certain of getting something usable. The sound was recorded on a separate machine and synced in the cutting room, where an Editor and his Assistant could spend several days doing a first assembly of a five-minute film.

In either case if I, the Director, so much as touched a piece of equipment, much less framed a shot, then the entire crew (and at least six people were needed even to record a one-man piece to camera on location) would be liable to walk out on strike.

Now, as often as not, much of the programme is shot by the Researcher on a camera you could fit in a handbag, the rushes can be carried home in a matchbox or squirted through a Wi-Fi connection direct to the cutting room, and you can fine-cut a five-minute film in a morning.

When I started there were effectively just two employers in the UK—BBC and ITV (though they were then, of course, fifteen or so different companies), and a television Director was a rare beast indeed. Now there are thousands of employers creating video for hundreds of outlets and the Producers and Directors who make them are as numerous as plumbers. Yet the job of directing television or video remains fundamentally the same as it was in the days of silent movies—it is telling stories using moving images.

With the advent of cheap digital equipment anyone can make a film. When I started you would need to invest at least £250,000 in equipment, all of which required highly trained operators before you could even think about it. Now most of us carry phones in our pockets which can record video and most laptops come with a basic editing programme ready installed.

So anyone can make a TV programme, surely? After all, we've all seen some. A quick glance through YouTube or even some of the lower-budget TV channels demonstrates clearly that this is not the case.

The problem is that when you do a job so much in the public eye the skills involved are not as readily visible as the end product. It's a bit like acting—actors learn lines, stand on a stage and say them. Anyone can do that, surely? A comparison of your local am-dram's production of *King Lear* and the RSC's again demonstrates that that is not true. In either case the average viewer has no concept of the amount of work and skill which has gone into what they are seeing, nor will they necessarily understand *why* one is a good watch and the other isn't. The work is, or should be, invisible.

If you look at a Persian carpet, an intricately carved cathedral or a well-painted picture you can see the work which has gone into it. With a film or TV programme all you see is the images which made the final cut. Unless you've actually worked in the industry you have little or no concept of how what you're seeing is just the tip of the iceberg. You don't know why only those images came to be chosen, how many were not chosen, or the considerations behind shooting them in the first place. It looks so easy. Making a film nowadays is easy, but making a good one is not.

With today's ready access to film-making equipment, many people are having a go without any training, or even study of the work they are seeking to emulate. They have either never considered, or they have forgotten that there are more than a hundred years of received wisdom to draw on, all of which will help make their work watchable. There is an accepted 'rule book', but how many of today's would-be film and programme makers even know it exists?

Of course there's nothing wrong with breaking the rules—all great artists throughout history have done that, and pushing the boundaries of any art form is essential if the work is not to become stale and derivative. But throwing away the rule book rarely results in something lasting—one glance at the architecture of the 1960s proves that. Each new generation of artists builds on foundations laid down by its forefathers, and if there are no foundations the building tends to fall down very soon.

So this book aims to look carefully at those foundations as well as to give a few insider tips which this particular brickie has discovered in a lifetime of building on them. I wouldn't presume to tell anyone how to make a TV programme, but I can explain how I have made them over thirty years in the business, and what I have learned from those who made them before me or with me.

I also wouldn't presume to suggest that this book is in any way comprehensive. I've never directed live news, on location in a war zone, light entertainment in a studio or a sports outside broadcast, for example. All of these have their own particular techniques which you will need to learn from those who have the experience. Then again, some aspects of the job are common to every programme you're likely to make.

1 What is directing?

When I applied for a job recently the Producer—perfectly understandably—asked to see an example of my work. He wanted to see my 'style'. I gladly sent him a programme I had recently made but found myself doubting whether he would be impressed by what he saw, and whether I would want to work with him. I sincerely hope I don't have a 'style'. I have directed drama, documentary—observational and scripted—and factual entertainment of all kinds on all subjects from cars and planes to houses and plants, aimed at audiences of all ages and interests. How appropriate would it have been constantly to use some kind of personal style to mark out my work in all these disparate areas? I hope that my 'style' is a good story well told, by whatever means.

That's not to say that I don't have methods I use to tell stories—methods that a diligent student who had nothing better to do than to study the spectrum of my work might detect. But with each programme I make I adopt a style suitable to that programme. It might be dictated by the subject matter, by the target audience or by the format if it's one in a factual entertainment series.

I never heard back from the Producer—he clearly wasn't impressed. And it's probably just as well as I doubt we would have seen eye to eye.

That experience highlighted for me what directing television is really about and one thing it isn't about is stamping your ego on everything you do. Of course there are screen Directors whose work you will seek out because their name is on it, but they are almost all working in feature films. Any regular cinema-goer is likely to be able to reel off at least half a dozen Directors whose work they admire, but how many regular TV viewers could name as many Directors in that medium? There are a handful—mainly working on those increasingly rare major one-off dramas or documentaries—but even then I suspect that though their names are well-known in the industry (and their work should most definitely be studied by anyone wishing to make such films) few of the viewing public would know them.

And that's as it should be. After all, the viewer has turned on the TV to see a story, to find out some information, to be entertained in some way or other, or maybe to see a favourite actor or Presenter. They have not turned on to watch the Director being clever. If they are amongst the cognoscenti who recognise a good Director's name they are likely to respect the fact that he tells a good story, not to admire the way he uses the camera or cuts his shots together. A Director who seeks to impose his arbitrary personal style on everything is interposing himself between the story and the viewer, who is not in the least interested in him or his work.

Many years ago I worked on a well-known series with a very young Director who had done astonishingly well to get to make films for the programme in his early 20s. During a long drive together we were talking about our work and he confessed that he made films not to please the viewer but to impress the Producer. His work was certainly visually striking but, in my view, too often failed to tell the story, his main aim being to create images which would catch the eye. It was all about him and not about his subject matter. I understand why he did that—as a young man trying to make his mark in a very competitive world he wanted to be noticed. Unfortunately for the viewer there are some Producers who are impressed by this kind of thing but a good, perceptive one will not be.

The fact of the matter is that good direction is invisible—a wholly transparent conduit between the story and its protagonists and the viewer. If the direction is noticeable it is usually bad, because it is clouding that transparency. That is as true on stage as it is on the screen. If I go to see *The Cherry Orchard* I want to see what Chekhov has to say, not how clever the Director is. If it's a play I know well I might be interested to see how a particular actor portrays a character, or how a particular Director illuminates the text, but it's still the author's play I want to see. And those in the audience seeing it for the first time expect to see the author's work as clearly as possible. If the Director's interpretation gets in the way of that then it is doing the piece a disservice. And the same is entirely true on screen. Just as you wouldn't stay long with a writer who is more interested in showing off how clever he can be with words than about communicating what he has to say, so your audience won't stay with your film for long if you are just trying to dazzle them with visual fireworks.

So directing is emphatically not about showing off or imposing your style on your work, but it is still very much about authorship. Just as a writer uses words to tell his story, so you use images and sounds. As soon as you frame a shot, ask a contributor a question or cut two shots together you have taken possession of your material and begun to fashion it in the way you want—you have begun to tell the story your way. But the big difference between directing for the screen and writing that book is that the former is rarely if ever a one-man job. There are a lot of creative people involved.

So how do you take control and author your piece? What is the job of directing television? As the name might suggest, it's the same as the policeman directing traffic. You're making sure everyone's going in the right direction. And just as the driver should not be watching the policeman's performance (hard not to in the case of some of the white-gloved Roman performers I observed a year or two ago on a shoot, I grant!) but merely seeing where his hand is pointing, so the viewer should not be watching the television Director's performance—but rather looking where he is pointing. Television is about teamwork and the Director is the team leader. The England football captain doesn't score all the goals himself, but he does make sure the team work together so that one member can deliver the ball into the net.

That said, of course the TV Director of today is expected to be able to shoot and edit as well as direct the piece. Some enjoy that overall control, but as a general rule I don't. I have learned so much over the years from the Cameramen and Editors I have worked with. They have made my films better and made me a better Director, and I have passed on ideas from one to another, just as I am now endeavouring to pass on some of what I have learned through this book. Even if you are the kind of all-rounder who can do all these jobs extremely well it's very hard to do them all at the same time. It would be wrong to say I don't enjoy using a camera myself—I do very much if that's all I'm doing. It's when I'm trying to interview the contributor, offer him an eyeline, keep the camera framed and ensure I'm getting good sound all at the same time that I feel I'm not as much in control as I would like to be. And while there are clearly occasions when one man and a camera can get a story in a way a full crew can't there always has to be a second, third, fourth pair of eyes somewhere in the production process for reasons I will discuss later in the book.

2 Telling the story

Almost without exception, any film you make, and any show you direct will be telling a story of some kind. It will have a shape and seek to engage the viewer's attention so that he stays with it till the end. Even if it's *The News* it is a succession of stories, with an overall running order designed to keep the viewer on board. If it's a quiz show it's the story of the winner's journey to the main prize. Even a comedy panel show has a structure in the form of the score, running gags, the relationship between the chairman and the panellists, and so on. *Gardeners' World* may be a show giving advice on how to make your garden look great, but each film within it will have a shape and will save the best begonia till last, and the most interesting or impressive film will be the last in the programme.

Storytelling is probably the oldest art form known to man. People have been telling stories as long as they have been able to communicate with each other, and although communication methods are changing and developing faster now than any of us could once have imagined, the job of the storyteller remains the same: engage your audience, involve them in the story, make them care about the characters in it, build it to a climax and offer some resolution or conclusion.

A television Director is working in the same tradition as Homer, Chaucer, Shakespeare, Tolstoy and Dickens. In a crazily fast-changing world, those are anchors to hold on to—and some of history's great storytellers might just have more advice to offer a television Director than YouTube does!

Who Does What?

The array of titles used by people in television can be bewildering. If I had a pound for everyone who has asked me the difference between a Producer and a Director . . . These titles often mean different things in different companies and it's often the case that one person will fulfil more than one role.

Here's a far from exhaustive guide.

Production

Commissioning Editor (Comm. Ed.)

An employee of the TV channel responsible for commissioning the production of programmes, and the final arbiter of the end product.

Executive Producer (Exec. or E.P.)

A senior position in the production company, responsible for overseeing the production of several programmes or series at any given time. The E.P. will have responsibility for budgets and staffing of the programme and will make editorial decisions about it, but should not be involved in the day-to-day process of making it.

They are likely to be employees of, or on rolling contracts with, the production company.

Editor

There are two roles associated with this title. Usually the Editor is the person who is responsbile for cutting the material in the edit suite.

In news and current affairs there are different kinds of Editor whose roles reflect those of their namesakes in print journalism—they may be in overall charge of a programme strand or news programme, or a senior on-screen journalist in a particular field.

Series Producer (S.P.)

Working to, and hired by the Executive Producer, the S.P. is in overall charge of a series, ensuring balance and consistency of its Editorial style, format and content. Usually a freelancer, they are responsbile for hiring the remainder of the production team and crew. They will sometimes go out on a shoot, and will look at each programme as it approaches completion. They will usually also oversee the online edit and the dub.

Producer

The Producer is the person responsible for getting a programme together—coming up with the idea, getting it commissioned and financed—and recruiting staff. He or she chooses the content of the programme.

Associate Producer

This is a variously used title which usually means someone with responsibility for one aspect of the content of a programme—either financially or editorially.

Director

The Director has overall responsibility for everything that happens on location, in the studio and in the edit suite. Hired by the Producer, they work to their brief to deliver the completed show but should not make decisions about its content—only the way in which that content is delivered.

On location, in the studio or in the edit the Director is the most senior person and well within their rights to ask the Producer to leave!

Producer/Director (P/D)

As the name suggests, this is a combination of both roles. Most often found in documentary and factual entertainment strands, they are responsible for both the content and the directing of one show in the series, having picked up a general brief from the Series Producer.

1st Assistant Director (1st or 1st A.D.)

Normally drama only.

On location the 1st works with the Director to ensure the smooth running of the shoot, looking after the organisational issues so that the Director can concentrate on looking at the work.

In the studio they are usually called Floor Manager.

2nd Assistant Director (2nd or 2nd A.D.)

Drama only. Oversees cast calls, transport arrangements etc. to ensure that everyone is on set when required.

3rd Assistant Director (3rd or 3rd A.D.)

Drama only. Works on set in support of the 1st. Responsible for directing extras.

Assistant Producer (A.P.)

Not drama. Works to the Director or Producer, finding contributors and setting up the shoot. May be required to shoot and direct some sequences.

Researcher

As the name implies, responsible for researching the content of the programme, internet and phone-bashing in the office in support of the A.P. On location they help out as required and may be required to shoot some material.

Runner

Known now by some companies as Location Assistant, the Runner is responsible for being useful in any way they can—from carrying equipment and driving to making the tea.

Floor Manager (F.M.)

In charge of the studio floor and communicating the Director's requirements to cast and contributors. In drama this is the 1st A.D.

Assistant Floor Manager (A.F.M.)

Mainly drama. Supports the F.M. and is mainly in charge of props, etc.

Floor Assistant

The Runner in the studio.

Casting Director

Drama. Works with the Director in casting a drama—responsible for assembling a list of actors for the Director to audition.

Script Editor

Drama. Works between the writer and the Producer to ensure that the script is ready for production. In a series, responsible for consistency through the different episodes.

Production Manager (P.M.)

Works to the Producer or Series Producer in overall control of the organisation and budget.

Production Co-ordinator

Works to the P.M., doing whatever is required, such as arranging transport and accommodation, etc.

Production Assistant (P.A.)

This role varies hugely and has changed greatly. In the studio she (usually, for some reason) is the Director's right-hand person and will maintain control of timings, logging takes and, if the cameras are scripted, calling shots. Apart from drama, the P.A. rarely goes out on location these days and tends to assume a similar role to the Production Co-ordinator in the office.

Location Manager

Mainly drama. In overall charge of operations on location.

Design

Art Director

Responsible for the all design elements of a film.

Production Designer

Responsible for the all design elements of a television programme.

Camera

Director of Photography (D.O.P.)

Mainly drama, or where there are numerous cameras. Responsible for all camera-work and lighting.

Lighting Cameraman

A D.O.P. working alone.

Camera Operator

Operates a camera under the supervision of the D.O.P.

Camera Assistant

Assists the Cameraman as required. If using film the assistant is responsible for loading the magazines.

Grip

Looks after anything—tracks, dollies, cranes, etc.—on which the camera is mounted.

Sound

Sound Supervisor

Responsible for all sound recording in a studio or on location.

Sound Recordist

A Sound Supervisor working alone.

Sound Assistant

Assists the Sound Supervisor or Sound Recordist, probably holding a boom.

Boom Operator

Swings the sound boom in the studio or on location. Might be a Sound Assistant.

Dubbing Mixer

Responsible for the final mixing of the sound track.

Lighting

Gaffer

In charge of the lighting rig in the studio or on location.

Electrician (LX)

Works to the Gaffer—or could be a Gaffer working alone on location.

Best Boy

The leading Electrician in a team working to the Gaffer.

Studio

Vision Mixer

Cuts and mixes the shots as called by the Director or P.A.

3 Being prepared

Whatever kind of programme you're directing, the pre-production period will require you to steer a careful course between the Scylla of unpreparedness and the Charybdis of tunnel vision which can result from planning everything too meticulously. Television programmes are about people and people are unpredictable things, so control freaks beware!

Of course you need to plan and prepare—to be clear what your programme is about and how you're going to tell your story. But even if you are shooting a scripted soap opera in a known and recced location with experienced actors with whom you've had the (rare) luxury of rehearsal there are a hundred and one things that can happen on the shoot which require you to think on your feet and come up with an alternative plan. These might include inclement weather or failing light, an actor off sick or delayed in traffic, or an actor with a very different view from yours of his or her character or the scene.

If you're shooting observational documentary your plan will have to be adaptable as you don't know what will happen. But even for planned and scripted shows I have regularly found myself turning up on location to discover that the story wasn't quite what I was expecting.

I remember a film I did for a daytime consumer show about some ramblers who were unhappy about the way farmers were obstructing their rights of way. It soon became clear to all of us during the shoot that the farmers were being entirely reasonable and the ramblers more than a little pedantic so we had to rethink our angle. Faulty research, perhaps, but it happens all too easily.

I once went to Italy to film a cheese-rolling competition which was washed out by a thunderstorm, and so the story ended up being about entertaining two fractious youngsters in a café.

Another Italian shoot found us turning up to film some Neapolitan folk musicians, one of whom allegedly spoke English and would be able to give us an interview. Except that he didn't. On the same trip we had planned a story to be filmed in the back canals of Venice using two traditional working gondolas, one for the Presenter and contributor and one for the crew. It was clearly going to be a tricky shoot with Health and Safety issues galore, which would take several hours. Then we found out that one of the gondoliers, without whom we couldn't do the story, had precisely forty minutes before he was due somewhere else. But more of that later.

The trick is to have a clear plan but to remain flexible and prepared, if necessary, to tear it up and 'shoot from the hip'.

2 Telling It Like It Is
Pre-production for factual

1 Developing the idea

Sometimes a Director is lucky enough to be able to follow his own idea from concept right through development and filming to the cutting room. If you do you are a Producer/Director, since you are responsible for content as well as delivery. But for a lot of factual work, especially in factual entertainment, as Director you are unlikely to be very much involved in the initial phase of putting a programme together.

You are one of the most expensive people on the crew, and so financial constraints will usually mean that you are brought in as late as possible. The programme content will already have been thrashed out between the Commissioning Editors and the Executive Producer. The Series Producer will have been hired and the structure or format pretty much nailed down, even if it is a new series. The Researchers and Assistant Producer will have been hard at work finding contributors and locations and, ideally, recceing. In this kind of work you will probably still be hired as a Producer/Director because you will choose the content of the shows you direct while the S.P. oversees them all. But you will be presented with a kit of parts from which to make a programme, and the extent to which the instructions on how to assemble them are written for you will depend on the level of creative freedom extended by the Commissioning Editor to the S.P. and/or how much he or she is prepared to pass on to you.

On heavily formatted daytime DIY shows I have turned up at the hotel the night before the shoot and been handed a script to shoot the next day. If, of course, you are directing a news or current affairs studio that is what you would expect. Remember that as Director you are not responsible for selecting content, merely for delivering that content to the brief.

Let us assume for a moment that you are lucky enough to be involved from the inception of a programme idea. Others can guide you through the minefield of getting your brilliant idea commissioned, but let me offer some thoughts about how you would put it together. Much of this will, of course, be discussed during the commissioning process.

The first consideration is your approach to your story, and the variety of ways you might handle this pretty much follows a continuum from the purely observational— actually very rare these days—where you construct your story from whatever happens in front of the camera without intervening in any way, right through to something entirely scripted and signed off before the shoot begins.

As you develop your idea there are a number of questions to ask yourself and the answers to these will dictate your approach.

- Is your story about a person or people or about something inanimate?
- Does it address an issue?
- Do you know what will happen or do you just think that something might?
- Is it happening now? Has it already happened? Do you anticipate it happening in the future?
- Will you have to make it happen?
- What is there to look at? What will television bring to the story that radio couldn't?
- How will you link your material to shape it into a coherent story?
- Is there someone who could tell your story for you?

The answers to these questions will steer you to a point somewhere along the factual spectrum.

The factual spectrum
Broadly speaking, this extends from objectivity to subjectivity, as follows.

Observational documentary
This style consists of simply following the subject(s) around and observing their behaviour to gain an insight into another world. Paul Watson is often considered to have pioneered the form with *The Family* in 1974, but in truth its origins go back much further to Direct Cinema and Cinéma Vérité.

Also known as 'fly-on-the-wall', observational documentary (or ob. doc.) is an appropriate approach for a story which is unfolding as we watch, be it the everyday life of a family or the events dealt with by the Emergency Services in the course of their work. The whole film consists of 'actuality'—the television jargon for stuff happening—and the film-maker cannot be sure how it will end.

In its purest form the story is told entirely by this means with no active intervention on the part of the film-maker. But in truth this is very hard to achieve as by their very presence the film-maker is affecting the events because the subject is going to be aware of the camera. Perhaps the only pure films of this kind regularly seen on television today are natural history programmes.

In practice most observational documentaries have the actuality supported by interview and linked by voice-over or captions. In some examples—for example Paul Watson's own award-winning *Rain in My Heart*—the film-maker will appear in the film, thus openly acknowledging the active part they have played in it.

Broadly speaking, however, these films will consist almost entirely of actuality, with perhaps a few GVs (General Views) to establish location, and some interview.

Observational techniques play a huge part in all kinds of factual programming, from news to formatted factual entertainment shows. They are essential tools in the Director's kit.

Reality television

This form began with *Big Brother* and has gone on to pervade our screens with such shows as *Wife Swap, Faking It, The World's Strictest Parents*, etc.

Although 'reality' shows use the same techniques as ob. doc. their genesis is fundamentally different in that the programme makers create an artificial situation and then film it rather than observing something which already exists. This will often include 'take-out' information to boost the show's educational credentials but its true intention is pure entertainment. The combination is often called 'info-tainment'.

A series I made which comes under this general heading, but which highlights both the blurred lines between the forms and the inherent falseness of the observational style, was called *The Boss is Coming to Dinner*. The premise was that the conventional job interview technique where the candidate comes into the office to meet the boss is flawed because neither party really gets to know the other in what is basically an artificial situation. Far better, therefore, that the boss should come to dinner with the candidate to meet him/her at home that they can get to know and understand each other better.

A series consisted of five shows. During each of the first four the boss would go to dinner with each of two candidates, interviewing them informally during the process, then choose one of them to go forward to the final. The fifth show had the four finalists put through further challenges relevant to the job so that the successful applicant could be chosen.

This was reality television inasmuch as we created the rules of the game, but it was ob. doc. in that once the dinner was under way we kept back and intervened as little as possible in order to give the candidates a fair interview. But a crucial difference between this and most reality shows was that we were unable to cast it—we could only film the candidates who had applied for the job. While they were cooking and getting ready for the boss, in order to build the story we would ask them whether they were nervous about the coming dinner. The truth was that most were far more nervous about having a film crew in their living room during a job interview than about the boss coming to dinner, but of course we couldn't say that.

This kind of show raises serious issues about your responsibility—and that of your company to its contributors. One could argue that those who put themselves forward for reality shows know what they are letting themselves in for and so deserve what they get. That said, I believe that a production company which fails thoroughly to brief people seduced by the prospect of ephemeral fame about exactly what they might experience is failing in its duty—and I'll come back to this later.

With *The Boss is Coming to Dinner* we had an additional moral issue—our contributors had simply applied for a job and we were gatecrashing their interview. What right had we to stitch them up or make fun of them? Far less than with people who put themselves forward for a TV show. It presented unique and very interesting ethical issues in post-production, which I will also discuss later.

Whether *The Boss is Coming to Dinner* should be described as reality TV or as ob. doc. is an argument which is largely semantic, but from the Director's point of view the techniques are largely the same for both. It is in the Director's integrity and the intention of the programme that the differences tend to lie.

Expositional

This is the film which seeks to tell a known story or explain something—it might be a human story or perhaps an explanation of how something works.

The story is likely to be told either by an anonymous voice-over or by a Presenter—the pros and cons of which I will go into later—and the footage could consist of anything from GVs, interviews and actuality to archive, rostrum and graphics.

A crucial question in preparing this kind of documentary is what visuals will be available. If it consists of someone telling a story about past events then it could be very dull—and might perhaps make a better radio programme than a television one—unless there is some way of illustrating these events. This might be archive or rostrum, but increasingly the tendency is to go for reconstruction, either by using actors and shooting it like drama—which is expensive—or by using some kind of generic or abstract shots which support the story. Another option available today is CGI (Computer Generated Imagery), but again this is very expensive.

An outline script will be written beforehand to give the structure, though this will almost certainly change during the shoot and edit. Where interviews are involved the script should reflect the information you would expect these to deliver, but again, more of that later.

Enter the Presenter

It's at this point in the spectrum that the question of whether or not to use a Presenter arises.

Ob. doc. will almost definitely not have one, though there are exceptions. Take, for example, the work of Louis Theroux, who enters into the situations he wants to observe in order to find the answers he wants. He directly manipulates what we see on the screen and therefore his work, arguably, cannot be seen as observational. Yet in a sense he is only one move on from Paul Watson who sometimes appears, and even does pieces to camera, and few would challenge his observational credentials. The divisions are, unquestionably, blurred.

Expositional documentary might have a Presenter, though most don't. All the other forms listed below will have one.

A decision must be made about what a Presenter will add to the film and whether the right person can be found. As soon as you use one, some objectivity will be lost and it will tend towards being an authored documentary. However, the use of an engaging guide with a passion for his or her subject (Simon Schama, Professor Brian Cox, Andrew Graham-Dixon, etc., etc.) can be the ideal way to tell your story.

On the plus side, a Presenter will give you more options when shooting your interviews, and this can be useful when it is a personal story with limited visuals to illustrate it. However, I have found myself on occasion working with a Presenter who does more to get in the way of a story than help it.

A crucial question to address in deciding whether or not to use a Presenter is what role they will play. Will he or she be the expert guiding the viewer through a subject area they know well or perhaps the enquiring layman entering into the world to discover it from the experts, taking the viewer along with them? If the former, there is the ever-present risk of one expert asking another a question to which he/she knows the answer, so that either the inexpert viewer is left out or the Presenter is placed in a false position. If the latter, the risk is that they will bring nothing which couldn't be better and more efficiently accomplished with a tightly scripted voice-over.

With some kinds of documentary Presenters are essential.

Journalistic

An investigation into an issue should be as balanced as possible, but will inevitably have a subjectivity about it. It is therefore normally better to have the investigator visible, thus acknowledging that subjectivity, but this is not universal. *Panorama* has an in-vision Reporter whereas *Dispatches* sometimes does and sometimes doesn't.

In other respects this will contain the same elements as an expositional documentary—interview, actuality, GVs, archive, rostrum, etc.

Authored

Sometimes a documentary will present an unashamedly personal view, in which case it is called 'authored' and will always have its author presenting in vision. The film excuses itself from the need for balance by declaring up front that it is this person's inevitably biased view.

Usually this person will be an expert in his or her field who has earned the right to such a personal statement. But sometimes they are simply someone the viewers want to see. Increasingly commissioners seek to improve ratings by building a programme round a name who will pull in viewers, irrespective of whether or not they have any particular expertise in the field. Sometimes, as in the case of the very engaging films made by Michael Palin on his various journeys, or Ewan McGregor and Charlie Boorman's *Long Way Round*, they are the story of a real and challenging journey which happens to have been made by a celebrity, but more usually they will be travelogues where the celebrity is basically a tourist discovering the country and its people on the viewer's behalf. The viewer watches because of the Presenter rather than because of the subject matter.

Factual entertainment

There is one other category—call it a branch of documentary or a category of its own —which comprises probably the majority of factual programming on today's television outside news and current affairs. Factual entertainment covers a wide range of subjects and styles and in general will use the same variety of techniques—observational, expositional, journalistic, etc.—as any other documentary. The only difference is that the emphasis is on entertainment rather than information, though there will usually be 'take-out information' woven in to lend the programme substance. These programmes will almost always have one or more Presenters and be formatted, providing a known pattern to which the viewer can relate.

Once you have decided on the approach which suits your programme, the next decisions are practical ones about how you will make it.

Studio or location?

Clearly the majority of factual programmes are made on location, and even when they do come out of a studio or outside broadcast (OB), unless they are discussion programmes like *Question Time* there will normally be a substantial amount of location material played in. So the decision as to whether or not to make the show on location or in the studio is usually pretty straightforward. However, some shows have migrated between the two, a notable example being *Top Gear*. When I did it back in the nineties it was all location and made in Pebble Mill but now it's a London-based studio show with, of course, location inserts. So it's worth looking at the pros and cons of both approaches to see why a decision such as that might have been made.

Location has many advantages, and for the majority of factual programmes it's the only option. It's real—the scenery is there—and you can meet your contributors in their own environments. You can take the camera to whatever you want to look at wherever it is to be found, and because you have a relatively small crew you can take your time (to some extent) to get what you're looking for. Cost-wise you have to factor in travel, overnights and longer shooting schedules but with your small crew that should still come to less than the cost of your studio. And if you're making a programme about cars you can't drive them far in a studio!

One of the principal drawbacks is that you cannot control your environment. The real world is a noisy and unpredictable place with planes overhead, police sirens, dogs and children in playgrounds which will drive your Sound Recordist and you nuts. Then there's the weather which can, of course, kibosh your whole shoot. Scheduling can be difficult if you have busy and expensive on-screen talent to ship across the country or across the world.

If you are shooting single camera it's hard to turn the material round quickly—you need a substantial amount of time in post-production—and it's impossible to capture a live event adequately.

So these are the areas where the studio wins—it's an entirely controllable environment in terms of both sound and light and is tailor-made for creating television. I think of its relationship to single-camera location work as the same as the combine harvester's to the lone reaper who toils by himself to cut the corn then hands it over to a thresher who separates the wheat from the chaff while someone else collects the grain and yet another process bales up the straw. In the same way a single Cameraman gets the shots before handing them over to an Editor who creates a rough cut, then a fine cut, then hands this to a Dubbing Mixer and an Online Editor to finish the programme. A combine harvester mows into the fresh crop, pumping out grain and ready-baled straw, just as a studio needs only talent and an idea which it will process into a finished TV programme complete with captions, music, and everything else if necessary.

For factual programming the studio comes into its own really only when some kind of live element is required, and that doesn't mean it will be broadcast live, merely that the event takes place, and must be captured, in real time. Sometimes it does have to be broadcast live to ensure it is up-to-the-minute, as with news and current affairs, or to allow some kind of interactivity, perhaps phone calls coming in, as in the case of *Crimewatch*.

The other live element which will send any programme—factual, fictional or entertain-ment—into the studio, be it comedy, variety, talent, chat or panel show, is the addition of an audience. As soon as there is any requirement for an audience to respond to an event then there is no option but to shoot it multi-camera, either in the studio or as an outside broadcast. Paradoxically the audience will normally predicate against broadcasting it live—audiences are unpredictable and may choose to disrupt the transmission.

The decision to make *Top Gear* a studio show was, I imagine, based on this addition. And the decision to add an audience to what had been an entirely location show was, I imagine, based on the desire to move the show more towards entertainment, driven by the realisation that the main Presenter, Jeremy Clarkson, had grown from a motoring journalist into an entertainment figure.

Hire a crew or go it alone?

Assuming the decision has been taken to make the programme on location, the next crucial decision, which needs to be made at an early stage in the development process and which will have massive budgetary implications, is whether to hire a full crew—these days that is usually two people, as compared to the busload once considered essential—or shoot your film yourself.

Too often, in my view, this decision is made entirely on financial grounds, and it isn't hard to see the accountant's preference for sending one man with a £5,000 camera rather than three accompanied by £100,000 worth of kit, especially when the trip will involve overnights and flights—the excess baggage costs for a film crew's kit are punishing! So it may be that you will have no choice in the matter.

But let us look at this decision from a purely creative point of view. There are advantages and disadvantages to both approaches, and I would urge any Producer to consider these carefully before simply going for the cheaper option.

A crew will always get you better-looking and better-sounding material—end of story. The Cameraman is using a camera costing upwards of £50,000 as opposed to your £5,000 toy. Each of his lenses is worth more than your whole camera, and no matter how sophisticated the electronic spec of your HD (high definition) recording, if the lens isn't as good, then neither is the shot. His carbon fibre tripod is worth around £6,000—and that will get you a steadier, smoother shot than you can dream of on your £200 pins. A professional Lighting Cameraman spends every day of his working life framing shots, lighting all kinds of different spaces, using different filters and different lenses, and will always get a better shot than a Director who picks up a Z7 or an EX3 with a couple of redheads once in a while.

In the same way, the Sound Recordist's microphones are worth more than your entire kit and he spends every working day concentrating fully on a job which you, at best, try to remember to think about while giving far more attention to the content and the camerawork.

Even if you are a brilliant Cameraman yourself—maybe that is where you come from—or an ex-Sound Recordist, it is very hard to do both those jobs while also directing. The minimum film crew will consist of a Director, a Cameraman and a Sound Recordist—three people skilled in their particular area and each focused exclusively on one aspect of the job. It stands to reason that the end result will look and sound better than anything achieved by one person trying to do three things at once.

But that isn't the whole story. A crew is cumbersome, very visible, and can be quite intimidating. In observational filming you want to be invisible, and that's hard with a full crew. You also want to react to events as they happen, and so the Director needs to communicate his or her wishes to the crew, and that can waste valuable time. If you're trying to get a contributor to open up about something, you're more likely to achieve that with just you and a small camera than with the whole team taking over their living room. Getting a full crew up a mountain, or in a car, boat or plane, is difficult if not impossible.

In all these circumstances you accept the poorer quality of the material because of the improved content—and content is king. So the creative decision should really be pretty simple. Can you get the best content with a full crew? If so, then that will make the best programme. If not, then self-shoot. In the end many programmes compromise, with a mixture of self-shot and crewed material.

The truth is that financial implications will always be a consideration, in terms of the duration of the shoot. It's very expensive keeping a full crew hanging around waiting for something to happen and it may be that you can buy a longer shoot by dispensing with the crew—and you might need that to get the content you want. Another consideration is that dropping a £5,000 camera off a mountain or into the drink will cause significantly fewer accountant's tears than losing a £50,000 one. And so on.

2 Casting

This is at least as important in factual programming as it is in anything fictional. The choice of people to tell your story will make or break it. Just as a good comic can make a bad joke fly and a bad one kill the funniest gag ever written, so an engaging Presenter or contributor can render a run-of-the-mill story into something special while a dull one can sap the audience's will to live, however fascinating a story they may have to tell. Casting is central to the development process.

Contributors

It's hard to imagine a factual programme of any kind without contributors—the interviewees. These might be experts in their field, entrants in a competition, people who have experienced something of interest, or volunteers who have signed up for a reality show.

Whatever they are they need some kind of charisma. They need personality and communication skills and they need to be articulate. Look for the light in their eyes and a desire to tell you their story. When you talk to them on the phone see if they will do the talking. If you're finding them hard work then be very wary. As any university student knows, the fact that someone is intelligent or highly educated and has written an authoritative doctoral thesis in their subject is no guarantee that they can communicate it well in person. The scientist, the economist and the lawyer may be as dull as ditchwater on camera, while the barrow boy can be hugely characterful and entertaining.

One of the problems we had with *The Boss is Coming to Dinner* was that it wasn't up to us to cast the shows. We could choose our bosses, of course, but the candidates were those who had applied for the job—and had agreed to the invasion of the film crew (something a large number of them wouldn't entertain). So we often found ourselves working with someone who was fundamentally 'not telly'—someone we wouldn't have cast in a million years if we'd had full control. As a result, getting some of the interviews was like pulling teeth! This can happen for all sorts of other reasons, but choosing the right contributors is absolutely fundamental to the success or failure of any factual programme. Get that right and you're rolling your snowball downhill instead of up.

The same basic criteria used for selecting contributors apply to your choice of Presenter.

On-screen talent

This is the name usually given to those you are paying to tell your story—the Presenter or Reporter.

Most Presenters come into television via their area of expertise—be it motoring, gardening, cookery, fashion, cleaning or selling houses, astronomy or—in the case or news and current affairs—journalism. Some, such as Alan Titchmarsh and Jeremy Clarkson, move on into more general presenting work having established their skills in their own field. Interestingly, even these often tend to gravitate back to their own territory eventually.

There are those who are simply professional Presenters, perhaps coming through modelling or acting, but generally they are fewer in number and often struggle to stay in work as long as the experts.

A good Presenter is someone charismatic, with an engaging personality, good communication skills and an enquiring mind, who is able to be themself in front of the camera. Actors often do not make good Presenters because their skill is in being someone other than themselves, and so there is a risk they will act the part of a TV Presenter. And there is a mistaken belief among some in the industry, desperate to up their viewing figures by whatever means, that anyone who is famous—or even just easy on the eye—can present television. Many a Director has struggled on location to get three coherent sentences out of the latest celebrity, resorting to every trick in the book to stitch something together.

Beware the ones who simply learn the piece to camera you have written for them and ask the questions you gave them. If they can't engage with the contributor, get to know them and befriend them—and that means putting in at least as much work off camera as on—then they will bring little to your film.

I once worked on a daytime make-over show—*Real Rooms*—with a Presenter who recognised that his job was to get contributors comfortable on camera and would spend every moment off camera befriending them. He knew what we needed and would go to any lengths to get it. On one occasion I was making a film about a mother and teenage son who were constantly warring and who couldn't agree about who the room make-over was for. Our show reflected this and offered a room convertible to either of their tastes. As we recorded the final piece the teenager put his arm round Mum—an utterly surprising event and the perfect end to the film. I was amazed and delighted, and only realised subsequently that the Presenter had been gesturing from behind the camera to suggest this. On another show, this time not mine, during the 'reveal'—the moment when the finished room is shown to the (hopefully) amazed and delighted contributor—he was observed clambering behind the camera in a cramped space, much to the surprise of the crew. His purpose? Quite simply to bring the contributor's eyeline round to the camera.

Presenting is a difficult job which takes a very special kind of person with a very professional attitude to their work. Genuinely good Presenters are hard to find yet they are often out of work, ousted by the latest cover star of a gossip magazine.

3 The recce

Although the bulk of the research and casting of your programme will have been done through the internet and phone-bashing, there is no substitute for a recce. I recalled some of the problems of shooting without one in Chapter 1.

It may not always be possible to do this. If your office is in London, you're filming in Aberdeen or Abu Dhabi and the schedule and/or budget is tight, then you might just have to shoot blind, but if this is the case I would urge you to try to get to the location at least half a day early and have a look around.

Equally it might not be possible for you to go (you are expensive) so you might be dependent on a Researcher or A.P. doing it for you, in which case be sure to brief them thoroughly.

There are several things you need to check on.

Contributors

As anyone who has been on an internet date knows, you can learn more about someone in five minutes face to face than in five hours of written communication or a long phone call. We communicate visually in so many ways, and television is a visual medium.

It's therefore unwise to commit to engaging any contributor until you have met them. See if they can hold eye contact—some people can't and it's very distracting to watch. Take a video camera with you—or use your phone—and see whether they do an impression of a rabbit in the headlights when you start to record them. Do you enjoy talking to them? If you don't, the chances are that your audience won't—and will be reluctant to listen to them. Are they on 'emit only'? Your Presenter won't thank you for lumbering them with a loquacious old so-and-so who could bore for England, and you won't thank yourself as you struggle to find a polite way of getting them to stop talking in order to preserve your crew's will to live.

Beware the performer—the person who acts for the camera. They will come across as phoney. Also beware the 'wannabe'. Today's celebrity cult, perpetuated by countless glossy magazines as well as reality TV shows, has created the possibility of being famous without any discernible talent, skill or personal endeavour. People make huge sums of money by being famous for being famous. Generally such fame is very short-lived, but it generates wealth and for some it is an unashamed ambition. TV reality shows in particular are a magnet for these people. Remember, you're far more likely to spot the wannabe face to face than on the phone.

Another important thing you—your A.P. or Researcher—need to discuss with a potential contributor is the possible effect that participation in your show might have on their life. Even if it's just an interview for a gardening show it's going to be a proud moment for them. But if, for example, they are going to enter a talent competition or be on *Big Brother* then it could change them completely, for better or worse. They might have such stars in their eyes that they are blind to the possible impact on their life, their job, their relationships, and so on. Certainly *Big Brother* used to brief their participants very thoroughly indeed on this.

When I worked on *How Clean is Your House?* I was astonished by the way people were prepared to reveal on national TV the squalor in which they lived—and there were regular difficult consequences of that show, especially when children were involved.

Remember that if you film someone they're going to tell their friends they will be on TV, so if you subsequently drop that part of the programme they are going to be devastated. Sometimes you have to do this—TV is not a philanthropic charity—but you owe it to the people you use to be up front about what you will do and how you will use the material, to moderate their expectations. It's certainly worth pointing out that even though you will be filming all day the sequence will only last five minutes in the programme. Most people have no idea how long it takes to make television.

The exception to this is, of course, the unwilling participant such as the rogue trader—but then you won't be recceing him!

Location

Because TV is a visual medium, you want the place you are doing your filming to add to the story. Generally you will choose to interview a contributor in their own environment—perhaps their office or their home—because it is likely to say something about them and so provide a good visual image. But this isn't always true. Just because someone is a millionaire it doesn't mean they live in opulent luxury—they might choose to spend their money on other things while living in a scruffy two-bedroom flat, or their multimillion-pound house might be next to an ugly tower block or electricity pylon which it will be very hard to frame out of the shots you need to get.

Conversely, the run-down housing estate in which you plan to film your story of social deprivation might be just up the road from Canary Wharf, whose icons of wealth and success will pervade every shot. This could of course add to the story, but it might not. You or your Researcher will have asked the contributor on the phone what the house or the area is like, but they might not have mentioned Canary Wharf because they no longer notice it—it's part of their lives. And even if they were aware of it, they're not TV professionals so they won't have realisèd its importance.

There is no substitute for taking a look yourself. I worked on the Channel 4 series *Room for Improvement*, where we would follow the progress of various home improvements from planning through to completion—a kind of mini *Grand Designs*. One of the regular elements was to take the contributors to a location which offered similar design features to what they were considering in the hope of inspiring their ideas. On one of these we were struggling to find an example of the kind of 'barn conversion' feel the contributors wanted close enough to them geographically to make filming practical. After some frantic last-minute phone-bashing the girls in the office came up with a place and off we went to film it. They had seen photos and assured us it was what we were looking for. We rocked up—crew, production team and Presenter plus contributors, who we left in the car while we took a look. (When you're showing someone something which you hope will impress them, if you want a genuine first impression always keep them away from it until they're on camera.) On this occasion we looked at the place in increasing desperation for anything which related to the project we were filming. We were there with a crew, the budget was limited and we had few if any filming days left, but there was nothing to talk about! I rang the Series Producer, who could only see the budget and the photos the girls had found—which simply did not adequately reflect the place we were looking at. We had a sharp exchange of views, but in the end, as Producer/Director of the show, I knew I was responsible for delivering something which worked, so I took the decision to abandon the location and shoehorn something more suitable into a subsequent filming day. We did find somewhere and the resulting programme completely vindicated my decision, but the experience emphasised the importance of a recce.

If you want to remain friends with your Sound Recordist, then stop and listen. I once went to film a beautiful, tranquil-looking garden in a pastoral setting where we planned to do pieces to camera with the Presenter and an interview with the owner. But it was in rural Berkshire, right under the Heathrow flight path. We could get at best thirty seconds at a time when we could record any usable sound. On *The Boss is Coming to Dinner* one of the candidates had planned a splendid South African barbecue in her garden. The weather was set fair and all seemed perfect for the event, even though we hadn't recced. We discovered when we got there that the house was right next to a busy road—the worst kind where there are regular cars and lorries but not continuous traffic. The contributor was entirely used to it so wasn't even aware of it any more. We might have got away with shooting an interview between lorries, but this was an observational show where we simply had to record what happened. My Sound Recordist shook his head, knowing that the Editor would kill both him and me if we continued as planned! We had no option but to collect the food from the garden and eat it indoors.

Think about the light, even if you are filming indoors. Paradoxically, a grey cloudy day will usually make your filming a lot easier, but let's assume it will be bright sunshine. Even today's HD cameras struggle to cope with harsh contrast between light and shade, and if you have bright sunlight pouring into the room where you want to film your Cameraman will struggle to get a usable lighting state. I have a compass in my watch and I use it regularly when filming. We all know that the sun rises in the east and sets in the west, though in fact that only happens in the spring and autumn. In the northern hemisphere in midsummer it's the north-east and north-west, in midwinter south-east and south-west. A quick check on the aspect of your location, be it interior or exterior, will give you hugely useful information to consider when working out your shooting schedule.

Parking, access, availability of power if you need to light or recharge batteries, as well as filming permissions and so on all need to be checked. If you are working in the middle of a field take a look at how far you will have to carry your heavy gear from the nearest parking place—it could seriously affect your filming schedule. If you are filming in London you have my sympathy. There are myriad additional problems to deal with, one of which is how far away is the nearest parking space which isn't 'Residents Only', and how many pounds an hour will it cost you even if it does happen to be available when you arrive.

A half-decent Researcher or A.P. will deal with most of this for you, but television is teamwork. They might have forgotten, or assumed you were dealing with it, so work together if you're recceing together, and don't be afraid to run through a checklist if they're doing it for you. They're unlikely to have much directing experience and may not notice the motorway, the oak tree which will cast a shadow across the garden between noon and 3 p.m. or, if they recced at the weekend, the building site next door which will be a hive of noisy activity between 8 a.m. and 5 p.m. every weekday.

4 Structure

Whichever approach your factual programme uses it will need a structure—a beginning, a middle and an end. And though the final structure will not be established until the edit, woe betide the Director who goes out on a shoot without at least some idea of what the end product might look like.

Script

Whatever it is you're filming, write some kind of a script.

If it's an observational documentary the script will be, to say the least, sketchy—perhaps no more than a checklist of things you need to get. But some idea of what you will shoot in the event that nothing remarkable happens is essential, if only to ensure that you look out for the kind of things that will make your story.

If it's an expositional documentary then you know the story, so write it. If there are elements which will be gleaned from interview that's fine, but write them down—this will serve as a useful aide-memoire on the shoot if nothing else. Either list the questions you want to ask (but please don't keep rigidly to them) or, better still, make a note of the information you want to get out of them. Your research—whether done by you or a Researcher—should have winkled out any stories and information which are pertinent or interesting. If you have these written down it will remind you and/or your Presenter to ensure you get them all from your contributor. If you are saddled with one of those Presenters who is likely simply to reel off your questions rather than engaging with the contributor then it's far better just to write the information down. It will ensure that at least some kind of thought process kicks in!

That said, unless it's that rare beast, an entirely scripted documentary, it's unlikely that more than a word or two of the script you write will make the final edit. So don't overscript. You run the risk of becoming so fixed in your concept of the programme that you lose the flexibility which is essential when shooting any factual programme. The intention is to focus your mind on the story as you shoot to make sure you shoot the right things. What you write in the edit will be a response to the material you have—which is likely to prove quite different from what you envisaged.

It's worth writing an introduction to your location, or subject, or any sequence if it's going to give you a clue as to what shots you will need. But otherwise it doesn't have to be written in full, or in beautifully stylish English—bullet points will do, or simply 'Link from x to y'.

If you have a Presenter doing pieces to camera then you need to write something—how much depends on your Presenter. A half-decent one will write their own from bullet points, a quarter-decent one will rewrite anything you have written in their own words. In Presenter-led or authored films the Presenter will have written the script and your job is to interpret it visually, decide what needs to be done in vision and generally edit it, casting a viewer's eye. Remember that's what you are—a professional viewer.

When working with a Presenter, the decision as to what should be in vision and what in voice-over can be tricky, but think about what you are trying to achieve in that section of the programme. Clearly you'll need some kind of piece to camera at the top to introduce your Presenter. Thereafter, if you are talking about something which can be shown then you're generally better off doing it in voice-over, but if you have nothing to illustrate what is being said then do it in vision or your desperate Editor will wind up having to use some of those meaningless wallpaper shots of buildings or trees or sky or whatever to cover the words. If the Presenter is giving an opinion about something rather than stating facts or telling a story then it's usually better in vision. And if it's a long film, or one which will be divided by commercial breaks, then you need a reminder now and again of who the Presenter is, especially at the top of each part. The general, and obvious rule, is: if in doubt, do it in vision. Chances are you'll only use some of the pieces you've shot. Some of them simply won't work and can easily be replaced in the edit with voice-over, but what you don't want is to have to go back and shoot some more.

The usual factual script format is to write in two columns, the left indicating what the visuals will be and the right the sound. It's a simple format and serves to remind you what visuals you will need to shoot, often clarifying at that stage what needs to be a piece to camera and what does not. If you like you can add a third duration column on the right which will give you a clue as to how long each sequence might last and prevent you getting 15 shots for a 5-second sequence, or 3 for a 30-second one. Typically this includes both the duration of each sequence and the cumulative duration of the programme.

Fig 2.1 is an example of a script I wrote for *Suggs' Italian Job* before we went out to film it. Note the careful distinction between pieces to camera and OOV (out of vision), largely dictated by whether we would be likely to have material to illustrate what Suggs was saying. For the interviews I have both suggested questions and the information I expected to elicit from the answer.

Working to format

If you're doing an episode in a formatted series chances are you'll simply take a script from a previous episode and rewrite it or fill in the blanks, but beware of this. It can lead you down an uncreative, box-ticking road which doesn't fully engage you with the story you are telling. This might be very different from the previous episode's even though it's in the same format. It's worth checking with your Series Producer at an early stage how strict the format is. Some will encourage the different approaches which different Producer/ Directors can bring, knowing how that can enrich the series, especially given that each story is going to be in some way unique. Others can be very prescriptive and will check at every stage whether you're 'on format'. Once I even had an S.P. coming on location with me and telling me how to direct the programme. This, I should add, is seriously out of order and did a great deal of damage to the shoot and the programme.

Storyboard

For some Directors a storyboard is more essential in the preparation for a shoot than a script. After all, television, as I keep saying, is a visual medium, therefore the script should

Fig 2.1 *Suggs' Italian Job*

Outline Shooting Script Prog. 2 (extract)

TITLES	Music	0.30/0.30
SUGGS in vision at wheel	**SUGGS to CAM** I've always had a thing for Italy—that's why I bought a house here—and it's not just the sunshine. Like so many before me I find the people, the tradition and culture, the style so irresistible I just wanted to find out more about it.	0.20/0.50
GVs northern cities + Cremona	**SUGGS OOV** I'm in Cremona, just south-east of Milan. There's been a settlement here since pre-Roman times and the history is all around you.	0.10/1.00
SUGGS up the Torrazzo GVs of Cremona	**SUGGS to CAM** And one of the best places to see it all from is the Torrazzo—the mediaeval bell tower of the cathedral—which, at nearly 113 metres—is the second highest in the world.	0.20/1.20
GVs Strad museum Music of Strad being played	**SUGGS OOV** But there's one name Cremona boasts which is unquestionably the best in the world—and that's Stradivarius. If you're a top violinist then a Strad is what you play—and it will have been made nearly 400 years ago. They've tried endlessly over the years to copy them but never succeeded in matching that unique sound.	0.40/2.00
Establishers Vittorio Villa in workshop	**SUGGS OOV** One man who is continuing that quest for the Strad sound is contemporary violin maker, Vittorio Villa.	0.20/2.20
Suggs and Vittorio Villa at Strad museum	**I/V Vittorio Villa** —What makes the Strad so special? *The sound.* —Why can't they reproduce the sound now? *Possibly the wood of the time grew very dense.* *Possibly the varnish.* —Why were the three greatest names in violins based in Cremona? *Pupils of Amati.*	2.00/4.20

be visual too. And that, effectively, is what a storyboard is—a visual script, and a preview of the edit.

I have to confess I have done only a handful of these in my entire career—that is to say, I have only drawn up a handful. One reason is that I am terrible at drawing, but it's mainly that I have not often found the need. That said, every shoot I do has a storyboard, but it's in my head and being made up as I go along. The job of television directing is one learned for the most part in the edit suite. There you find out which shots you need—and should have got, and those which you don't need but wasted hours on. When directing on location I am editing in my head, and therefore drawing an imaginary storyboard.

However, there are some jobs for which a storyboard is essential—a carefully scripted and constructed advert, for example, will be built around one from the word 'go'. Any complex action sequence or stunt will need one, and a drama scene with multiple characters where there is an inherent risk of crossing the line (of which more later) will also benefit hugely from one. It will clarify your thoughts and, like a script, provide a checklist to help you ensure you get everything you need.

The downside of storyboards, as with overscripting, is that they can cause tunnel vision. You sit at home with the action going on in your head and create your imaginary film, then go on location and discover, inevitably, that it doesn't look quite how you thought it was going to. Your Cameraman will almost certainly have some suggestions about alternative ways of getting what you need—remember, he is likely to have shot far more such sequences than you have—but your carefully prepared storyboard might make you reluctant to listen to him.

Storyboarding successfully in your head takes experience, so if you are new to directing and don't have that confidence, and certainly if you have a complex sequence to shoot, then my advice is to do a storyboard. It can do no harm as long as you keep it as your servant and don't let it become your master. Discuss any storyboarded sequence with your Cameraman the day before the shoot, or at least over lunch or coffee. The last thing you want is a discussion on location while your contributors or actors hang around getting impatient and confused. If the Cameraman has seen and thought about what you are trying to get from the sequence he can make suggestions to help you get what you want, rather than using his instincts on seeing the action. And if your storyboard does get torn up, don't worry—it has served its purpose. One thing I can guarantee is that you'll do more storyboards at the start of your career than later on!

5 Equipment

If you are booking a two-man crew then the kit which will normally come as standard will include the following:

- camera
- standard + wide-angle lenses
- tripod ('the legs') + (probably) low angle tripod ('baby legs')
- sound mixer
- 1 or 2 boom mics + 2 or 3 radio mics
- basic lighting kit

It will vary from crew to crew but you can expect this as a minimum, and frankly it's perfectly adequate for most location filming needs.

Toys

However, we all like to add a bit of pizzazz to our shots and it is very tempting to book out as many toys, in the form of jib arms, tracks, jimmy jibs and steadicams, as the budget and the P.M. will let us. And if we're filming outdoors, how about a helicopter?

The truth is that toys take up time, and so add to the cost not only in terms of their hire but also in terms of shooting time. They take time to rig, and extra time to set up the shot. They will add a certain something but the temptation will be to use them because you've paid for them even though the shot, quite frankly, would have worked just as well on the legs. And thus you waste even more time.

My advice is to consider very carefully how much you will be able to use them before you book them. Bear in mind, for example, that tracks and jib arms take up a huge amount of space and so are not going to be much use indoors unless you are filming in a very large room. If you think that one or two really dramatic jib or tracking shots will add something then just go for those—allocate time to rig the kit and get them, then put the toys away. If you can get away with hiring for just one day out of a multi-day shoot, or even half a day, then go for that. The acid test, as with all directing decisions, is whether the extra cost will be visible on screen. Will it enhance the viewer's experience or do you just like playing with the toys?

Helicopters

Helicopters are a classic case in point. Who isn't going to jump at the chance of a trip in a chopper? But they are very expensive, and although they undoubtedly add something spectacular to any film they take up huge amounts of time. If you are going to get value for your money you need to plan your flying time very carefully.

My first helicopter filming experience was an object lesson in how to get it wrong. I was doing some climbing shoots for the BBC2 programme *Tracks*. This film was of a climb on Buachaille Etive Mor in Glencoe, to be done by the lady Presenter and her female instructor. We all headed up into the mountain to film the walk-in and the climb, then the crew and I embarked on the two-hour walk back down the mountain to rendezvous with the helicopter, leaving the girls with a box of sandwiches, a walkie-talkie and instructions to drop down the last section of the climb in order to repeat it for the helicopter shots.

This was just a standard helicopter, with no gyro-rig, so we were using the standard camera. We removed the starboard door and strapped it and the Cameraman firmly in, then took off. The idea was to get some GVs of Glencoe then head in to the mountain to get some dramatic shots of the final stages of the climb. We got the GVs OK, but when we tried to get into the mountain we realised, far too late, that we had a tailwind of some strength when we offered our starboard side to the mountain. We had a devil of a job even spotting the climbers on the mountain, and when we did we could do nothing but fly past at about thirty knots. We managed only one shot, where they could just be glimpsed briefly in the corner!

Had we thought about the wind before we took off we could have rigged on the port side and been able to fly into the wind and therefore much more slowly. But there was no time to land and re-rig—and the girls had been on the mountain quite long enough!

It would have been well worth the additional expense to hire a chopper with a gyroscopically mounted camera. These are designed for the job, get far better, steadier pictures, are more flexible and are flown by people who spend their working lives filming so, although you will spend more, your chances of getting value for money are much greater.

I once used this arrangement to get some aerial shots of trees for *The One Show*. The chopper was based in Denham and we had booked one hour and, with the Chiltern Hills at our immediate disposal, it might have been tempting simply to head off and look for what we wanted from the air. But, perhaps chastened by my earlier experience, I was determined to ensure that we got what we needed and so had spent the previous day driving round the Chilterns armed with a hand-held GPS plotting the positions of suitable trees, not only of the right kind but sufficiently separated from their neighbours to get a decent shot of the whole thing. I also had to bear in mind the law which prevents flying within 500 feet of any person or building.

I was therefore able to direct the pilot from tree to tree, using my GPS, ticking off the shots methodically. Even so we only just had enough time to get what we needed. Had I not done this planning we would have struggled to get half of it.

6 Studio and O.B.

Although the end product looks in many ways the same, the job of directing multiple cameras in the studio or on location is really quite different from directing with just the one camera, and it is not surprising therefore that Directors tend to specialise in one or the other. Although both jobs require creativity and organisation, on location the ratio between the two is 50/50 while in the studio it's 5/95.

The Studio Director needs good spatial awareness and an ability to think quickly and calmly in any situation. Most of his creative work will be done beforehand because all he has time for in the studio is to put it into effect. He also needs a commanding presence. A quiet and retiring Director can function perfectly happily on location through a good understanding with the crew and an easy way with contributors, but in the studio he or she needs to keep a much larger group of people constantly informed and heading in the same direction. At the university where I teach I have observed student studios directed by people who lack this basic quality of leadership, and it is painful to watch. Nothing happens!

The preparation and planning required for a studio or OB shoot is basically the same as for a location shoot, only more so! Remember that a studio crew is normally substantially larger than a location crew and therefore time spent in the studio is vastly more expensive—waste it at your peril! Whereas an hour or two's overrun filming single camera on location can probably be handled by the budget and only needs to be agreed with two people, overrunning a studio or OB is, for most programmes, out of the question. Twenty or thirty people, maybe more, must agree to this, and overtime needs to be paid. Fifteen minutes can cost thousands of pounds.

Antiques Roadshow is done by an outside broadcast unit, and I remember vividly that while recording an item about an object would normally take 20–30 minutes, as the 1900 scheduled wrap time approached they would regularly be dealt with in 10 or even 5—and usually none the worse for that. Needs must when the Devil drives and overrunning 1900 was simply not an option.

Make sure that when booking a studio you only book what you need. Studios come in very different sizes with anything from two to six cameras or even more, and therefore at very different costs. It's pointless and wasteful to book more than you will actually need.

Most smaller studios and OB units are 'self-op', meaning that the Director does his or her own vision mixing. For small-scale Presenter shows or unscripted interviews this is often preferable, given that the Director will be calling the shots anyway so he may as well cut them. But for a scripted show, factual or drama, hiring a Vision Mixer (a person— confusingly the operator and the equipment have the same name) will enable you to concentrate on what is being recorded rather than worrying about which buttons you need to press. And certainly if there are complex graphics or other visuals involved you will need someone else to deal with them, preferably someone who is well acquainted with that particular piece of kit. They are all different and many are quite complex.

Organising an outside broadcast—whether to cover a pre-existing event such as a football match, theatre performance or state occasion, or an event staged specifically for TV such as *Question Time* or *Antiques Roadshow*—will require a great deal of additional technical planning in terms of cabling and power supplies as well as the logistical requirements of bringing a large number of people into the location. You will have a Production Manager and Technical Manager as well as a Location Manager to get all this organised, but it is down to you to choose your layout and camera positions. Your schedule may well be dictated for you on events such as these, but you need to check it.

As every event will be different and impose different restrictions it is impossible to advise beyond a few basics such as remembering the line (see Chapter 5)—while accepting that it is totally impossible to direct, for example, *Question Time* without crossing it!—and giving yourself a chance of remembering where your cameras are by ensuring a logical arrangement of their respective monitors in the scanner.

The script will usually need to be more exact and detailed, but this is by no means always true. *Antiques Roadshow* has a skeleton script only. The show features objects of interest which are found on the day, so all the Director will have is a blank Running Order sheet on which the slots are filled in as objects are found.

Other factual shows—magazines, news or current affairs, for example—are likely to consist of scripted pieces to camera, probably on autocue, and unscripted interviews. The script will therefore need to identify which camera takes which shot and where in the script it is to be cut to. For an unscripted interview or demonstration it will say 'cameras as directed' but may still give an indication of which camera is to offer which shot. It should also give timings for each item, especially if the show is live, when these will be crucial.

If it is a fully scripted drama or comedy the process is slightly different and I will discuss this in the next chapter.

The important point to remember about the multi-camera script is that it has to inform many more people than is necessary with a single camera on location. Making it up as you go along is simply not possible. Even with a loose running order as in *Antiques Roadshow*, the areas where the pieces will be shot are predetermined and pre-lit.

At the end of the day the quality of the programme you direct in the studio will depend far more on your preparation beforehand and organisation on the day than it will on brilliant creativity in the gallery.

7 Filming abroad

Making programmes in foreign parts sounds like the glamorous end of television, and in some ways it is. Few Directors, or any other crew members, would turn down the opportunity for an expenses-paid trip to an interesting place abroad. Certainly many of the foreign programmes, films and series I have made stand out as the most memorable of my career, but they have also been by far the hardest work.

Maintaining film crews abroad is an expensive business, not least because they have to be accommodated even on their off days, and you will generally find your days very long and arduous. The crew will usually include the minimum number of people for the same reason. If the shoot is more than a week or so you will be very lucky to get more than one day off in seven. You might find yourself filming in some exotic, perhaps sun-soaked place, but because of the pressure of the work you will struggle to enjoy it. You will trudge across the beach full of holidaymakers in 85-degree heat carrying heavy kit to shoot your piece, then carry it back and move on, probably not getting back to the hotel before 8 p.m., then spend dinner discussing the next day's schedule before collapsing into bed exhausted with the prospect of a 7.00 a.m. start and another equally full day.

My trip through Italy filming *Suggs' Italian Job* was certainly a highlight of my career—in retrospect! It was a four-week trip covering the length and breadth of the country, visiting some of the most fascinating places to be found, but I remember being utterly exhausted for much of the time. We made eight half-hour episodes filmed in around twenty different towns or locations. I remember coming to the end with enormous relief, then thinking I'd like to go back and do the trip again, only without having to film it!

The crew was the nicest bunch of people you could hope to work with, but inevitably there were tensions and sharp words on occasion, and that's an important aspect to consider on foreign trips. You will be thrown together with a group of people who might be complete strangers and living with them 24/7, regularly in stressful situations, for maybe weeks on end. You might have the luxury of a hotel room to go back to at night, but you might equally be in a tent in the desert. Your people skills will be paramount, and if you have any say in the choice of crew think carefully about this. You may know a Cameraman who is the bee's knees in terms of his work, but is he easy to get on with? Generally TV people who get a lot of work are amenable and easy-going because you have to be to survive, but beware the exceptions, especially on foreign trips. The trick is to recognise that you will all need your own space from time to time, so though there's a good chance you will usually eat out together, don't be afraid to get room service now and again, and don't take it personally if others do that. I would always endeavour to spend any days off by myself.

There should be at least one person in the team who is a native speaker of the country you are visiting—probably the A.P. or the Researcher—and it will certainly help if there are more. If you can speak another language with any degree of competence make it clear on your CV—it could well get you work. If you don't have a native speaker available, and sometimes even if you do but they are not acquainted with the particular place you are visiting, then you will need an additional member of the crew—the Fixer. These are people native to and with a good understanding of the place you are visiting. Sometimes they do this job fulltime, sometimes they are part-timers or just a local you have found—but they should have a close understanding of anything you need to know, be it transport arrangements, local culture, where to eat and how to eat safely, and so on. A good Fixer is worth his or her weight in gold, can save you time and trouble, and generally make your life a great deal easier. In Europe, if you have a native speaker with you, you might not need one—but although we had two Italians with us on *Suggs* we still booked a Fixer for Naples, which can be a tricky place if you don't know which areas are safe and which not. If you go to somewhere further afield there's more chance that you will need one.

It's pretty unlikely you will get a recce for a foreign trip, so be prepared to adapt your ideas in the light of what you find. As suggested earlier, try to build in time for a quick visit to your location the night before, if it's feasible, or at least get your native-speaking A.P. or Researcher to. Then you'll have the evening to rethink if necessary, which could well save the time, not to mention the stress of rethinking on your feet on the day while everyone waits for you to make a decision.

I'm sure you will look back on your foreign trips, as I do, with fond memories. Just don't expect them to be fun at the time!

3 The Word to the Action
Pre-production for drama

The great advantage of shooting the drama over shooting the documentary is that you have—or should have—pretty much complete control over what will happen in front of the camera. But the requirement for this to look good and truthful is far greater, so it takes as long or longer to shoot, the budgets are higher and the crews, in general, larger. As a Director this means that you are more supported, and should be free to concentrate on the quality of the work while others deal with the organisational aspects. But with more people involved and more money at stake your responsibility is considerably greater.

Drama stands or falls by the quality of the script and of the cast. High production values might make it look glossy, but they cannot redeem bad writing or poor acting.

It is a common complaint of actors working in television that screen Directors do not understand what they do or properly engage with them. Too many hide behind the camera, leaving the actors to do that clever thing they do over there while concentrating on making it all look lovely.

To be a truly successful drama Director—and that means one who will create dramas where even as a professional viewer you cease to notice the camerawork, the editing or the budget and become utterly engaged in the story—you need to understand not only how to tell a story effectively with the camera but also how a script works, how actors work and what they need from you. My drama work has been informed at least as much by my work in the theatre as it has by my work in television.

1 The script

It is to be hoped that by the time you get on board, the script you are to direct has been knocked into shape by the Script Editor and the Producer. But it might not have been, and you should certainly go through it with a fine-toothed comb to make sure that it is actor- and camera-ready. The writer writes, the Producer produces and the Script Editor edits. None is likely to be a Director. You are the one who has to make the script work visually—to make images of the words. So your input is vital.

A good script will be laid out in the conventional way, and will contain extensive stage directions to indicate the visual content, remembering that a screenplay should be roughly 80 per cent visual, 20 per cent verbal. On the stage the proportions are directly opposite—80 per cent verbal and 20 per cent visual. Some writers, whose wrists should be firmly slapped, will give camera directions:

'Wide shot of school playing field where a game of football is in progress. MS Daniel as he runs towards the ball. CU ball as he kicks it into the net.'

It is not the writer's job to tell you how to do yours. What he should have written was:

'On a school playing field a game of football is in progress.
Daniel sees the ball and runs towards it.
He kicks it firmly and it lands squarely in the back of the net.'

If he's a clever writer with an idea of what the shots might be he will indicate each one by starting a new line. But all his job entails is to provide the story which needs to be told. It's up to you how you tell it. And if you choose to do the sequence by tracking in on a steadicam then that's your prerogative.

The problem for writers is how to indicate simply through dialogue and stage directions exactly what is going on. How can they write subtext and be sure you have seen that it is there? In the theatre there will normally be three or more weeks of rehearsal during which the actors and Director will explore the text in search of characters and relationships, giving plenty of opportunity to extract all the nuances. For this reason stage scripts tend to be much lighter on stage directions—there is time to find these out organically. Screen work rarely offers that luxury—for many low-budget dramas rehearsal is something that can only be dreamt of. And so the writer will seek to find ways of spelling it out for you.

This will often manifest itself in overwritten dialogue, for example a line to say what a look could say more quickly and better. An experienced actor will edit that out for you. Indeed a glance at the TV screen any night of the week will demonstrate what a good actor can do to make a dull or badly written line work. But how much better to offer them a good script to start with. Although they will, as often as not, bail you out, remember that their job is primarily to make what they have been given work. They will be wary of criticising the script in case they upset the writer or gain a reputation for being difficult, and if they had to make a choice between developing the script to perfection and working again they would be likely to choose the latter! Unless they are working with Mike Leigh (a Director famous for devising his scripts organically with his actors) their

DRAMA SCRIPT EXTRACT—SHOWING CORRECT FORMATTING

For other examples see: http://www.bbc.co.uk/writersroom/insight/script_
archive.shtml

1   INTERIOR. SQUALID HOUSE. NIGHT

        ALAN - 50 and looking haggard - waits in his flat.
        He seems agitated.

        Suddenly he reaches behind some books on a cluttered
        shelf and takes down a bottle of whisky.

        He starts to open it but the doorbell rings and he
        puts it back guiltily.

2   EXT. FRONT DOOR

        HELEN - 23 - & JOE - 27 wait outside.

                        HELEN
        I so need this one to work. Sounded
        great on the phone. But then so did
        that old dear who threw a wobbly and
        chucked us out.

                        JOE
        Not your fault Babe. Glad it wasn't
        my shoot mind!

                        HELEN
        I can't help thinking how much mon-
        ey's gone down the pan - and that I
        should have seen it coming.

3   INTERIOR

        ALAN seems undecided whether or not to answer the
        door.

4   EXTERIOR

        HELEN & JOE are getting impatient.

                        HELEN
        Do you realise I've only found one
        so far that worked?

                        JOE
        Well this one's looking like another
        bloody timewaster.

        He rings the bell again - a long ring. Then hammers
        on the door.

inclination will be to take the script as a given—the bedrock on which the drama is built. And so it should be.

So it's crucial to get it as close to absolutely right as possible before it gets to the cast. And if you are going to do that it's essential to be aware what they will be looking for.

How an actor works

The am-dram concept of learning the lines and not bumping into the furniture is a very long way from the professional actor's approach to a script. The line is not some stunt that needs to be performed like a song or a conjuring trick, it's a product of the character's thought process.

There's a famous theatrical story of a Director addressing a young actor at the back of the stage and asking him what he is doing.

'Nothing' replied the actor.
'Why nothing?' asked the Director.
'I have nothing to say.'
'On the contrary—you have a thousand things to say, you are just choosing not to say them.'

The message is clear. A character's lines are merely the audible symptoms of his or her thought processes. On stage they have to carry the story to the back of the auditorium, and so more words are necessary. On screen the twitch of an eyebrow can be seen and can convey as much as a paragraph of words. And this is what the actor will seek in the script—the thought process which gives rise to the lines written, and a myriad other thoughts which don't get as far as verbal expression but might well show on his face. If he cannot find that process, cannot find the way from one written line to the next, then he will have a problem and will question the script. And he should be able to look to you, the Director, for help.

So if you are going to prepare fully to direct a dramatic piece you need to have an idea of those thought processes, to have gone through the script from each character's point of view to ensure that their thoughts cohere and that there is a consistent throughline. And as you discover those thought processes you keep looking out for occasions when they can be conveyed without speech.

The actor will look in every scene for his 'objective'—the reason he made his entrance. It is that which will focus his performance and give it veracity. We never do anything without a reason. If we enter a room there is a reason why we are doing it, even if it is only to make a cup of tea or veg out in front of the TV. And it is a bad writer who gives an actor an entrance merely so that other characters have someone to talk to. The actor will want to establish his objective—what he wants to achieve. He will then look for the means by which he will achieve it—the 'activity'. What does he do to achieve his objective? It could be practical or verbal activity. If his objective is to make a cup of tea then his activity is to fill the kettle and switch it on. If his objective is to bed the girl then his activity might be to flatter and charm her, and so on.

Editing the script

If you, the Director, understand how the actor works then you are far better placed to get the script right before he sees it. And, given that you will have to realise the script visually, you also need to look at it from a practical viewpoint. Perhaps the scene is written to take place in a crowded room—a doctor's waiting room, for example. This will complicate the shoot and add to the cost by requiring extras. So you need to consider whether the extras add anything to the scene—whether they have a part to play in affecting what the characters at the centre of the scene are doing. If they don't, if the scene just reads like a private conversation, then it will be far easier, and cheaper, to shoot it in a private place—or even outside the surgery door.

As you study the scene in detail, make sure that each line tells us something new, either about the character, their backstory, or a development in the plot.

When you come to shoot the scene, each shot must do this too. Look at every line and see whether it needs to be said, or whether its information could be portrayed visually. If you approach the script believing that dialogue is only to be used as a last resort—for information which can be given in no other way—then you will be on the right track.

Does every scene contain conflict? Without conflict there is no drama. It can be internal conflict—it may only be someone wrestling with a decision about whether or not to make a cup of tea—but conflict there must be. If a woman comes home and makes herself a cup of tea as usual, that is not drama. If she has sprained her ankle and must struggle against pain to make it, that is. If we know she has developed an allergy to tea but is at the same time addicted to it, the scene has real conflict and we will watch it.

Is there a clear story arc for each of the main characters? They will need to be changed by the events of the drama. If they are not, then why do we want to hear their story?

Do we know and understand each character? If we don't then we won't care about them, and if we don't care what happens to them we won't keep watching.

These are some of the fundamental things to look out for in a script. Unless you are working with a very experienced writer then my guess is that with your perspective, which will differ from that of all the others who have seen it, you will find something to improve in it—something to add or take away. And even if you don't you will have improved your acquaintance with it so that you are better placed to tell the story, as well as being a great deal more use to your actors.

Timing

One crucially important thing you need to do with any script before you go into production is to time it. If you are making a TV show there will be a fixed duration for the commission, and if you miss that duration either way you are in trouble. If your assembled drama is overlength you have wasted everyone's valuable time shooting stuff which ends up on the cutting room floor, and it's far harder to cut material from a filmed drama than from a script. On paper it might just be a line or two but in the film there could well be continuity problems—actors may have changed position or taken a swig of their drink or a drag on their cigarette.

There's a very rough rule of thumb that one A4 page of double-spaced script equals one minute of film, but that is definitely not good enough to go into production with. You need to read the whole script out loud, either by yourself or with friends or colleagues, including the screen directions. Envisage these happening as you read them. It's likely that in production the time you calculate in this way will expand by 10–20 per cent, depending on how carefully you did it.

Timing a script accurately is a skill which should be acquired by any good drama P.A., and if you have such a person in your team then use them.

Of course you'll be doing some tweaking in the edit to achieve your correct duration, but you should not be cutting whole scenes or writing new ones.

2 Casting

Casting is the next job and it's utterly crucial. Miscast and you are rolling a snowball up a hill—and it's impossibly steep. Get it right and it should be a downhill ride all the way.

If you're making an episode in a running series then a lot of the casting will have been done for you, but you will be responsible for choosing any actors who appear only in your episode. So if you are doing a *Casualty* or *ER* or a police show it's crucial that you are choosing the people in the story of the week.

Remember that on screen you always cast to type. Obviously you are looking for someone of the right type who is also a good actor, but that isn't always possible. If I have a choice between actor A who looks and sounds perfect for the role and actor B who is not quite right but a much more interesting actor, then for the theatre I will choose B but for the screen always A. There are two reasons for this.

Firstly, the theatre actor needs consistency, commitment and a professional technique which will engage a theatre audience reliably over two hours or more. On screen, if you have an actor who doesn't always get it right then you can construct a good performance in the edit if you have to. Note the number of celebrities who have made a reasonably successful transition from sportsman or pop singer to screen acting. Few, if any, have made it into the theatre, and if they are wheeled into the Christmas panto to up the bums on seats, note that they are often atrocious!

Secondly, remember that a theatre audience expects to suspend its disbelief far more than a screen audience does. We will therefore readily accept a 40-year-old Romeo there, or a black Juliet born to white parents. The screen audience, on the other hand, expects a high degree of naturalism. Because the camera can go out and see real places, we expect to see real people in them.

It is for this reason that although many, of course, do both, actors tend to specialise in one or the other medium. The jobs are actually quite different. Stage actors at all levels of experience and ability are regularly required to play many and varied parts, often within the same production, but even at the top of the profession it is hard to find a genuinely versatile screen actor. There aren't many Daniel Day-Lewises, Johnny Depps or Julianne Moores. At the same time many a TV star has made a very good living starring in a succession of vehicles where he or she plays a very slight adaptation of him or herself.

Fifty years ago most actors were middle class and we were subjected to a cockney accent which was little more convincing than Dick van Dyke's in *Mary Poppins*. But now we live in an age where people of all backgrounds go to drama school and learn to act, so there is no excuse for not finding the right person for any part. If at first you don't see them, then look further afield. You should have a Casting Director who will do the legwork, but beware the one who also wants to make your choice for you. Some are unadventurous and will only allow you to see someone who has been in something on TV recently, but the truth is that there are thousands of excellent actors out there who haven't yet had their TV break—they just need finding. Equally there are far too many who regularly pop up on our screens without ever setting them alight, simply because they got a lucky break once and Casting Directors with no real perception of what acting is all about assume that because they've been on TV they must be good.

It's the Casting Director's job to find interesting new people, but don't be afraid to go looking for them yourself. When casting *Doctors* once I needed to find a 16-year-old boy for a leading part. The Casting Director found me a selection of lads with an impressive list of credits to their names on mainstream TV shows. All were competent, but none inspired me. However, I'd seen a lad in the local youth theatre who I felt had something special and got him along. He acted the others out of the room. And it wasn't just my opinion—the Producer and Casting Director agreed. He got the part and did a superb job.

What is good acting?

Good acting is truthful—it's as simple as that. Do you believe in the character portrayed? Does he or she inhabit the role, the environment? Do you forget that you are watching an actor? Are you engaged by what they are saying? A truly good actor could make the telephone Directory interesting but too many a bad one has made *Hamlet* seem a dull play.

If you need to cast children then it is even more important to cast to type. They are either natural performers or they're not right. They don't act—they just play. Never ever try to cast a youngster who is anything other than as close as possible in reality to the character in the script. Getting a performance out of them is another matter I'll go into later.

Auditions

Auditioning is the usual way to find your actors, unless they are major names to whom a direct offer can be made. And do beware of this practice. Producers and Casting Directors will have an eye to the ratings and a well-known face can do wonders for these, but bankability is not the same as good casting. Take a look at John Madden's film of Louis de Bernière's *Captain Corelli's Mandolin*—a magnificent novel in the hands of a very experienced Director but ruined, in my view at least, by the complete miscasting of Nicholas Cage in the eponymous role, presumably shoehorned in by the Producers to get US money and audiences.

Anyone who is not a major name is likely to be found through interview or audition, and there is a certain etiquette to this as well as ways in which you can make a very tiring process easier.

There are four things you need to know from an actor's audition:

1. Can they act?

This should have been established by the Casting Director before you get to see them, but some slip through the net. If you've seen their work before then you'll know the answer, but if you haven't then you can always get them to bring something along. All actors will have at least one Shakespeare and one modern audition piece which they have worked on, so ask them to do one of these for you and you'll know they're not struggling with dyslexia or a lack of sight-reading expertise. If you want them to bring something then tell them in advance. It isn't fair simply to pitch this at them in the audition—they will not have revised and prepared.

If you are interviewing an established actor, even if you haven't seen their work, then you would not normally expect them to do an audition piece and they would not expect to be asked to do one. If their CVs list several respected theatre companies and TV shows, with named parts (not extra work!), then you can reasonably assume they can do the job.

2. Are they right for the part?

Even a well-known actor should be perfectly happy to read a scene from the script. If they're not then think carefully about whether you want to work with someone who might be difficult or have an inflated opinion of themself. There are some excellent actors who are difficult to work with, and it may be that the quality of their work will encourage you to cast them anyway, but be aware of the toll they will take on you, your crew and the rest of your cast and think carefully whether they are worth it. My experience has been that the difficult actors are either the ones who are more successful than they should have been and are afraid of being found out, or the ones who feel they are not as successful as they should have been.

If there are other characters in the scene get your Casting Director, who is likely to be with you, to read the other part(s). Don't do it yourself. You want to look and listen, not bury your head in the script. Then see if you believe what the actor is doing, whether they inhabit the part, whether they engage you and, most important of all, whether they would fit and be believable with any other actors already cast.

Sometimes, when you are casting a bit part, their lines are so few that it's not useful to get the actor to read them. In such a case don't be afraid to get them to improvise, maybe to develop the scene in their own way, or you could suggest another relevant scenario. Any half-decent actor can improvise. Alternatively, if it's literally a two-line part and they look right and have the right sort of voice, you can probably take a chance without too much risk.

3. Are they directable?

A good actor will grow into a part as he or she becomes more familiar with it, and in conjunction with the rest of the cast. But with some you will see the same performance on the screen as you did at audition, come what may. When they have read the scene once give them a note which should change the performance. It doesn't need to have anything to do with the actual story—you're merely trying to see whether your actor can do anything different. Give them some kind of immediate backstory—'your mother's just died', 'you've just won the lottery', 'you've just had a major row with your partner'—and see if that affects the way they read the scene. If you get the same as before you have a very dull and immovable actor on your hands.

4. Do you like them?

You might think that as a professional you should be able to work with anyone, whether you like them or not, and you would be right. But when you can choose who you work with, why make life harder than it needs to be? If you find an actor irritating at audition when they are trying to impress you and get the job, imagine what they might be like in the middle of a stressful shoot when they know you can't readily sack them?

You will usually have a preliminary chat before you get into the readings and this is where you begin to get some sense of the person. Don't underestimate the importance of this—it's not just chit-chat but a crucial part of any audition.

Seeing fifteen or twenty people in the course of a day is an exhausting process, but there are ways in which you can ease the burden.

Get some outlines of the script and the show, along with character breakdowns, a synopsis, shoot dates and any other relevant information printed up and leave them in the waiting area. It will save you having to explain everything to each candidate and give them something to do and think about while you overrun!

Take a short video clip of each of your auditionees—it will help you to remember what they did after you have seen a dozen others.

Always allow a minimum of fifteen minutes per actor, more if you are not planning recalls. Sometimes it pays to have a short meeting to begin, just to weed out those who aren't right and save you going through the motions for a full half-hour when you know you are wasting everyone's time, but if you are casting a major part you will need a lot longer, and it's better to do this only with people who are on a very short shortlist. Actors will not object to recalls. They understand what you are trying to do and would rather not waste time at a lengthy first audition for a part they're clearly not going to get. If they have been recalled they'll know they're on a shortlist and will read for as long as you want them to.

Always give yourself coffee and lunch breaks. You will overrun, especially if you see several actors who you are really interested in. They will accept being kept waiting up to a point, but to avoid keeping them hanging around too long and to preserve your own sanity, build in some buffers.

When you have made your decisions do please get back to everyone who has taken the trouble to come and see you, or at least ensure your Casting Director does. There is an increasing tendency simply to ignore anyone who has been unsuccessful and in these days of email there is simply no excuse. Actors are often under consideration for more than one job and it is utterly unfair to leave them lingering till they give up hope, by which time they may have lost the other job too. Even if basic courtesy falls outside your remit then remember that the acting community is a small world where it's almost impossible to assemble a cast without at least two actors having a friend or ex-colleague in common. Treating someone badly can easily bite you on the backside later.

3 Rehearsal

It seems to me fundamental to creating successful drama that the actors should have an opportunity to work together exploring the text before committing themselves to performance. How else can they discover their characters and relationships and deliver the truth we expect of them? Yet when it comes to television work increasingly this procedure falls victim to a tight budget, or possibly to the problem I referred to earlier— too many screen Directors don't understand how actors work and therefore cannot be of much help in rehearsal, and perhaps even feel threatened by the process. All too often a low-budget soap or serial will expect its actors to turn up on set word-perfect, meet each other for the first time and then go straight for a take.

Two different problems will result from this. The newcomers will struggle to feel part of a world they have only just joined and to relate convincingly to actors they have literally just met, who might be playing their wives, husbands, parents or children. And while the regulars should be better acquainted than you are with their characters and relationships they may well be struggling to remember which episode they are filming, what has just happened and what hasn't. In both cases actors may fall back on survival instincts or go on to a kind of autopilot. What they are unlikely to do is take the kind of risks or do the surprising things which make a performance interesting and engaging.

So if you possibly can, make time to rehearse. You don't need the three to six weeks a stage production does but you do need to get the cast to know each other, to explore their characters' relationships with each other and to find out what is going on in the scene, especially where it is laden with subtext. So if you can get at least a day or two, depending on the length of the piece, then your screen drama will be all the more convincing. Even if you are doing a show which eschews rehearsal there will be moments you can snatch on set. On *Doctors* I would use the few valuable minutes while the D.O.P. set and lit to examine basic relationships or find the structure of a scene.

A rehearsal room should be a place where actors can explore and experiment without fear of failure—where they can try things in different ways, see what works and what doesn't, and so steer a path away from the safe but predictable decisions. Your job as Director is to make the room a secure place to do that, and to offer the actors support as they find their way.

Actors need an audience—a response to what they are doing, be it laughter, tears or a tangible silence. In the theatre they get that once they are on stage and will hone their performances in the light of it, which is one reason why they never want critics there on opening night. On screen, unless they are doing studio-recorded sitcom, they never get it, so it's down to you. You are the professional audience and you need to give your cast the same confidence they would get from an appropriate response among a theatreful of playgoers. They need to trust you and it's in rehearsal that you must establish that trust. Just as a trapeze artist will try something more adventurous and dangerous if he knows there's a safety net, so an actor will push the boundaries into exciting new territory if he knows he can trust you to recognise and, more to the point, tell him whether or not it's working.

Many books have been written exploring the relationship between actor and text, between actor and Director, and it's beyond the scope of this one to offer more than a few basic pointers, but here are a few dos and don'ts.

- Do always offer a response to what an actor is doing, including when it's working—it's far too easy only to give notes when it's not. An actor needs an audience.

- Do respect what an actor is doing even if it wasn't what you were expecting. Keep an open mind. Creating drama is teamwork and your actors are, or should be, as creative as you. Ignore this to the detriment of your work.

- Don't under any circumstances say 'Do it like this'. Even if you're an Oscar-winning actor yourself the best you'll get is an impression of you, not a truthful performance. If you're not an actor yourself you are insulting them beyond words. Imagine how you would feel if they came behind the camera and started framing your shots for you!

- Don't give a blocking if you can possibly avoid it. It's far better if the blocking comes out of the actors' work rather than being imposed on it. The am-dram habit of moving counters round a set plan is so deadening and anti-creative. That said, if you're working on a low-budget, no-rehearsal show you might have to pre-block in order to expedite things on location, but even then offer it to your actors—don't force them into it.

- Don't confront an actor you disagree with. It creates negative energy which will damage the work. Find a compromise, or a way to get both what you want to see and what they want to do. Remember that at the end of the day you can get what you want in post-production, so you will have the final control.

- Don't play mind games. Some Directors, wanting an actor to be angry or upset, for example, will make them angry or upset by any means and then record the scene in the hope of veracity. By doing that they destroy the trust the actor has placed in them and also insult them, the inevitable implication being that they don't trust him to be able to act angry or upset. They might get what they were looking for in this scene, but at the cost of the rest of the piece.

Common actor faults

Actors can fall into many bad practices. Here are some of the more commonly observed ones.

1. Working too hard

If an actor is uncomfortable or not confident in what they are doing, the tendency can be to work harder—to do more with face, hands or voice in the hope of making it work. In fact this is counterproductive and will usually make matters worse, and it's all the more visible when it happens on screen, for obvious reasons. It can result from not getting feedback from the Director, especially if the actor is young and inexperienced.

The remedy is quite simply to give them confidence. Tell them it's working fine and they can pull it down a few notches. 'Less is more' may be an old cliché but it's so often true, especially on the screen.

2. Playing the emotion

This is another kind of overacting, when an actor portrays an emotion without demonstrating where it's coming from. The words are just fodder for the emotion and could as easily be Chinese. It's often seen in bad Shakespeare performances where the actor doesn't really understand what the words mean but recognises that the character is angry or upset. So we get a lot of 'sound and fury, signifying nothing'.

When we're angry or upset the things we say are redolent with meaning, and come from the thoughts of hurt or grief or whatever it is we are feeling, perhaps fuelled by adrenalin. If the actor simply plays the hurt or grief or anger without finding the meaning then the performance is hollow and false. Again this shows on screen even more than it does on stage.

One remedy is to get the actor to play the scene without the emotion, simply to find the meaning of the words. If that doesn't work you can always point out that big displays of emotion don't work in close-up. You have to cut wide and then you lose the screen's intrinsic advantage. On screen suppressed anger, a tear hurriedly wiped away or a look will usually carry far more power than a stream of invective or screaming.

3. Autopilot

This is when an actor simply delivers the lines without engaging the thought process behind them. It can happen when you have done too many takes, or when a regular in a soap or serial has done so many different scenes from so many different episodes that they're just concentrating on remembering the lines in order to get through the day. In the same way you could drive fifty miles along a motorway without any recollection of the road or where you've been.

One remedy, which can also work when a scene goes stale or doesn't seem to come alive in rehearsal, is to throw something entirely different into it, which could be physical or emotional. Get the actors to play it while chucking a ball about or running round the room or, as in audition, give them some dramatic immediate backstory. It doesn't have to be relevant—it's just a device to kick the scene out of its torpor. If you do a couple of runs like this and then go back to a more suitable reading of the scene, it should have some kind of new life.

4. Inconsistency

One technique a screen actor must acquire is consistency, especially if it's a single camera shoot. On stage the performance can, and indeed to an extent should, be different every night, but on screen your Editor will be driven to drink if your actor doesn't get up, swig a drink, wave his arms or move his head in exactly the same place in every take.

It's hard to correct this fault in any way other than have a P.A. who's hot on continuity and not afraid of keeping your errant actor up to the mark. If at all possible avoid drinks and cigarettes—they're continuity nightmares. This is much less of a problem on multi-camera shoots, of course.

Directing actors is really a lot about psychology. All actors need direction, but they are all different, have different levels of experience and need different things. Some need building up, others reining in. Even Anthony Hopkins would want to know from you how you see the character and whether what he is doing accords with your image and works with the other characters. Just don't tell him how to do his job—you wouldn't like it if he told you how to do yours!

Your job as a Director is to get your cast working together and all going in the same direction, just like that traffic cop.

Once you've assembled, rehearsed and made friends with your cast, your next job is to ensure that the incredibly stressful period which your shoot will be goes as smoothly as possible—or those friendships might prove short-lived!

4 Planning the shoot

In terms of the planning, your Production Manager and First and Second A.D.s will take care of a lot of the practicalities, such as when you get to which location, how long you need to be there and which actors need to be called when. Your main job is to work out how you will shoot the scene.

Scheduling

In an ideal world you would shoot your drama in story order, but this is extremely unlikely to be possible and all kinds of considerations will have to be borne in mind. A move from one location to another is hugely time-consuming, so first and foremost your schedule will be dictated by that. Time of day and the weather, the need for an actor to be unshaven in a scene or to have their hair cut, make-up and costume—a thousand and one things will affect the schedule. Your P.M., your 1st A.D. and your 2nd A.D. will all contribute but you will be the final arbiter.

Design, costume, props and make-up

You will have people in charge of all these areas and the extent to which you will influence them will depend firstly on whether you are doing one show in a series or a one-off drama, and secondly on how specific a vision you have of these things.

What is important is to ensure that you have a meeting with each of them, either together or separately, to discuss any relevant issues well before the shoot. What you don't want to do is to discover on location that your actor is dressed entirely inappropriately or driving a completely unsuitable car.

Give all these areas due and careful consideration in the relative quiet of the office well before you start the shoot and your life will be so much easier.

Special requirements

If you have stunts of any kind then they will require a registered Stunt Director, stunt doubles, and a great deal of meticulous planning which is beyond the scope of this book.

You may well find that you have to film a scene in a car, which can only realistically— or at least safely—be done using a low-loader. This enables the actors to concentrate on their work without worrying about driving the car, and also allows you to light the scene properly and film a full set of shots from different angles. I have seen dramas where the actors are really driving but this is fraught with danger, and the shots you get are very limited—a single of the driver, a 2-shot from the back seat, and that's about it.

Anything like this will need careful planning and a lot of time set aside for it.

Camera plans

You should have recced all your locations with the same thoughts in mind regarding aspect and light that you would have for a documentary, and that should have informed your schedule. Make sure you have a plan of the location. If the Location Manager hasn't provided you with one then draw your own. It doesn't need to be entirely accurate or to scale, but it does need to indicate where doors and windows are, and you need to decide where furniture will be. Draw a rough plan at the recce then a fair copy when you get back to the office. Then make several photocopies.

Ideally you will have established a blocking in rehearsal. If you haven't had that opportunity you will have to impose one as discussed. Then you need to work out where to shoot the scene from, bearing in mind the light sources and any points in the location the actor will need to visit during the scene. Draw a camera on your plan in each position you think you will need to use it and number the position, remembering that each time you move the camera the D.O.P. will need to relight, which will take time. Don't forget where the actors will be looking—you don't want shots of the backs of their heads. If you're on the ground floor of a house consider shooting through the window, especially if the room is small. It might restrict your choice of position but it will give you a lot more choice in your length of lens and depth of field and will free up space in the room. If necessary you can always adjust the blocking to fit.

On some drama shoots, *Doctors* being an example, two cameras are used. It's different from a multi-camera studio in that both are recording their material separately and it will still need to be edited like single camera, but it does mean that time can be saved by running each scene only half the number of times. So a decision you have to make at the planning stage is how you will use those cameras. Your D.O.P. will urge you to 'stack them up', i.e. put both cameras next to each other looking the same way, one on a loose shot, one on a tight one. That way he can light for just one angle. You may only need to take the scene once for each camera position if your actors, or more particularly the actor you are looking at, get it right. You then move both cameras across, relight and shoot the other way. But if you have a busy scene with lots of comings and goings then your Editor will thank you for cross-shooting—i.e. putting one camera on either side and shooting the whole scene in one go. If it's the kind of scene where you don't need close-ups you might feel that's a better use of your resources, and certainly it's more likely to match in terms of continuity. However good your 3rd, the extras will hardly ever coincide with the dialogue in exactly the same way every time, but your D.O.P. will be grumpy because the lighting will be a compromise. The choice is yours, but whatever you do try to avoid cross-shooting with cameras at ninety degrees to each other—that is the lighting nightmare!

Have a look at the studio plan in Fig 3.1. Your location plan will look much the same, except that the shots will be taken one (or two if you have two cameras) at a time, and you won't normally have the worry of cameras getting in each other's frame.

Storyboards

As I suggested in Chapter 2, storyboards are a very useful tool for any complex scene and particularly when you are starting out. They are far more commonly used in drama than in factual for the simple reason that you know exactly what you want to shoot and can therefore plan in much greater detail, and they are essential for any stunt or action sequence. If in any doubt, do one.

Shooting multi-camera

Very little drama these days is shot multi-camera in the studio, although with the advent of HD relays of theatre plays and operas there is a resurgence of outside broadcast drama work.

The main reason the multi-cam studio drama—which comprised the vast majority of television drama only thirty or forty years ago—has fallen out of vogue is as implied above. Lighting for more than one camera angle has to be a compromise. Add to that the impossibility of getting a decent eyeline shot (see Chapter 5) of both characters during dialogue without the cameras getting into each other's shot.

However, if you are doing one of those few soap operas still shot multi-camera then considerations in terms of camera positions and planning will be much the same as for single camera, bearing in mind these restrictions. The main difference is that you will need to be a great deal more organised. As with any studio it becomes much more of a logistical exercise. The Director does most of his work before the studio starts, honing it at the camera rehearsal.

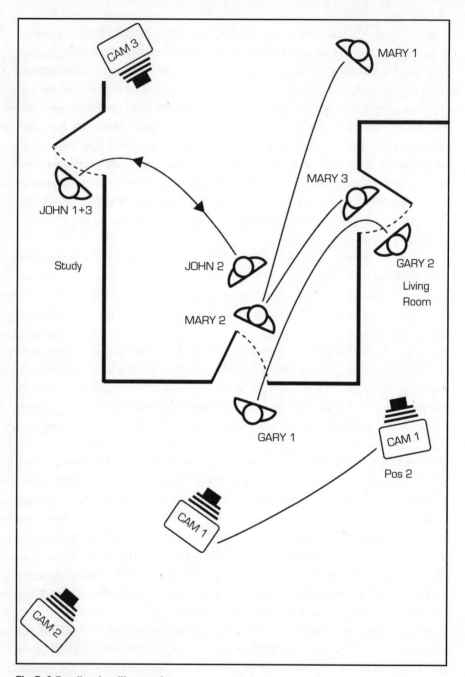

Fig 3.1 Studio plan illustration

One advantage you will have is that the set will (or should) have been designed to accommodate camera positions, which your location will not.

Camera script and cards

In addition to your camera plans you will need to prepare a camera script (see Fig. 3.2), where every shot is numbered and described and allocated to a camera, with the cut point indicated in the script, whether this is on action or dialogue. A properly drawn up camera script of this kind is going to enable you as Director to focus totally on the performances.

Fig 3.2 Studio camera script example

1 CAM1 C/U Bell _____ / The doorbell rings

2 CAM3 MS MARY _____ / MARY walks down hall + opens front door to reveal
GARY.

3 CAM2 MS MARY _____ MARY: ___/Yes?

4 CAM3 MS GARY _____ GARY: ___I— er—/I've come to see John Douglas.

5 CAM2 MCU MARY A/B ___ MARY: ___/I don't think you have an appointment do you?

6 CAM3 MS GARY A/B ___ GARY: ___/No, I . . .

MARY: ___It is rather late . . .
JOHN has overheard and comes through.

7 CAM2 2S MARY+JOHN ___ JOHN: ___But not too late . . ./It's never too late!

8 CAM3 MCU GARY _____ You are . . . ?/

GARY: ___Gary.

9 CAM2 3S _____ JOHN: ___Gary—/come on in!

GARY enters.

I'm just with another client—I won't be long.

To Mary

Mary my love, would you . . . ?

Track in 2S _____ / MARY ushers GARY into the living room.
JOHN returns to the study.

MARY: ___John does the sympathy. I just do the tea.

```
10 CAM3 MS GARY                            Would you like a cup while you wait?/

                        GARY:        Thanks. You were in bed?

11 CAM1 MS MARY         MARY:        John doesn't mind./
    Pos 2

12 CAM3 MS GARY A/B                        How did you find out about the service?/

13 CAM1 MS MARY A/B     GARY:        You've been in the paper./

                        MARY:        Yes.

                        GARY:        Busy night!
```

From this script camera cards will be prepared for each camera, listing the shots they need to offer (see Fig. 3.3). Your first job in the studio will be to do a camera rehearsal, working through this script shot by shot, adapting and improving it as you see what shots you can get. Remember to encourage your Cameramen to offer shots they might see which you had not envisaged. Visionary as you may be, you will not have imagined every shot exactly, and there will always be better ways of getting what you want.

Your actors will be 'marking it' during this rehearsal—don't expect them to deliver a performance while you stagger from shot to shot. This is a technical rehearsal and no experienced actor will do more than ensure he or she's in the right place looking the right way, saying the right words and doing the right actions.

This is the process by which you ensure you are going to get what you need—that you will have a camera catching every line, every look, every action or reaction you need to tell your story and that your Vision Mixer knows what you are looking for. Working single camera you can make the decision where to cut in post-production. In the studio it's going to be done as live, and if you missed the shot or the cut point it's a retake. And, as with any studio show, time is of the essence.

Correct and update your script and get your P.A. to update the cards, if the Camera Operators haven't changed their own, and your creative work is pretty much done. When it comes to recording the scene the P.A. will call it, the Vision Mixer mix it. All you need to do is watch to ensure you are getting what you want.

Whether you're shooting single or multi-camera there is one consideration which needs to be uppermost in your thoughts while planning your camera positions, far more so in drama than in documentary, and which will involve you in endless discussions with your D.O.P.: the line. This is explained at length in Chapter 5, and if you only have time to read one chapter before you go out on your first shoot, that is the one you should read. It will inform your planning as well as your shoot.

CAMERA 1

1 C/U Bell

11 MS MARY - Pos 2

13 MS MARY A/B

CAMERA 2

3 MS MARY

5 MS MARY A/B

7 2S MARY+JOHN

9 3S Track in 2S

CAMERA 3

2 MS MARY

4 MS GARY

6 MS GARY A/B

8 MCU GARY

10 MS GARY

12 MS GARY A/B

14 MS GARY A/B

Fig 3.3 Camera cards

Before You Leave Your Desk ...
The essential paperwork

Whether shooting factual or fiction, location or studio, there are two crucial documents in the preparation of which you, as Director, must be closely involved. You should also check them thoroughly and keep them with you at all times on the shoot.

1 Call Sheet

Your P.M. and/or P.A. will have compiled most of this—phone numbers, addresses, travel arrangements, etc., but it remains your responsibility to check it all. It's too late to berate the P.A. when you are on location and running out of time and your contributor or Presenter is not there.

Your principal contribution will be the schedule—what you will film and when. That will depend on many factors.

In factual, it will include the availability of contributors and Presenters, travel arrangements, access to locations, or timings of events which you are attending. Bear in mind daylight hours, the position of the sun and the aspect of the location and the weather forecast. You will curse yourself if you shoot all your interiors one day with your Cameraman fighting ferocious sunlight, then spend the next day doing your exteriors in the pouring rain.

If you are going to be interviewing inexperienced contributors—i.e. any member of the public—then think in terms of doing the interview as early in the shoot as possible. They are likely to be nervous and apprehensive, and will only get more so the longer they have to wait and watch you filming other things. If you need to get some establishers for them then it might be worth scheduling those first and the interviews as soon as possible thereafter. It's also good for you and the crew to get interviews done early so that you know which cutaways you need rather than shooting everything you can think of, and you don't have to worry when the council road works team move in with their pneumatic drills outside the front door.

In drama your 1st A.D. should do the bulk of this scheduling for you, but, as with factual, this will be driven by actor and location availability as well as time of day and light. Often with soaps or long-running serials there are several episodes being filmed concurrently and the actors' schedule will be a hugely complex jigsaw which others will be putting together, but which may well have an impact on your shoot order.

If you can film in story order, then great. It will help everyone involved and you most of all, enabling you to see how the story is shaping up. However, although this might happen in factual, it never will in drama.

The problem is the time it takes to change location. Even with a two-man crew and basic lights you can reckon an absolute minimum of half an hour to clear out of one location, and the same to set up in the next. Add to that the time taken to drive between them and park, then carry all the gear in. So normally—and certainly in drama—you will film everything at one location before moving on to the next.

Your P.M. will have agreed a deal with the crew in terms of hours—normally either 10 or 12 base to base. So remember that if you are a 45-minute drive from the crew's base or the hotel your 12-hour shoot—say, 0800 RV and 2000 wrap—is actually a 14-hour day by the time they have done the get-out, which means two hours of overtime. Be sure to allow enough time for the whole process. It's scarily easy to find yourself up against a scheduled wrap time with half an hour's work still to do and knowing that picking it up tomorrow is not an option. Your P.M. won't thank you for running up overtime bills, and though your crew might be glad of the extra money they will not appreciate being expected to work those extra hours without being asked first. At the scheduling stage it's always best if at all possible to keep within the agreed hours, and demonstrate that you are being realistic about what is achievable. If you know there are one or more days which will be killers then contact the Cameraman in advance, explain the situation, and ask whether they're happy to do the overtime. And if it is humanly possible, schedule lightly the next day.

Always schedule a lunch break and, if possible coffee and tea breaks. Crews know the pressures of filming and will normally understand if lunch has to be a sandwich grabbed between takes, providing that you ask them first and don't assume their compliance. If you don't even schedule a break then they will arrive on location already hating you!

The important thing to remember is that while the shoot is a special and vital time for you—the culmination of all your preparation and creativity—for your crew it's just a day like any other. Yesterday was someone else's special day and tomorrow will be someone else's again. A good crew knows how important it is for you, but they get very tired and grumpy when it's casually assumed that they will work round the clock without a break just because you want that BAFTA, and especially if you have not scheduled well or used your time efficiently.

If I have one piece of advice more important than any other when heading off on a crewed shoot, it is to get the crew on your side and keep them there.

The Producer I mentioned earlier who felt it necessary to come on my shoot and tell me how to direct also rode roughshod over crew breaks without a second thought, then berated me for considering their needs. The effect on morale, and hence the productivity of the whole shoot, was nothing short of catastrophic!

2 Risk assessment

Whatever you are filming, wherever and however you are filming it, there is one more vital piece of paperwork you need to deal with—the Risk Assessment form.

This is a chore which everyone hates. Yes, they have a lot more to do with the risk of litigation than with anyone's health or safety, and it's a sad reflection of the world we live in that suing people is seen by some as an income stream, but as a Director on location or in the studio, you do need to take this seriously. Neglect it at your peril.

The fact of the matter is you don't do it just to avoid litigation. As the person in charge of the shoot you are responsible for the safety of everyone on it, and if an accident of any kind befalls anyone as a result of where or what you've chosen to film or asked someone to do you then you are personally liable and could be prosecuted. Thinking through what you are going to do and how you are going to do it will focus your mind on accidents which could happen.

The incident when Anthea Turner was seriously injured as a result of confused cueing—she was presenting a motorcycle stunt with a pyrotechnic involved and the stunt controller mistook her cue for his—is now the stuff of legend. But that was the Director's fault and the Director was prosecuted.

The truth is, most accidents during filming happen because things are being done in a rush, on the spur of the moment or without proper planning. The 300 m.p.h. crash which very nearly cost Top Gear Presenter Richard Hammond his life occurred when they were trying to squeeze one last run in before the wrap. It's all too easy to get carried away when you are under pressure on location, either because some exciting new activity or shot suddenly occurs to someone or because you are up against the clock or the light.

The Risk Assessment form won't prevent an accident but it will force you to think clearly and carefully through everything you intend to do and highlight areas where there is the potential for things to go wrong. Most of it is a box-ticking, covering-your-back exercise, and yes, before going out to film in a zoo I did write, in all seriousness, 'I am not aware of any specific risks involved with filming penguins', but at least I'd thought about it and done my research. If I hadn't and had subsequently discovered the hard way that an angry bird can seriously peck a Cameraman I would, rightly, have been for the high jump.

I'm pleased to say I have not yet had any significant accident happen on one of my shoots, but I have had to think carefully about Health and Safety issues at least a couple of times. On one occasion I was filming in December in the Brecon Beacons. It was cold, wet and miserable and we were doing a piece about hill-walking with a family which consisted of two teenage lads, an eight-year-old girl and their parents. The pressure was fairly intense—at that time of year you run out of light at around 3 p.m.—and the crew and I were working flat out to get everything shot in time. But while we were running around, totally focused on what we were doing and keeping warm, some of the family were finding themselves, inevitably, doing a lot of standing around. After a couple of hours the young girl was shivering and turning blue with cold, and I simply hadn't noticed. Nor had her parents, or if they had they were reluctant to say anything for fear of ruining the shoot. It was the A.P. who raised the alarm, and fortunately she could be spared to take the girl back down to the cars without causing too many continuity problems. We had taken due precautions and ensured that all were properly dressed before setting out, plus her parents were on hand, but even so, that was my responsibility and I should have been aware of a possible problem.

Another time I was filming a lad doing some fairly hairy-looking skateboarding. The temptation was to get him to do it one more time, maybe a bit faster, maybe a bit closer to the lens. Had I done so, and he had come a cropper, then he or his parents would have been entirely within their rights to sue me. Had I set my camera where it got in his way or caused him to be distracted the same would have applied. You could even argue that my very presence with a camera would encourage a lad to show off and risk hurting himself, and had I detected that happening I would have been well advised to stop filming. Fortunately all went well, but it did bring home clearly to me just how easy it would be to land myself in trouble.

The bottom line is that safety on a shoot is largely down to common sense, but a serious approach to the Risk Assessment form when you are at your desk and not under pressure could save someone an injury or worse, and you a lawsuit. In the unfortunate event of something untoward happening, proof that you have considered all potential risks and taken sensible precautions to minimise them will be crucial not only to your defence, should litigation ensue, but also, far more importantly, to your conscience. People have died on location because of avoidable accidents. Imagine how you would feel if this happened on your shoot just because you hadn't thought something through.

5 Looking Good
The importance of screen grammar

During the hundred plus years that moving images have been joined together to tell stories a huge wealth of received wisdom has been generated about what works and what doesn't, although to look at some of the video offerings available on the internet and on TV these days one could be forgiven for not realising that. Fashions change, of course, and a liberality has come into screen work just as into everything else. But architecture, music, art and writing which ignore their heritage and throw away the rule book tend not to last but to be seen as some kind of experimental aberration, and I advise anyone directing on the screen to acquaint themselves thoroughly with what has gone before. You will break the rules—of that there is no doubt—but you will do so from a position of knowledge rather than ignorance. There is always another way of doing things, but if your new approach is built on a sound knowledge of the tried and tested ways then there is a whole lot more chance that it will work and be genuinely innovative rather than simply different for the sake of being different.

1 Describing the shot

The first thing to do is to acquaint yourself with the names for shots and moves as outlined in Fig. 5.1. This is not so much about making it look right as about learning a shorthand language which will enable you to liaise quickly and effectively with your Camera Operator—or Operators if you are in the studio, where it is vital knowledge. The desired result will be achieved much more quickly if you say 'Camera 2, crab left and give me an MCU of John' than if you say 'Camera 2, can you move left—no, move the ped don't just swing the camera—I want a shot of John—in a bit—out a bit—head and shoulders . . .'

Long shot (LS)—shows a person full length

Medium long shot (MLS)—knees to head

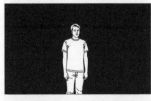

Mid shot (MS)—top half of body, i.e. above the waist

Medium close-up (MCU)—head and shoulders

Close-up (CU)—head only

Big/extreme close-up (BCU/ECU)—tight of the face, excluding hair and chin

Wide shot	**WS**	the whole room/landscape or whatever
2-shot, 3-shot, 4-shot	**2s/3s/4s**	shot containing 2, 3, 4 people
Low angle	**L/A**	shot looking up at its subject
High angle	**H/A**	shot looking down at its subject

Fig 5.1 Name that shot

What's the move?	
Pan left/right	Camera swings left/right on its tripod or pedestal
Tilt up/down	Camera swings up/down on its tripod or pedestal
Crane up/down	Camera raised/lowered on its tripod, jib arm or pedestal
Track	Tripod or pedestal moves—in = forwards, out = backwards
Crab	Tripod or pedestal tracks left or right
Zoom in/out	Camera changes lens length, so tightening or loosening the shot without moving

2 The line

Generally speaking the best camera direction is that which offers us what we want, or expect to see. It isn't surprising therefore that the most fluid direction is guided by what we would see if we were in the scene ourselves. For example, if we are looking at two people talking to each other we are likely to see them facing each other—one facing to the right, one facing to the left, and this is what we would expect to see on the screen. If they are both facing the same way then the presumption is that they are not seeing or speaking to each other.

From this most basic of realisations has developed the concept of the line—also known as the 180 degree rule (see Fig. 5.2). Any scene has at least one line in it—if it's two people talking the line simply connects them. If it's one person looking at something then it's between the person and whatever they're looking at. If there are three people talking to each other then there are three lines, basically the sides of the triangle which they form. If there are five people sitting round a dinner table (see Fig. 5.3) there are ten lines—if you don't believe me draw it out and count them. Then think how many lines there are in a show like, say, *Question Time*.

Let's begin with the simple one-line scene—two people facing each other and talking. The line joins them and continues to infinity from their backs. Assuming you will shoot the scene from more than one position, you can set your cameras anywhere in one of the two 180 degree arcs created, but not in both. As soon as you cross that line—i.e. take one shot from one side of it and another from the other—you will destroy the sense that these people are talking to each other. They will both appear in frame to be facing the same way. That's reasonably straightforward. But add a third person and it immediately becomes more complicated. You can make your life easy and stand them in a line, but it will look odd. Or you could stand them in a triangle and shoot it all from behind the baseline, as it were, but your eyelines won't be great—there will be a lot of profile shots. So you need to think carefully which lines of dialogue or looks you need to get from which angle.

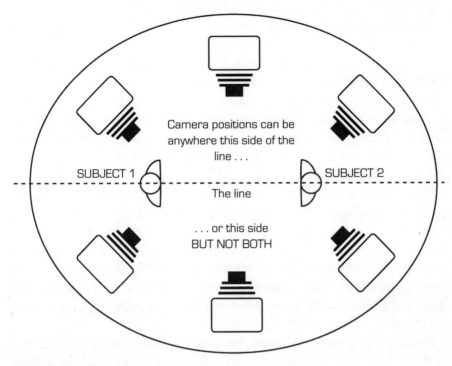

Fig. 5.2 The line

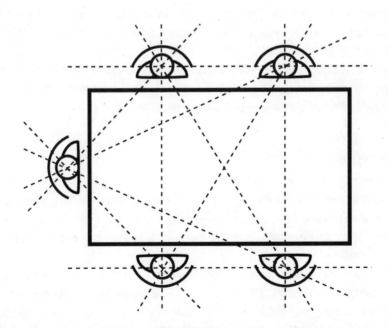

Fig. 5.3 The dinner table scene: with five guests sitting round a dinner table there are no fewer than ten lines to observe!

The dinner party scene is a nightmare and needs careful planning before you start your shoot. The only sure way to do it is literally to draw it all out on a piece of paper and tick off the shots. On *Question Time* it is quite simply impossible to avoid crossing the line on a regular basis, but if the line cross is preceded by a wide shot of some kind then it softens the impact by giving the viewer the geography of the scene.

There are other ways of taking the viewer across the line when you need to—tracking across behind one of your subjects, for example, or getting the subject to move across frame, but remember you will then need to take the next shot across the other side of the line too.

The line also applies when people move in and out of frame, for the same reason as before. Imagine yourself in the scene. If the guy being chased runs left to right and you cut to a shot of the guy chasing him running right to left, then the assumption is that they will collide! That's how you set up a car crash, for example. If they are chasing each other then they need to be running the same way. You can change direction by inserting a shot of them running towards or away from the camera, but once they leave frame they generally need to enter the next shot from the opposite side to the one they departed from.

If you watch television any night of the week you will see the line crossed. Sometimes, as with *Question Time*, it's unavoidable. Sometimes, as with observational documentary, it's deemed acceptable because of the ad hoc way the material has to be gathered. Sometimes it's done for effect in drama in an attempt to emulate an observational documentary style in the hope of adding veracity. Sometimes, I suspect, it's done by mistake or through ignorance!

Generally speaking the more you can stay on the right side of the line, the easier on the eye your work is going to be. Your audience will maintain a sense of the geography of the scene and feel comfortable with what is going on.

3 Eyeline

There is another convention which stems from the normal way we talk to each other— i.e. looking at each other face to face—which is that the best shot of someone talking is as close as possible to square on to their face. The direction your subject is looking is referred to as their eyeline, and getting that right is another very important aspect of screen grammar.

Looking into the lens is reserved for the Presenter in a documentary, or a Newsreader who is giving the impression of talking directly to the viewer. Very occasionally it's used in drama to achieve the same effect—in a soliloquy or an aside to the audience, for example.

The conventional best eyeline, for an interview or for drama, has the subject looking just off camera to the right or to the left, creating the sense that they are talking to someone there. When we cut to the reverse and see that person in shot then their eyeline should match—from the opposite side, of course. They should be framed similarly, using the same length of lens, and looking the same distance off-camera. If one person is standing and the other sitting then again the camera position should reflect that, at all times being right next to the head of the person being addressed, looking up or down as appropriate. This supports the illusion of reality and helps us to understand the relationship between the characters in the scene.

Again this is a convention which is regularly, often rightly, flouted. Profile shots are often used to great effect, but do be aware that you will never see a facial expression as clearly in profile as you will looking straight into a face. Think about what your audience will benefit most from seeing—and remember that they want to follow the story, not to see how clever you or your Cameraman can be!

4 What cuts and what doesn't

When you come to put shots together there is only one criterion at the end of the day—does it look right? An Editor I worked with many years ago used the delightful expression 'I felt no pain!' when assessing an edit as acceptable, and he was absolutely right—that's all it is.

Generally speaking, in order to cut between two shots of the same person or thing you need to change size by at least one step as listed in Fig. 5.1. Preferably also change angle by at least 30 degrees, though sometimes a 'punch down the line' can be effective.

Changing size dramatically—i.e. from WS to CU—is likely to jar.

2s to 2-shot, or 3-shot to 3-shot tend not to work, though there are exceptions, for example in panel shows. And any 2-shots where the same subject is in frame but in a different position will look terrible. For example, if you have 2 x 2s of three people sitting on a sofa and cut them together the guy in the middle will leap from left to right of frame, with disastrous effect! Imagine two 3-shots in a panel game, each including the chairman and one team. Cut them together and the chairman will leap across frame. Generally speaking, when cutting round a group of people go from a single to a group shot then back to a single.

Cutting from a moving shot to a static shot will jar—let it settle first, or cut to a static shot and then let it move. Cutting between two moving shots can work providing they're going the same way—cutting a moving shot to one going the opposite way will look ghastly.

Don't use a dissolve to cover a duff cut!

Just as Picasso's work was enriched by his skill as a representational painter and Mozart's by his knowledge of the Baroque tradition which preceded him, so I would advise any new Director to gain a thorough grasp of screen grammar. Follow the rules till you know what you are doing—then break them if you will, but from a position of knowledge, not ignorance.

PART 2
The shoot

PART 2

The shade

6 Camera Direction

1 Basic principles

Once on location the Director has two fundamental responsibilities, with all that they entail: you need to make sure the people in front of the camera are doing what you want and that those behind the camera are getting the material recorded the way you want it. The first job varies according to the type of programme you are making and I will deal with that under the different headings. As far as the second goes, there are some general principles which apply to everything.

The basic responsibility when you are directing the camera is coverage. Whatever is in front of the lens, and is a part of the story you are telling, needs to be seen clearly. It could be an actor's performance, the ball at a soccer match, an artefact in a museum, a landscape, a city or a microscopic organism. In some kinds of programme—observational documentary, for example—this basic coverage is normally all you can aspire to, and it's a challenging enough job to get that, particularly when you are filming in a situation where you don't know what is going to happen next. You also, of course, need enough material to assemble the story in the edit, maintaining visual interest and avoiding ugly cuts.

But when you do know what will happen there is a higher level you can aspire to, which is to use the camerawork to enhance the story, to add value to whatever it is you are looking at—to tell the story in a different way.

When shooting actuality or an interview, or anything unscripted which you know will be edited, it's usually a waste of time creating some beautifully crafted shot to start the piece because chances are you'll cut out the beginning in the edit! To ensure you have enough material to cut it with, shoot all the cutaways you can think of and then the same number again, but different ones this time. Any Director will tell you that documentaries eat cutaways. Sometimes it can be very hard to think of relevant shots if your story is essentially abstract or non-visual, or you simply can't access the visuals you'd like to. You should, of course, have addressed this at the planning stage, but as you observe what is unfolding in front of you, keep in your head some sense of how many cuts you will make in it—and you will need at least one cutaway for each!

If your documentary is scripted then you should certainly be looking at ways you can do more than simply show what needs to shown, but this added value—call it visual artistry—is more often seen in drama because it is always scripted and therefore predictable. It's about using the camerawork to enhance meaning, to contribute to the story. It can be about energy and movement and the pace of cutting—you can introduce those even to unscripted material and actuality—or it can be about framing and the development, or treatment, of shots. Volumes have been written on the subject of cinematography and it is beyond the scope of this book to explore all that it entails. But as a Director, whenever you have the opportunity you should be thinking how you can use the camera to underscore, enhance or clarify your story, be it factual or fictional.

There are countless ways that different lenses, different depths of field, different kinds of framing can add more information about the relationship between characters or about the story. There are any number of ways the juxtaposition of shots can reveal information or position the viewer in terms of what he knows about what is happening as compared to what the characters know. Then there is lighting, colour temperatures, grading, lenses, filters, and so on. All I can offer here are a few examples of the kind of thing I mean.

You might want to tell the story of a man who is sad and lonely. Ideally you will have a good script and a good actor to interpret that script, and so if you get him delivering the lines or the facial expression within the frame you might consider the job done. But there's another way. If he is portraying emotion your first thought might be to be close up on his face, but you can tell his story perhaps better—certainly more visually—by setting him in a wide shot devoid of other people so that he looks lonely. Although we can't see his facial expression, if, say, he puts his head in his hands, we know he's sad.

Two people in a relationship which is not working might be portrayed very effectively—as on the stage—by two actors doing good work on a good script, both kept in the frame. But you can underline the nature of their relationship if, perhaps, they never occupy the same frame or the same space in the location.

Generally speaking a long lens will add intensity to a shot because it reduces the depth of field and so only certain parts of the shot are in focus—perhaps a subject's face while the background is blurred. This draws attention to the face not the background, and is also a particularly useful technique when doing an interview where you don't have a suitable or relevant background. Defocus it and we don't notice it.

Using a 'dirty' shot, in which you include the shoulder or cheek of one character at the side of an eyeline shot of the other in a dialogue or interview, also adds intensity and enhances the sense of confrontation by drawing the people closer together, especially if you use a long lens. It works far better in the modern 16 x 9 standard framing than it did in the old 4 x 3.

The fine line a Director has to draw when directing camera is to add his visual imagination to the material and enhance it, but in such a way that the audience picks up the message without noticing the direction. Good direction, as I have said before, should remain invisible.

In the Oscar-laden 2011 film *The King's Speech* there are some interesting examples which illustrate the point I am trying to make. The first scene between the future King George VI, played by Colin Firth, and the speech therapist Lionel Logue (Geoffrey Rush) takes place in a large studio which oozes faded grandeur. It is an awkward meeting with both men feeling acutely uncomfortable. Both actors are consummate (they both got Oscars for their performances) and convey this sense admirably. But director Tom Hooper took the decision to enhance that feeling with the cinematography. The shot of Rush is oddly framed—he's positioned at one side looking out of frame rather than into it, and the shot of Firth is low angle and tilted. The classic rules are broken—the eyelines don't match. I assume the intention is to exacerbate the feeling of awkwardness, but for me this strays into the territory of obtrusive direction. Looking at it I asked myself, 'Why has he shot it like that?' and came to the conclusions I did. I was therefore noticing the direction. If I had simply felt more uncomfortable watching the scene without realising why then perhaps it would have worked for me.

Now I have to accept that as a professional Director I am always going to notice these things more than an ordinary member of the audience—indeed my criterion for a good film or television programme is that I cease to notice the work and just become engaged in the story because it transcends the mechanics of its making. And clearly all such judgements are subjective. If the unschooled members of the audience simply felt uncomfortable without realising why, then I have to pipe down.

However, there have been occasions when audiences have famously noticed the direction, and in my view this has to be the detriment of the show. A case in point is the 1990s drama series *This Life*. It was a well-written, well-acted and generally very engaging series about young professionals sharing a flat in London. The camerawork was, certainly for the time, revolutionary. It was mostly hand-held and constantly on the move, presumably to reflect the energetic, bustling lives of these young people. Instead of cutting between shots of two people talking to each other the camera would swing between them. Whole scenes would be filmed with the camera snaking around the room catching whoever was talking, but inevitably this resulted in a lot of screen time spent simply swinging around the wallpaper. For me it was utterly distracting and got in the way of an otherwise very laudable series. Many others, not TV professionals, were talking about the style. The very fact that they noticed it indicates to me that there is a problem. Interestingly, subsequent series of the show calmed the direction down quite significantly.

I suspect that the thinking behind the *This Life* style, and indeed many other dramas which have followed in its footsteps, is that it enhances the sense of veracity. It's fascinating to observe how drama and documentary styles have chased each other in circles over the decades. When observational documentary first came along the intention was to shoot it as far as possible like drama—steady, well-framed, matching shots and eyelines all observing the line and so on. But because the Cameraman is trying to grab what he can as a real-life situation develops it's rarely possible to do this, especially since the material will invariably be edited, making any kind of attempt at continuity a non-starter. So this kind of work has developed a style of its own, jump-cutting all over the place with scant regard for continuity or the line. Audiences have come not only to accept that style but to recognise it as evidence that it's documentary they're watching not drama—real life, not fiction. So now some drama directors emulate that style to bring an added sense of veracity to their work. A recent example of this is Armando Iannucci's brilliant comic drama series *The Thick of It*. There's no doubting that the camera direction on this show has an extraordinary, visceral energy. Whether it would work less well if it obeyed the line is an interesting question. Personally, I think it would add elegance to that energy if it did, and perhaps run less risk of being noticed by the audience.

So the challenge of good camera direction is firstly to ensure the audience sees clearly everything they need to see when they need to see it, and secondly to find inventive and innovative ways of enhancing the story without the audience being aware of your work.

2 Shooting styles

Whatever decisions you make about each shot you need to give some thought to the overall style you want to use. In truth there are as many shooting styles and camera techniques as there are Cameramen and Directors making programmes, and I can do no more here than offer some general hints about what works where. But you should certainly begin your day with a discussion with the Cameraman about how you want your material shot. If you don't he will have his own ideas and do it his way, which may be fine, but if you have a view then share it at the start of the shoot. If you are doing one show in a series then you should have a discussion with your Series Producer during pre-production about any 'house style'—and this applies to drama as much as to factual work.

Leaving aside any 'toys' in the form of tracks or jib arms, the first decision you are likely to make is whether to put the camera on a tripod or go hand-held. Each method creates a different feel and both have their practical advantages and disadvantages.

Tripod

Putting the camera on the tripod will give you a steady, well-framed shot and enable you to change lens length to suit your needs. It will give a feeling of stability and order and will tend to draw attention not to your camerawork, but rather to the content of your shot.

It will enable you to light your subject properly and, all in all, it will look better than going hand-held. You should think of it as the norm.

For drama, where you always know more or less exactly what is going to happen, it will enable you to make the actors' work, and everyone else's, look as good as it possibly can. There is nothing which cannot be shot on a tripod in drama—as demonstrated by the films of fifty years ago where the size and weight of the camera precluded any other approach. There are different styles you can use on the tripod. *Doctors,* for example, is all shot on a long lens to reduce the depth of field and so defocus the background, drawing attention to the actor. This works because it is a low-budget drama and the actors' work is all-important—there are no stunts or special effects, no tracks, jibs or steadicam to make it more visually interesting. This style gives it a consistent quality which helps to belie its budget.

In factual work the tripod should pretty much always be used for GVs, for static interviews, or indeed for anything where you know the subject is staying in the same place. The shot will be steady, the framing better, and you can go in as tight as you like. You can also light interior shots properly, and because the Cameraman will not be carrying the camera it's much easier for him to keep it in focus. For montages of cutaways you have the whole range of moves, focus pulls and zooms at your disposal.

The problem with the tripod is that it is inflexible. You will not readily be able to grab shots of something which occurs unexpectedly, or to follow fast action. In a situation where you don't know what is going to happen the tripod will hamper you. On a practical note it's also heavy and cumbersome and no fun to lug around if you have a lot of distance to cover on foot. In these days of small crews it is regularly you, the Director, who carries it and I have come back from many a shoot with a bruised shoulder!

It will restrict you to a fairly conventional style of getting your shots one by one and cutting them together, and while there's nothing wrong with that it might not deliver the energy you are looking for.

Hand-held

With modern, lighter cameras the hand-held style has become much more popular, and in some contexts is now seen as the norm—not always appropriately in my view. It's flexible, you can go anywhere with it, and it gives your work a sense of energy along with an edginess, an uncertainty, a sense that no one knows what might happen next. This can be intrinsically exciting and engaging. For a lot of actuality and observational documentary it's more or less the only sensible approach.

The drawbacks are that it will always wobble to an extent, you can pretty much only use a wide-angle lens and the lighting will be a compromise. The framing will inevitably be more ad hoc and though the focus should be reasonable because you're on a wide lens there will be little or no flexibility in your depth of field.

75

Because of its intrinsic energy there is a tendency to believe that going hand-held will give your work a more exciting quality, and there are certainly some dramas—the recent spy series *Spooks*, for example—where this approach has been adopted. Without question it gives the work a certain style, but beware the belief that waving a camera around will automatically render something more interesting. If you are doing a sit-down interview then a wobbly shot of someone sitting still is not going to make what they have to say any more engaging—it's far more likely to alienate your viewer.

Let me add a word of warning about using today's smaller, lighter DV cameras hand-held. Because they are too small to go on your shoulder—and considered too light to need to—you will tend to hold them rather like a domestic camcorder, on a bent arm in front of you, and the result will be a lot more wobbly. To get decent hand-held shots you need a camera with some weight in it and the support of a shoulder under it. There are some DV cameras designed for the shoulder but I really don't understand why they aren't all like this. The other problem is that though they are made to be used like a domestic camcorder, the better ones are a great deal heavier. I used one of these for extensive observational shooting a few years ago and ended up with a serious case of tennis elbow from which it took me six months to recover. Shoulder mounts are becoming increasingly available for these cameras now and I would highly recommend their use, but in general, contrary to what you might think, I would suggest that a lightweight DV camera, i.e. the one a self-shooting Director is likely to use, needs a tripod more often than a full broadcast one.

You don't need to stick to tripod or the shoulder for the whole programme. The two styles mix perfectly well. If you're shooting a factual programme you might go on the shoulder for the actuality but on the tripod for the interviews. In drama it works perfectly well if you shoot a static scene on the tripod then go hand-held when someone gets up and runs out of the door, for example.

Steadicam

The advent of Steadicam in the mid-1970s seemed to bring the ideal combination of the flexibility of hand-held with the steadiness of a tripod—the ability to do tracking shots without the constraint of tracks or the lengthy process of rigging them. It has become so popular that every new camera that is brought out now seems to have its own version of Steadicam as an accessory.

It certainly is a great tool, but it is not really an alternative to a tripod—think of it more as an improvement on the standard 'on-the-shoulder' technique. The lighting remains a compromise, and although you will get less wobble you still can't go far down the lens or guarantee your framing.

One shooting style which has developed with the advent of Steadicam is what I think of as the *ER* style, having seen it used a lot in that series. Unsurprisingly it's used regularly in *Casualty* and *Holby City* and it's particularly suited to the kind of busy, lots-going-on ambience of a hospital Accident and Emergency department. The camera is driven by carefully choreographed action from the actors, typically two or more people talking as they walk through a busy emergency room with the camera tracking them, then one of them peels off to talk to someone else, taking the camera with them. Perhaps these two then leave frame and the camera tracks in on the scene taking place behind them, and so on. It's very elegant and pacy, the actors love it because they play whole scenes, and it can have a tremendous fluidity. It takes rehearsal, of course, and it can be done on tracks, but Steadicam makes it a great deal easier.

I remember an episode of *The Bill* made in the nineties when it was a half-hour show with one ad break in the middle. The whole show was shot using this technique and there were just two shots in it, one each side of the ad break. It had a remarkable, integrated, almost theatrical feel to it.

There are many other ways of mounting your camera and moving it around, although the above are the most common. Your decision as to which to use should be informed by the material you are shooting and the effect you want to create. It will also, inevitably, be constrained by your budget, both in terms of hire costs and shooting time, but please don't let it be informed by a desire to impress!

Lenses and filters

The standard **lens** you are likely to get when booking a crew or a camera from a facilities company will be something like 17 x 6.3, meaning there's a 17-1 zoom with the widest end being 6.3 mm. You might additionally want to get a wide angle lens—typically 11 x 4.7. This would be appropriate, for example, if you are filming in a house where you want to see as much of the rooms as possible. If you know much of your material will have to be shot a long way from the camera then a longer lens, say 22 x 7.6, is going to be useful

You can, of course, book additional lenses—a telephoto or a super wide or fish-eye—for special purposes.

A compact DV, or 'point and shoot' camera will normally have a 12 x 4.4 or 14 x 5.8 lens, perhaps with a wide angle adapter which might give 20–30 percent extra field of view. These are fitted directly to the front of the camera lens.

Filters enable you to change the quality of your shot by adding a piece of glass in front of the lens. There are dozens of different filters available for all kinds of different purposes, and they all come in different strengths. These are some of the more common ones:

Neutral Density (ND)

These reduce the amount of light falling on the camera sensor, allowing you to work with the exposure range which is most suited to the camera. Most compact DV cameras have at least a couple of these built in.

Graduated (Grad.)

These filters have a graduated ND effect across the filter glass and so allow you to affect specific parts of the frame. These are most popular for reducing the sky light to match darker parts of the frame in typical landscape shots and so reduce the overall exposure range to a more workable level. They enable you, for example, to bring out the clouds in a bright sky without losing the details of the land beneath. They can be used just to enhance what is there, or to add a special effect. The most popular range is 0.3, 0.6, 0.9. They come in soft edge and hard edge (soft/hard graduation).

Ultra-Violet (UV)

These remove the UV light which can create a washed-out effect when shooting outdoors in bright sunlight.

Polarising

These remove glare and reflections on glass, shiny surfaces and water by separating the light into horizontal and vertical components. They work in exactly the same way as Polaroid sunglasses and are also good for creating deep blue skies and reducing contrast on skin tones.

Pro-mist or Diffusion

These create a special 'atmosphere' by softening excess sharpness and contrast. They can be used to soften wrinkles, or perhaps for a dream-like quality. Black Pro Mists are great for video as they take the 'electronic look' edge off. They also reduce information in the shadow areas. The secret is to use the effect lightly, so use a 1/8 or 1/4 but no higher.

Star

This creates a starburst effect when a sharp point of light is in frame, typically a studio light. It adds pizazz, especially to Light Entertainment.

7 Getting It in the Can

The shoot, whether on location or in the studio, is inevitably the most testing and stressful time for the Director. During pre-production you have your Producer and your Production Manager to hold your hand. During post you have your Editor, then your Dubbing Mixer—who can get on perfectly well without you much of the time. During the shoot you will have your team to support you, but it is up to you to make things happen and if you are not constantly proactive, they won't. Much of the time you are dealing with people and, whether they are professional actors or amateur contributors, trying to elicit from them that most fragile of things—a performance. You need to exercise your 'people skills' constantly and often to be an amateur psychologist, while also being utterly organised and efficient.

If you are working with a crew then you need them as your allies—they are creative people who can bring much to your work. Get to know them, respect them and treat them well and you will earn their respect in turn, which will make your life so much easier. Treat them badly and you will have a very miserable experience. Take a look at what my colleague Mark Bond has to say on p. 82.

Once you get on location time will invariably be tight. And if it happens that one day it's not, that'll be the day you overrun, on the age-old principle that work expands to fill the time available.

There are two rules to constantly bear in mind: take charge and keep things moving.

1 Take charge

Directing is not a democratic process, it is a dictatorship—albeit, hopefully, a benevolent one. From the outset you need to assert your authority, not by throwing your weight around but by earning the respect of your crew. You do this in the first instance by demonstrating that you know what you want. As an inexperienced Director you might not be entirely sure how to get it, but an experienced crew will understand and respect that and offer their expertise.

However, television is a competitive industry full of people trying to prove themselves, so be prepared for those who will seek to demonstrate that they can do the job better than you. One to watch out for in particular is the Producer who comes to your shoot and interferes, or tries to take over. A Producer's job on location is to support you, to get the coffee, keep hangers-on out of your hair and get the drinks in at wrap, not to boss you around. They should have briefed you thoroughly before you set off, and if you have any questions about the content of the show, then make sure you ask them before you get to location. If you are having discussions on location then your Presenter/contributors/cast/crew will wonder who's in charge and the effect will be disastrous. If you are new it's understandable that the Producer will want to be there for your early shoots, but it is very important that they behave themselves—and the good ones, of course, will.

If your Producer is on location and is not happy with what you are doing then the appropriate behaviour is to take you aside at a convenient moment and tell you, then let you communicate any change of plan to all concerned. If they don't do that, but start directing over your shoulder, you are perfectly within your rights to ask them to leave the location, but understandably you will be reluctant to do this when they are paying your wages. My advice is to take them aside and ask what their concerns are.

You will encounter such Producers. I can recall several occasions where this has happened—usually with Producers who have been, or still are, Directors themselves. Not so long ago I was working with just such a Series Producer who had left me blissfully alone during the two weeks of the shoot but came down the night before the final day, which was going to be a very complex and multifaceted set-up with two full crews and a DV camera—a full-on day with room for more than one Director when the crews were working separately. Sensing the possibility of trouble ahead I spent the evening before in the hotel bar trying hard to establish what was wanted, how we would achieve this and who would direct what, but the Producer was tired and intent on enjoying a drink as well as catching up with old friends on the crew.

The next day, with the crew and Director allocation not agreed I was constantly finding my plans changed behind my back, or getting phone calls with alternative ideas. For one sequence we were using both crews together to cross-shoot, but hadn't agreed who would direct. I went to brief one of them only to find they had already been briefed by the Producer in a way that made nonsense of what I had in mind.

I could have stood my ground but chose in the end simply to step aside, keep my mouth shut and let the Producer direct the sequence. It was galling at that stage in the production to relinquish my control, but it was the only way that the very heavy schedule was going to be achieved.

That Producer was no better or worse a Director than me, but did things in their way while I do things in mine. Co-directing simply does not work. I have had many students come to me and assure me that, despite my contrary advice, they are going to work with a friend and direct a film together. I have had a more or less equal number reporting in the analytical essay they write later about the production process that it didn't work.

One of my leisure-time activities is yachting and exactly the same applies there. It is said that if someone is parachuted on to the deck of a boat at sea they should immediately know who the skipper is. There might be six yachtmasters on board with six different ideas about the best thing to do, but only one can be in charge. He may not be the most experienced, and may well seek advice from his crew, but he must make the final decision—and the safety of the yacht and its entire crew depends on that.

The same is true on any shoot, on location or in the studio. The Director, and the Director alone, is in charge.

2 Keep things moving

As Director on a shoot it is your energy which will drive events. If you flag or are indecisive or, worse still, arrive late, then things are likely to grind to a halt.

I used to do a daytime garden makeover show called *Garden Invaders*. They were killer shoots—a 30-minute programme shot in one day, with all the makeover work being done as well. The trick was to hit the ground running on arrival at 8 a.m. and get all the 'before' shots in the can as quickly as possible so that the lads could start digging. It all had to be shot before dark, whatever the weather. There was no time for finesse or fancy camerawork—getting it shot was the order of the day.

The worst time was around 3 p.m. when everyone was hitting their postprandial energy dip and it seemed as if the world had gone into slow motion. We were always waiting for the next bit of makeover to be finished so that we could shoot the following sequence. I was as ready for forty winks on the sofa as everyone else, but knew I would wake up to find that little or nothing had happened. I simply had to keep gently encouraging everyone, and trying to keep things moving.

On one memorable shoot on a hot summer's day we seemed to be getting alarmingly behind schedule, largely owing to the construction of a rather ambitious pergola which simply had to be completed before we could shoot the next sequence. One of the lads was slaving away getting the posts fixed and I was hovering, trying to get an estimate of how long it was going to take, offering to help—many was the time I'd be getting my hands dirty with a shovel or paintbrush as the evening rapidly approached—and gently urging him on, or so I thought.

In the end I had no choice but to leave him to it, while the DV Cameraman got some working shots of his efforts. Viewing these rushes later I was amused to hear the lad saying, 'If that —— Director doesn't get off my back I swear I'll deck him!' Clearly he had forgotten that all cameras have microphones, and that Directors look at rushes. Then again, maybe he hadn't!

But I make no apology for my actions. I was doing what any Director has to do to maintain a sense of purpose and urgency. It's human nature to work more efficiently when you know what the deadline is, and on a shoot you are Head of Deadlines. If you are doing a drama and have a 1st Assistant then he takes that responsibility off your shoulders, but on most factual shoots it is down to you.

I remember many years ago at school a science teacher demonstrating the principles of inertia by pulling a toy lorry with an elastic band, showing how the band had to stretch far more to get the vehicle to start than it did to keep it moving. The same principle applies to getting your shoot under way and keeping it going—it takes far more energy to get a team motivated and into action after they've been sitting around for an hour waiting for something to happen, or for you to make a decision, than it does to keep them going once they're off to a good start.

At the end of your long, hard day, in the studio or on location, you will say the words your crew is longing to hear: 'That's a wrap.' Don't use the words lightly, especially with a big crew. They will trigger a frenzy of packing up ready to go home, and if you suddenly remember that one last shot you have been meaning to do all day but forgot in the heat of the moment you will not please your colleagues. If it's a small crew and you have a good relationship they might let you get away with it once, but make a habit of it at your peril. It's a surefire way of destroying that crucial relationship you have spent so much time and effort establishing. Everyone likes 'going home time' and it's usual for the Director who 'unwraps' to buy all his crew a drink.

Many of the principles of running a good shoot apply whatever kind of programme you are making, but let's look first at the one that's likely to be less predictable.

Q. & A. with Mark Bond, Lighting Cameraman

Q. *What do you find most and least helpful in your working relationship with a Director?*

A. Different Directors work in different ways—some are very 'hands off' and happy to let me do what feels right while others are very prescriptive and 'hands on', with very specific ideas about what they want.

I'm very happy working with either, but it really helps if the Director has clear vision of what they're trying to achieve. Sometimes young Directors trying to make a name for themselves will try to achieve too much in too short a time without really knowing what it is they want. They'll get you to shoot every imaginable shot because it 'might come in useful' rather than because they know where and why they need it. That wastes so much time.

One of my favourite Directors will often surprise me by saying 'That's a wrap— we've got it' before I think we have. He's very experienced and knows what he wants and that's so reassuring to work with.

A good Director is calm, concise and pragmatic, with a good sense of how long it takes to do something and when it's time to move on. It's important to know when you've got what you need—don't shoot for the sake of it.

It's really annoying when a Director interrupts when I'm in the middle of doing something and gets me to shoot something else. We finish up with a bit of this and a bit of that and nothing shot properly.

It's important to agree the style before we start—do we want it rocking and rolling? With twitchy moves? Or steady, on the legs and carefully framed? And if we're going to communicate properly it's important to learn the language—know the difference between a pan and a tilt, between a mid-shot and an MCU.

It's important to be aware of what's going on and what the crew are trying to do. Don't get in shot! Don't have your head so buried in the monitor that you're unaware of what's happening around you.

Keep your crew well fed and watered if you want them on your side.

It's nice when a Director trusts you to get what is wanted without breathing down your neck the whole time.

Q. *What has annoyed you most in a Director's behaviour?*
A. I once had a Director who started moving my lamps! And another had the habit of pushing my lens while I was shooting towards what he wanted me to shoot. I even had one who had picked up the camera in my absence and did some shooting!

Q. *When choosing a camera for self-shooting, what are the considerations?*
A. You have the choice between a larger body broadcast camera with interchangeable lenses or a 'pro-sumer' camera—basically a professional version of a 'point and shoot' domestic camera. It all depends how comfortable and familiar you are with cameras.

As an experienced Cameraman I always prefer a full broadcast camera sitting on my shoulder, where I have full control of everything and all the controls fall easily under my hand.

With modern 'pro-sumer' cameras you can put everything on automatic and the results are quite usable, if not necessarily good. If you want it there is a high level of control on these cameras but it isn't easy to access. You have to fiddle about in various menus.

Another disadvantage of them is that they usually don't sit on your shoulder, unless you buy a shoulder mount. As a result people tend to hold them at waist level and shoot upwards, giving a very strange eyeline on interviews, or give themselves strain injuries by holding them up like a domestic camcorder.

DSLR cameras are becoming very popular, and with their huge sensor and high resolution they give cracking pictures with lovely colours and so on. The prime lenses will give the possibility of a much shallower depth of field than the main range of 'prosumer' cameras, and used with great care they can deliver fantastic results.

But it's important to remember that they are basically stills cameras, not designed for shooting video. So you can end up spending loads more on extra bits such as a shoulder mount, different lenses, viewfinder, matt box, follow focus and a monitor, so that in the end you would have been better off buying a purpose-built movie camera.

Other problems with them are that they don't record timecode, which complicates editing, nor do they record decent sound. The on-board microphone is not up to the job and there's no way of monitoring sound, so you have to record this separately and sync it up manually with a clapperboard or sync software such as 'PluralEyes'.

You can get great results with them, but they are far less forgiving than a 'prosumer' movie camera and you do have to know what you're doing.

An important thing to remember if you're self-shooting is that you're trying to do three jobs at once—frame up the shot and keep it in focus, listen to the sound to ensure it's clean, and watch and listen to what is going on in the frame to make sure that you are getting the narrative you want. It's hard to do this, and so a camera which is automatic and forgiving can make life considerably easier, but do remember it will always be a compromise solution.

When choosing a camera, speak to facilities companies and see which ones have survived hard use in the field. Cameras that are consistently being hired are popular for a reason. Your camera choice will also be driven by the format and codecs required by your clients. There are new cameras with great new features coming out all the time. They are reviewed, but the reviews are written by carefully chosen people. Newer isn't necessarily better—older cameras have been market-tested.

Q. *How do I light a simple talking head or interview?*
A. I would use four lamps—key, fill, backlight and one to light the background.

It all depends on the look required but with a conventional lighting set-up we are often trying to recreate a natural light, so light from above—ideally around 45–30 degrees down on to your subject. If you light from below it looks unnatural and slightly spooky because this is different from what we are used to seeing.

The key light is the strongest, and should be on the side of the face away from the camera, i.e if your subject is looking right to left then the key light should be positioned on the left of the camera to light the right side of their face. Aim just off to the side of nose to avoid nasty shadows and get right amount of modelling. The backlight should be directly opposite the key light, and the fill light at around 90 degrees to the key and at around half the level depending on the degree of modelling and contrast you are aiming to achieve.

When you have a high contrast between the key and the fill such as in 'film noir' this is referred to as 'high key'. When the strengths of the key and the fill are nearer to each other, such as on a Newsreader's face, this is called 'low key'.

Q. *And what about more general actuality?*
A. If you are filming actuality where people will be moving around then a more general light is needed. You can bounce a light off a white ceiling and this will raise the general ambient light level. Or better still you can bounce the light in off a white polystyrene board, or a white wall—preferably a corner—if there is one available, and in this way we can still achieve a degree of modelling. If the walls are coloured then any light bounced off them will take on that colour.

There is a fundamental difference between daylight and artificial, or tungsten, light. Your camera can be balanced for one or the other but if it's balanced for tungsten then any daylight will look blue, and if daylight any tungsten will look yellowy orange. If you are working with a mixture of the two then you need to correct one or other light source with a colour correction gel—blue to correct tungsten light and orange to correct daylight. You should carry both kinds of gel at both half and full strength, remembering that if you put a full strength colour correction gel in front of your light it will substantially reduce the level of that light, so sometimes you have to use half strength just to maintain the level of light needed.

A basic kit I would take on any shoot would consist of:

Lights (all with stands)
1 x 800w Open Face (redhead)—powerful but harsh
1 x 650w Fresnel light—a better quality of light with far greater control
1 x 300w Fresnel light

Gels

Colour correction—Blue and Orange full + half

Fx gels—any colours as required

Neutral Density—0.3 & 0.6 reduces the intensity of any given light

Diffusion—Frost 1, 2, 3—to soften a hard-edged light

Kinoflo and LED lights are useful for general lighting and have the advantages of low power and low heat output. They give a lovely soft, less directional light but don't have a very long throw.

The important thing is to learn to see the effect you are creating. Don't just put up the standard lights—pay attention to results you are getting. And remember the conventions are just that. Once learned and understood they are to be there to be challenged and broken.

8 Factual Location

With all shoots, but especially factual, it's very easy to waste time at the beginning of the day. You'll be getting to know your crew and looking round the location with them—even if you've seen it before they are unlikely to have done so. Your hospitable contributors will have put the kettle on after your long drive and since this is probably a new experience for them they'll be looking forward to an exciting day and want to know all kinds of things. Before you know it an hour and a half has slipped by and you've not yet turned over.

At the same time you don't want to rush into filming something just for the sake of getting going. You might need time to get to know your contributors, to decide what your interview approach will be and, indeed, the best location to film it.

If we need, as we invariably do, to hit the ground running, my preferred approach is to meet and brief the crew before we go in to meet the contributors, outlining the story and what I expect to get out of the day, then telling them what GVs or cutaways I know we will need. In this way, while I am getting to know the contributors and briefing them—and sometimes doing a belated recce!—I know that there is useful work going on. Of course the crew can enjoy a brew, but they know what they need to do and will follow their own timetable. This sets the pace for the rest of the day. Your contributors will recognise the professional approach going on around them and get used to the idea that while it might be a day off work for them it's a hard day's work for you. If you begin it with a coffee break it can be very hard to get things under way as everyone is getting into an interesting conversation about something with someone.

The normal routine

As a professional you should at least be aware of the normal routine for initiating a take. It's a routine which has been developed over years through experience, and though it dates back to film days it remains a useful basis on which to work.

When everyone is ready to go for a take the Director says 'Turn over', which means he wants the Cameraman to start recording.

The Cameraman replies 'Speed' or 'Set'. He means that he is not only recording but also framed and focused on the agreed shot.

The Director then calls 'Action!' having, of course, previously agreed with all concerned what will happen at this point.

Whatever is happening will then be filmed until the Director—and no one else—calls 'Cut!'

It's a simple routine but sticking to it when appropriate—and that certainly means when a large number of people are involved in the take—saves a lot of time and trouble.

I once worked on a reality show with a Presenter who, despite having completed three series of this show, had never grasped this basic routine but would just start talking when ready and then look indignant when asked to stop and wait. It wasted so much time. I suspect the fault lay with the inexperienced Directors who had previously worked on the show and never taught the routine to this particular Presenter.

In practice the routine is often bypassed with good reason—when doing GVs it isn't necessary and when you're working with nervous or inexperienced contributors it can be intimidating. When shooting actuality it might be a positive disadvantage in that it draws your subjects' attention to you filming. In these circumstances the Director will usually simply catch the Cameraman's eye, point, and then do a circular finger-wave.

So be aware of the routine even if you don't use it. As with screen grammar, a professional Director will know what the rules are even if he chooses not to follow them, and his crew will respect him for that.

The material you will be filming will, broadly speaking, fall into one of the following categories.

1 GVs

A half-decent Cameraman will know how to get you the GVs you want and you shouldn't need to direct him. That said, if you are working with him for the first time it's worth keeping an eye on the monitor, which he should offer you. In the old days this was tricky as the monitor was a medium-sized cathode ray TV set, very heavy to carry around and attached to the camera by cable. Nowadays it's usually a lightweight, radio-linked LCD, sometimes small enough to sit in your pocket. It means you can keep a discreet eye on what you are getting while chatting to the contributor and without breathing down your Cameraman's neck.

Even without looking at the monitor you can get an idea of what you are likely to get from seeing how the Cameraman sets up. If he's looking at the house, garden, car, boat or whatever from different angles, and moving the legs from place to place—perhaps using the baby legs from time to time or resting the camera on the ground—then the chances are you're in safe hands. If on the other hand he simply parks the legs in one place and swings round, zooming in and out, then beware. There is an unfair stereotyping of news Cameramen as behaving in this way. It stems from the idea that in news it's not about the framing or originality of the shot, simply about getting some wallpaper to cover the Reporter's words. A news Cameraman comes into his own chasing the action, whether in a war zone or in a press pack outside Number 10, and may not be stimulated by the idea of getting an unusual shot of the semi where you're doing a makeover show. Most news Cameramen are far more creative than that, but watch out for the one who just gets you one shot of everything you asked for and is back in ten minutes. You're going to have to put in a lot of work directing him—and you'll try not to work with him again.

The words 'general views' might seem to imply a collection of wide shots and landscapes. They shouldn't. The truth is that wide shots and landscapes rarely work on the small screen unless they are framed with something. If you look at your holiday snaps, how many of those scenery shots you took are half as impressive as the view you remember? If you are going to get these then look for some 'dingle'—a branch of a tree, a shrub, or perhaps overhanging eaves—to frame the shot and give it depth.

The true purpose of GVs is to establish a location, and that is more effectively done with a collection of details than with wide shots, added to which wide shots rarely cut together well. Next time you take in a view of any kind note how you look at it. You begin by seeing the whole panorama, but soon you focus on details—a particular building, a rock with waves breaking over it, a clump of trees or perhaps a group of people. Your GVs should do the same. If you are trying to tell a story about your location then the detail will tell it more quickly than the wide shot. If it's a story about a rundown council estate, a few close-ups of litter, boarded-up houses or graffiti will say far more than an empty street. If it's a street full of expensive designer shops, the wide shot will tell you little or nothing whereas close-ups of a handbag and its price tag will say it all. And however many cutaways you think you need, shoot twice that number. Factual programmes devour them and you can never have too many.

You will need to discuss with your Cameraman if you want your GVs in a particular style. Some movement will always make them more interesting, especially if you envisage a montage of some kind, and different kinds of programmes aimed at different audiences will suggest different approaches. Maybe whizz-bang whip pans and crash zooms would suit something aimed at youngsters, while careful pans and pulling focus might suit the beauty of a garden in a programme aimed at the over-50s. Beware long lingering pans, though. Cameramen tend to love doing them but in my experience there's rarely space for them in the programme, especially in formatted factual entertainment. If you are going to do one, make sure there's a good long hold front and back so that if there isn't time for the whole thing at least you have two usable shots.

You might be lucky enough to get that rare luxury—a GVs day. If you do, savour it. It can bring a welcome semi-break in a busy schedule given that your duties are largely organisational and you're not having to deal with contributors or Presenters. You'll feel you can breathe and be yourself. You'll have time to take coffee breaks—and you should, for your crew's sake as much as your own. This is a comparatively easy day for you, so avoid the tendency to be so hyped-up and determined to direct that you never sit down or shut up. It's easy to be like that on your first shoot and you'll annoy the crew. By all means tell the Cameraman what you would like and keep an eye on the monitor. If you see a great shot, suggest it, but remember that your Cameraman has a very creative eye of his own and you will do nothing for your relationship with him if you don't remember and respect that. Concentrate on keeping an eye on the schedule and the weather, let the crew know when you are happy that you have enough for your purposes and, if you don't have a Runner with you, don't be too grand to get the coffees!

In fact, as often as not the GVs will be done while you are preparing for the first of those sequences which are likely to form the backbone of your factual programme.

2 The interview

On the face of it, what could be easier than pointing a camera at someone and asking them to talk? If you've chosen the right contributor it should be a straightforward process, but there are a number of ways you can make your life now—and, more to the point, in the cutting room—a great deal easier.

There are two main things you need to ensure:

1 that the contributor says what they have to say clearly and concisely
2 that you get enough of the right shots to cut it all together.

There's a simple bit of jargon you'll need when talking to your crew about interviews. If it's one person talking to one person it's a '1+1', if they're talking to two people it's a '1+2', and so on.

When I did my first film for *Gardeners' World* many years ago my first interview was with a middle-aged lady. She was very pleasant and personable as well as articulate and knowledgeable about her subject, which was the plants in her conservatory.

For some reason we had rather a lot of time to prepare for the interview—I forget now whether the crew had been delayed or were busy doing GVs. I was nervous, and determined to get my first film right, so spent the time chatting to the lady about what I wanted her to talk about and what I didn't. She too was a little apprehensive, so happy to accept my guidance.

When we finally got her on camera this articulate lady was reduced to a gibbering wreck! She was trying so hard to deliver exactly what I had asked her to that she couldn't get a sentence out, and the more takes we did the more angry she became with herself for not getting it right and the Law of Diminishing Returns kicked in with a vengeance.

It was entirely my fault—I had 'over-chatted' her. An interview will always be better for being as spontaneous as possible. You may get some irrelevancies, but that's what the edit is for.

On another occasion much later in my career I found myself sitting in an office listening to a Producer explaining to my young Assistant Producer that the only way to get what you want in an interview is to give your contributor a 'script'—to give them the words you want them to say. To avoid an awkward confrontation I tried to disguise the steam coming out of my ears. Fortunately the A.P. and I spent the rest of that day together on a long drive and I was able to disabuse her of that concept. If I undermined her respect for the Producer I make no apology. Contributors can only be themselves and say what they have to say in their own way. If you want to write a script, hire an actor to perform it.

The chat with your contributor while the crew are doing GVs is important, but absolutely not as an opportunity to nail down what they will say in more than the most general terms. What you need to do is to get to know them so that they feel comfortable with you, especially if you will be doing the interview yourself. Once on camera they will then be able to talk to you like a friend. The most you should do is to give them the questions, or at least the kind of questions which you will ask them. That will get them thinking about what they want to say without actually rehearsing it.

If you are working with a Presenter then get them to do the bulk of the chatting—or even leave them to it if there are other things which you can be attending to. This is assuming you are with an experienced Presenter you can trust, which will not always be the case. If they are inexperienced then stick around, and if you start to hear some kind of rehearsal of the interview then intervene and stop them, likewise if you find your contributor starting to pour out, without prompting, what they have been thinking about ever since you booked them.

This is part of the reason why you should do interviews as early in the day as you can. Your contributor will be nervous and become increasingly so as the day wears on, so spend a few minutes over a cup of tea or coffee befriending and reassuring them, then set the shot up and get stuck in.

Asking the right questions

If you have an experienced Presenter or Reporter doing the interview you should be able to leave them to it, having primed them with the appropriate research. If they are inexperienced you might need to brief them.

There will be many occasions when you are doing the interview yourself so this is very much a job you need to know how to do. When it comes to it, in the absence of a Reporter or Presenter you might choose to get your Researcher or A.P. to ask the questions, especially if they made the initial contact with the contributor and did the research. This has the double advantage that your contributor is dealing with someone they have already got to know and you are free to concentrate on what you are getting without worrying about engaging their eyeline or framing the questions.

A few bits of advice to your contributor should help you get what you need:

'Just look at me—I'm the only one in the room—the camera doesn't exist.'
When we are speaking to a group it's polite to acknowledge everyone, so you need your interviewee to break that habit or the result will be eyes wandering all over the place, which is very distracting to look at. You can help them by ensuring that none of the rest of the crew—and that includes you if a Presenter or A.P. is doing the interview—engage their eye. All look away, or down at the equipment. If the interviewee doesn't catch someone's eye it's easier for them to ignore their presence. If I'm doing the interview I sometimes make a corny crack like 'Just look at me—I'm the best looking' on the principle that a laugh helps relax people.

'We're going to edit this, so don't worry about repeating things.'
You will regularly be driven mad in the cutting room by people saying 'as I said before . . .' If you over-chatted them before you started they'll be doing it from the word go. It's sometimes worth explaining why they don't need to say that.

'Try not to overlap with me—feel free to take time to think about your answer.'
The interviewee's instinct will be to fill in any silences, as at a job interview, but if they start their answer before you've finished the question your Editor will have a nightmare. If you give them permission to take their time you will help them and yourself and, as a bonus, you are likely to get a more coherent and considered answer.

If you, or any member of the production team, are doing the interview then you should be thinking in terms of cutting the questions out of it afterwards. They are irrelevant—a means to elicit the contributor's story, no more. So it's important to ensure you can do this easily.

There is an increasing tendency these days to allow the Director's off-screen words to stay in the cut. To me this is messy, lazy and inappropriate. The viewer will, quite rightly, want to know who is asking these questions. It may be that they are particularly challenging, in which case they become part of the story and so the person asking them is part of it too and should appear in the film, but if it's just an anonymous off-camera voice then there's a mystery extra person lurking in the film. Good direction should be inaudible as well as invisible. The viewers don't want to know how you got the story any more than you want to know what size spanner the mechanic used when he fixed your car. They just want to hear the story.

All too often these off-camera questions result from the Director's failure to ask the right questions or to listen to the answers being given. There are some standard techniques which can help you here.

If your interviewee seems comfortable and you sense they're not going 'rabbit in the headlights' on you, you can say 'Try to repeat the question in your answer, so that if I ask you "What did you have for breakfast?" you don't just say "bacon and eggs" but "for breakfast I had bacon and eggs".'

It's surprising how quickly people get used to this idea, but if you feel your contributor won't cope then leave out this last bit of advice and begin all your questions with 'Tell me about . . .'

Both techniques help to achieve the desired result of an answer you can cut straight into without having to write a convoluted voice-over to reconstitute the question.

As suggested in Part I, you should have a clear idea of the information you want to elicit from the interview and have some prepared questions, but don't stick slavishly to them. They are tools to extract the information and there will be others which work as well or better. Listen to the answer you get and phrase the next question accordingly, always remembering the information you want. Far too many interviewers don't listen to the answers they are getting, but merely wait for a gap to throw in the next question and consider the job done when the list is all ticked. You should be having a conversation with your contributor, constrained only by the rules of not overlapping, and the more comfortable they feel, the better material you will get.

It's possible, probable even, that the first couple of answers will be hesitant and not get you what you want because the interviewee is getting used to what is likely to be a new and alien experience. Resist the temptation to retake them straight away—you risk destroying their confidence and making matters worse. It is usually better to charge on and then go back and retake those answers you felt weren't what you wanted once your contributor is comfortable and happy that the experience is not the nightmare they had feared.

The take 2 rule

When it comes to retakes I have what I call the 'take 2 rule'. Generally speaking when interviewing a non-professional contributor, and by that I mean people other than politicians or professional spokespeople who have been trained in the art of being interviewed, if you don't get a clear, concise answer it might well be worth having one more go, but no more. The first answer might find them struggling to clarify their thoughts or find the words. By take 2 they should have sorted these and might well give you a clearer answer. After that they are likely to start confusing themselves, forgetting what they have said and what they haven't, and saying 'As I said before'. I have often seen an inexperienced Director doing take after take because they can't elicit a whole clean answer. The contributor gets more and more flustered and even if they do get the words out eventually they have lost any semblance of spontaneity, yet they had given a perfectly good beginning to the answer in take 1 and a good end in take 2. That's what cutaways are for. You'll have to get some, so that's where you'll use them. I'm not saying never go for take 3, but be aware that you could well be on to a loser.

Bear in mind that when you come to put the show together you often will need to put a 'strap' up—a caption of the interviewee's name at the start of an interview. You will need a mid-shot or MCU of sufficient duration to take this. I find it useful to retake the first answer at the end of the interview on that MCU or MS. On the 'take 2' principle there's a good chance you will get something more articulate and concise, and since the contributor will have relaxed and got used to things by then that will also help you get what you want.

Apart from that, I tend not to retake an answer just to get it more concise. Sometimes it can be worth a try, especially if the original answer was so rambling that to edit it into anything useful will make it resemble a patchwork quilt, but often what you get is the opposite extreme—something so short as to be useless. It's usually better just to cut down the original answer.

As with all directing, what I am doing when listening to an interviewee is editing in my head, listening for the cut points, including the intonation, and once I've heard what I need that's it. The interviewee feels as though they have just had a nice chat and they will come across on screen as natural and unforced.

There are some psychological techniques which can be used in interviews, depending on how devious you want to be. An obvious and harmless one is to kick things off with a gag of some kind—possibly, if you know them well enough, at the crew's expense. It will make the whole experience less intimidating if you give the impression you're a bunch of guys who get on really well with each other.

If you're trying to get some deep personal revelation then try just shutting up and leaving silences. Your subject will feel the need to fill them and might just open up and go further than they had intended to, while if you keep interrupting and trying to steer them they will constantly be aware of your presence.

Take a look back at the work of those two doyens of the chat show, Michael Parkinson and Jonathan Ross, and compare their techniques. Parkinson would be perfectly happy to prime the guest with a simple question and let them do the rest, while Ross tends to interrupt constantly and engage the guest in some kind of banter. Though Ross might argue that his motivation is pure entertainment, it's clear who gets the more revealing interview.

There's nothing revolutionary here. Keeping quiet is a technique used by some psychotherapists who will usher you into a room then remain completely silent, waiting for you to say something, however long that takes. In that way they can be certain that the conversation is about something in your mind rather than a response to something they have said.

This technique is used regularly when the subject matter of the interview is likely to trigger an emotional response. Once the territory has been entered you leave a silence. Your subject remembers the event or the person in question and, when they cease having to control their emotions in order to get the words out, those emotions rise to the surface and tears often follow. It's manipulative and you may feel uncomfortable with it but it works.

Getting the right shots

Over the centuries people have come up with assorted novel ways of transporting an object over land, but somehow the wheel still reigns supreme. Similarly there are dozens of ways of shooting an interview and you will probably come up with ideas of your own, but there is a conventional way of doing it which has served for decades and still delivers the goods. Other approaches can bring in all kinds of different elements, create different moods and energies within your film and maybe even score you brownie points for novelty, but if you simply want to engage the viewer in what someone has to say then there's a lot to be said for the good old-fashioned way—and it is still used in probably 80–90 per cent of television interviews.

First and foremost an interview is about looking at someone's face. Consider the conversations you've had with strangers—on the telephone, typing on a computer and face to face—and think which have brought you most quickly to a knowledge and understanding of that person. Words are just a part of the communication process— visual communication is at least as important, arguably more so. A silence on radio is a silence. On television it is an opportunity to see the person behind the words as they maybe squirm with discomfort or register an emotion beyond words.

So, starting from the convention outlined in Chapter 5, the main shot you are likely to use is an MCU with an eyeline just off camera one side or the other. This will mean positioning your interviewer, be it you or the Presenter, with their ear brushing the camera.

When choosing your location or background try to find something which will set your contributor in context—be it their workplace, their home or the perhaps the location of the events about which you are talking to them. That said, avoid the temptation to loosen the shot to show more of this location. It's not about the location, it's about the person in it. Offices, however interesting and/or evocative of their occupant, don't have facial expressions or communicate with their eyes.

A mid shot is generally the loosest shot you should be using and more often it will be an MCU or CU. If you can't find a relevant location then look for something neutral, like greenery, or use a long lens to reduce the depth of field and defocus the background.

It's tempting, especially if you are doing a relatively chatty, non-intense interview, to get your contributor doing something while they talk—if it's a cookery show, you might chat to them while they're cooking. This is great for adding visual interest and putting your contributor in context, but there are two important drawbacks. They won't be looking at you but at what they are doing, so you lose the visual communication, and if they are doing something which requires them to think or concentrate then they will only have half a mind on answering your questions. What they will probably then do is stop what they are doing and look at you, so you finish up with your standard interview shot. This can be great—it can help your contributor to relax and feel comfortable as well as setting them in context—but what you will not get is an interview while they are doing something.

Your choice of shots will largely be dictated by the edit you are almost certainly going to be doing on your interview. A standard technique is to change the shot size on each answer. This can enable you to cut directly from one answer to another by 'punching down the line' and so save a cutaway. If the interview becomes more intense, more personal or more emotional then a tighter shot will draw the viewer in. A general rule would be to start on an MS or MCU then go closer, on the principle that the interview is likely to get more intimate or intense rather than less as it goes on. There's also a courtesy issue here, particularly if the likelihood is that the interview will be used in roughly in the same order as it's shot. If we are chatting to someone we should be getting more interested in what they have to say as we get to know them better. If the shot is getting looser the implication is that we are bored now and want to move away!

If you're doing the interview yourself then that's about as far as you can go. You need, of course, to think of what you will use as cutaways. If the interview is about something we can look at—a place, a person, a thing or some actuality—then you have no problem. If it's about something abstract, about the interviewee or about some events of which you have no visual record, then you have to be a bit more inventive. A standard technique is to get some 'establishers'—these are basically shots of your contributor doing something in their environment, whether making a cup of tea in the kitchen, weeding or strolling round the garden, typing on the computer in the office or just walking down the street. Obviously if there's an activity you can find which is in some way relevant to the interview than that's better, and you should try to shoot this in a location other than where you are doing the interview—it will cut better. Either that or keep the establishers tight—fingers on a keyboard or mouse, perhaps, or eyes looking at the screen. It's a good idea to do some of these before the interview—it helps to get your contributor used to the camera in an easy way.

Another thing some people do for cutaways is shots of hands or eyes, but in my view these can look a bit desperate. Unless these are saying something—a twitching hand betraying nervousness or tension, perhaps, or a wedding ring if talking about a spouse— then they serve no purpose other than to cover the edit and that's very obvious, so it draws attention to the edit rather than disguising it.

If you are interviewing two people together—a '1 + 2'—then by all means start on a 2-shot, but, as soon as you can, go into a single of whoever is speaking and then stay on singles as far as possible. If they're talking over each other or to each other the 2-shot is better, otherwise you have the ever-present risk of the person who is not speaking looking elsewhere absent-mindedly, or, worse still, at camera, or maybe picking their nose! Personally I am allergic to those Presenter 2-shots so beloved of daytime shows and some news channels for the same reason—the second person adds nothing to the shot, keeps it loose so you can't see the speaker's face so well, and often looks uncomfortably like a spare part.

Using the 2-shot for a '1 + 2' also gives you fewer editing options. So shoot singles as far as possible, then simply get some looking shots of each looking at the other and at you, and get the turn of the head between, and you probably have all the cutaways you need. If they are holding hands, perhaps, then that's worth a shot because it says something about them.

There is a school of directing which seems to take as its starting point that any steady, stationary shot or any shot held for more than two seconds is intrinsically dull. So you get a hand-held close-up wobbling for no good reason, or the shot wanders from mouth to ear or cuts to the interior of a nostril, or tracks constantly from side to side. It is particularly prevalent among young Directors trying to get noticed or impress their Producer. If I were their Producer they would be sacked. If what your contributor has to say is not interesting then no amount of chucking the camera around or closer acquaintance with their nasal hair will make it so. And if it is interesting then all this nonsense will make it far harder for the viewer to engage and listen. I have found myself closing my eyes in front of stuff like this so that I can concentrate on what the interviewee is saying. Hardly a demonstration of a visual medium well-used!

A standard and very useful technique when shooting several interviews which you know you will be cutting between is to change the eyeline. Say you are interviewing two people with opposing points of view or two different memories of an event. If you shoot the two interviews with opposite eyelines—i.e. one looking camera right and one looking camera left—then it will look much more elegant when you are cutting them together, as if the two people are talking to each other. So always remember, or better still make a note of which eyeline you use. If I forget to write it down I try to recall whether the camera was brushing my right ear or my left!

If you have a Presenter conducting the interview then you immediately have far more options of how to shoot it. The standard technique of an MCU with an eyeline just off camera remains, but there are also some variants on the shots you can use during the interview to good effect. The 'dirty single'—where you have something of the interviewer in frame but out of focus as you look over their shoulder—can add intensity, particularly to an interview with an element of confrontation. It also works well with today's 16 x 9 aspect ratio. But be aware of your interviewer's head position—it can catch you out in the edit.

Make sure that either you or your Researcher or A.P.—or your P.A. if you are lucky enough to have one with you—takes a note of all the questions asked. Your next job is to turn the camera round and get reverse questions and 'noddies' from your Presenter. Noddies are basically listening shots and frankly it's far better to avoid any nodding at all—it usually looks phoney. Just get your Presenter to look interested—serious if it's a serious interview, smiling if it's light-hearted, laughing if they did so during the interview. Reverse questions are, as you might have guessed, simply the questions asked during the interview repeated as accurately as possible. Try to make sure you shoot them on the same size shot as you did the answer. If you can't remember then shoot an MS. Somehow it always looks rude to have a tighter shot of the interviewer than the interviewee—it implies we are more interested in them than the contributor—but if it's the same or looser then that's suitably courteous.

You then need to get your 'non-sync wides'. These are, as the name implies, shots of your Presenter and contributor which are sufficiently wide to disguise lip-sync. Keep them as nearly as possible in the positions they were—that said, you'll be surprised how much you can move them around to get a decent shot without it being obvious. You'll need to make sure they both speak—even if you can't read lip-sync you can see who is talking and who isn't. They can talk about whatever they want to, but sometimes I get them to rerun the interview, especially if I wasn't 100 per cent happy with the answers—it's surprising how often a nervous interviewee relaxes and opens up once the pressure is off. And if there has been any visual activity during the interview—looking at something, pointing, turning of heads or walking in or out—then I get them to repeat all of that in the wide. It doesn't take long, and certainly don't repeat all the interview unless you think you need to. If you can find them, two non-sync wides will come in handy. If you're in a small room you might get something through the window, but do remember the line. There are those who will throw the line to the winds for these shots, but your work will look less elegant if you do. Another technique favoured by some is to focus on something near the camera with the subjects blurred in the background. I'm not keen on this, but it can be a fallback when you can't get far enough away to lose lip-sync.

If your interviewee is pressed for time, and particularly if he/she is a VIP, do your non-sync wides first and then get your reverse questions and noddies with a stand-in after they have gone. The Prime Minister will not thank you for keeping him standing around to give your Reporter someone to look at!

When you have your interviewer in vision it opens up so many more possibilities for different approaches to the interview. The walking 2-shot is a favourite and can work well, with the Cameraman walking backwards or perhaps tracking on some kind of dolly, improvised or otherwise (I have got some great supermarket interviews using a shopping trolley). But spare a thought for your Cameraman if you're planning a long chat. Ten minutes is not a long interview but you can easily walk half a mile in that time. You try walking half a mile backwards with a heavy box on your shoulder! And remember he'll have to do it again for the reverse questions and noddies. As with activity interviews mentioned earlier you will often find that your subjects will naturally come to a stop if they want to talk with any degree of concentration, so encourage or even prescribe this, and make sure you repeat it all in the non-sync wide. This is a classic technique for a stroll round a garden, for example, and it works really well for that kind of thing where it's an interesting chat rather than an in-depth interview. The two naturally stop now and again to look at the next plant, and the non-sync wides are great because it puts them in the context of the garden that the piece is about.

A technique which some favour for shooting interviews is simply to do it all in one hand-held shot, shaking around from interviewee to Presenter to cutaways. This gets it all done quickly and is fine for a live inject to a magazine show where you have no other option or when shooting observational documentary and picking up snippets in the middle of something else, but you will curse it in the edit. My advice is don't do it if you don't have to. You will find that the shot is mid-pan just where you want to cut the sync, or looking at the Presenter when the interviewee is saying something crucial, and so on. You end up having to cover the whole thing with cutaways to make it look halfway decent.

Don't do what so many of my students seem to do—shoot the main interview take on a 2-shot of Presenter and contributor. It will give you nowhere to go in the edit, and even if you do listening shots afterwards your continuity is likely to be all over the shop. And in any case we probably already know what the Presenter looks like. It's the interviewee we want to see—they are the ones with the information to offer.

If you keep the basic elements you need in your head then you can adapt them in all kinds of ways depending on the circumstances in which you find yourself. Necessity is the mother of invention.

At the end of one of the climbing shoots I did for *Tracks* our lady climbers had 'topped out' at the end of an ice climb on Aonach Mor—the mountain next to Ben Nevis—in a 60 m.p.h. gale. I needed to get a final chat between them to complete the piece, but a glance at my Sound Recordist was rewarded with a laugh. He was barely able to hold the pole much less record any usable sound through the mic. The climbers were both muffled in anoraks which hid all but their eyes, so we did the shot and recorded the sound when we got back to the car park at the bottom. When you don't have to worry about lip-sync you can cut it like radio.

In the introduction I mentioned an interview shot on a gondola in Venice. We turned up at a boatyard in Venice to do a piece with Presenter Suggs interviewing Jane da Mosto about Venice in Peril, the charity which addresses the problems the city faces as it sinks into the sea. The plan was to do it on a traditional working gondola round some back canals. It was a glorious day, it had the potential to be a great piece and it would clearly take a lot of time to set up and shoot, but when we arrived we were told that one of the gondoliers on whom we depended had to be elsewhere in forty minutes. Nothing daunted we fitted Suggs and Jane with radio mics, loaded them on to one gondola and the crew on to another, and off we set. The Cameraman simply shot what he could get—2-shots, singles, non-sync shots—according to where the gondolas happened to be in relation to each other. I was listening to the sound on headphones, and when we found ourselves out of radio range we stopped them talking and mopped up GVs and cutaways. Forty minutes later we had the five-minute piece in the can, and to be honest if we'd had four hours to shoot it I'm not convinced it would have been significantly better. It's not hard to get nice shots in Venice, but what enabled us to do it in the time was knowing from years of experience what shots we would need and, rather than carefully setting them up, simply snatching them as and when we could.

Ultimately, the trick to getting a good interview is to direct your contributor as little as possible. The more you can make them feel comfortable on camera the more they will reveal themselves. If you have a Presenter they should do that job for you—they should befriend the interviewee before going on camera, and it's important that you let them do it. Brief your Presenter beforehand and make sure you are singing from the same hymn sheet about what you want from the interview, but once he or she meets the contributor you should keep a low profile or you will confuse the latter. I mentioned earlier how disastrous it is to have more than one Director, and this is a similar situation. Let them develop a trusting relationship which should then deliver the interview you want. You are still directing the show, and that includes the Presenter and contributor, so if you need to retake parts of the interview then tell them both, but by then the Presenter will have become the contributor's friend and will help him or her deliver what you want.

Vox pops

If you make factual television you will almost certainly at some point find yourself shooting vox pops (*vox populi*—'the voice of the people', if you didn't study Latin!). These are basically mini interviews and many of the same rules apply. The difference is that you are only likely to be taking a short clip from each so you don't need to do all the reverses and non-sync shots. Normally you will cut them together to form a montage, so swap the eyelines regularly. Because you will be cutting from face to face you won't have jump cuts so you don't need to worry about cutaways.

Whether you are working with a Presenter or doing this yourself the trick is to get on with it as quickly as possible. If you arrange people carefully and make them wait while you set up the shot you will lose any spontaneity, and your contributor is likely to become increasingly nervous as they wait for you to get organised. If you approach them camera in hand, all you need is the basic courtesy of a quick 'Hi, I'm X and we're making a film about Y. Could we have a quick chat?' and if they say 'Yes', get on with it. I don't recommend coming at them with the camera already rolling—it's rude and intrusive and you will alienate people. As with all interviews, the more relaxed you can make it, the more like an ordinary, friendly conversation, then the more relaxed your contributor will be and the better the material.

Get some general crowd shots of wherever you're filming, and if you are chatting to a group of people get looking and listening shots from those who aren't talking, and the job's done.

Before you walk away, there are some important things to remember.

Release forms and respect

For you this is a job and your interviewees are people you deal with in the course of a day's work. But remember what I pointed out in Chapter 2, that for a lot of people the idea of appearing on television can be life-changing. It may be more and more common for members of the public to appear on TV, but it's still a big deal for most people, especially if they are the subject of a whole programme. Ideally your contributor will have been briefed beforehand as I suggested, but that doesn't give you the right to ride roughshod over them.

Many years ago I did a series about people losing weight. Over the course of a few weeks we filmed a family, all of whom needed to lose a few pounds and were trying a well-known diet. The shoots all went well with no problems and the films were transmitted. A week or so later we had a call from the employer of one of the family members. Apparently he had called in sick for a few weeks, so when his boss spotted him on our show looking hale and hearty they had cause to be suspicious. It transpired that the man had been mercilessly ribbed by his mates about appearing on a daytime TV show to the extent that he couldn't face going in. He very nearly lost his job—but we knew nothing of this before that phone call.

All was well in the end, but this demonstrates clearly how, as users of people, we TV Directors need to be sensitive to the possible effects of what we do. We have a duty of care to the people we use which needs to be taken very seriously. I will address this further in the post-production section, particularly in terms of how we present the people we have filmed.

With this in mind, before you say goodbye to your contributors there is a crucial piece of paper you need them to sign and that is a Release Form. It gives you permission to use the material you have filmed in any way you want, and could be vital if you have any comeback after transmission from a contributor claiming you have misrepresented them. Additionally, if you have filmed in their house or office, you should get a Location Agreement form signed. Normally your Researcher or A.P. will take care of all this for you, but make sure they do. If they don't and there's a subsequent brouhaha then it will land fairly and squarely on your desk. Even with vox pops it's worth doing that if you have the time, though there is a shorthand way to get consent if you don't—and that's to get it on camera. Just record them saying 'I am happy for you to use this material' and you are covered.

3 The piece to camera

If you are working with a Presenter then you will usually, but not always, do at least one or two pieces to camera. These are the Presenter's opportunity to communicate directly with the viewer and establish the relationship which will hold the programme together. He or she will address camera directly to introduce the story or an element of it, to express an opinion or to link two sequences together.

It is to be hoped that the Presenter is experienced and professional, in which case you will have a very useful ally in your job. If they are new then try to brief them and offer any direction out of any contributors' hearing to avoid the risk of destroying the confidence of both.

You should have scripted the content of these pieces if not the exact words. If you have written the words then encourage your Presenter to rewrite them. Better still, just give them the bullet points and let them say it in their own way. If they simply read out what you have written then they are bringing nothing to the film. Some Presenters have the ability simply to stand in front of the camera and give articulate voice to their thoughts on a subject or place and the results can be very effective. I have known professionals, such as Alan Titchmarsh or the late Geoff Hamilton, who could deliver two minutes or more to camera without hesitation, deviation or repetition, and if the shot didn't work, or a police siren went by, they could do it again. They might have been prompted by the plants they were walking past but even so, it's no mean feat. I have also known dull-eyed celebrities who struggle to get one sentence out at a time. You need to know how to deal with both.

If you are working with an experienced professional don't tell them how to do their job, but do give them direction. If what they are saying is not clear to you, then say so.

This is particularly true of the passionate expert who might forget that the viewer is not as well up on black holes, diff locks or F1 hybrids as he is. Get them to run through what they want to say—which will enable them to clarify in their own mind how they will say it—and you can decide what shot to use, where you want them to move, and so on.

If your Presenter is new to the job then try to guide them towards the idea of chatting to the camera as they would another person. It's best to avoid complicated moves with someone inexperienced—just let them sit or stand and maybe walk in and/or off at the end. If they really are struggling to get the whole piece out in one then do it in two shots. Decide on an appropriate point in the piece when it would work to break it and get them to look in another direction at that point. Take your camera round to that new position, change the size of the shot and get them to turn from the old direction to the new, then say the rest of the piece. Or you can get them to leave shot and pick up the next sequence as they walk in, always remembering to maintain the line of movement.

If you choose a walking-to-camera shot then tell your Presenter to take two or three paces before starting to speak, otherwise you might find in the edit that you cannot avoid seeing them take their cue and start walking.

Sometimes it's best if they enter frame at the beginning and/or leave frame at the end, other times a hold on them looking to camera at the end can get you into whatever comes next more effectively. If you are doing a tailpiece at the end of your film it's usually best either to have them walk away at the end or to look away, maybe giving you the opportunity to cut to their POV. That way it feels like the end.

4 Actuality

Actuality is stuff happening—basically it's anything which isn't a piece to camera, GVs or an interview. Since it could be anything from machinery in a factory through cookery or gardening to events in a war zone it's impossible here to give anything more than the most general hints about how to shoot it successfully.

The crucial thing to clarify in your mind—and communicate to your crew—is what you want your actuality sequence to say, just as with anything else you film. Why are you shooting it? What information will it offer in your film? It may seem obvious, but that clear thought makes the difference between a focused sequence and bland wallpaper. If you are filming in a factory, do you want to suggest that it's a hive of industrious and purposeful activity or a place where robot-like people are bored to distraction? You could film either in the same location—it's what you focus on that will tell the story. In the first instance you look for energetic people doing things—purposeful activity of any kind. You might go hand-held to keep it energetic. In the second you look for blank faces and repetitive activity and you might on the tripod to get a sense of stasis and boredom.

If you are filming a high street, is your film about shopping, about the buildings, about crowds or about individual people doing things? Again you could get all these in the same location and on the same day just by concentrating on different things. This is why you need a script giving some idea of where your sequence will come in the film, and what the voice-over will be saying, or whether it's a music sequence. If it's the latter that could inform the way you film it, especially if you have chosen specific music or at least the kind of music you want to use.

Sadly, I fear that there are inexperienced Directors out there who approach the job rather as a farmer approaches watering his crop—by spraying the camera around sufficiently far and wide that they will somehow capture enough vaguely relevant shots to wallpaper their commentary, which they will write later. If you do this the result will be bland and unfocused. Every shot you use needs to say something—to be framed to convey its meaning as effectively as possible. The more clearly you know what you want to say the more informative your work will be.

If you're working with a crew, then any half-decent, properly-briefed Cameraman will know perfectly well what you need and will go out and get it for you. Much of the time you can't direct him because he'll be busy covering what's going on, and you shouldn't really need to. If there's a particular way you would like it shot then brief him beforehand. Other than that the most you are likely to need to do is to tap him gently on the shoulder and indicate if there's something happening other than where his camera is pointed which you need him to get. Normally you will have a monitor in your hands, so just keep checking to ensure he's getting what you want, then suggest at the end anything he might have missed. Whatever you do don't stand next to him telling him what shot to do next—at least not if you like your teeth arranged the way they are!

It might be that you are self-shooting, in which case there are some basic principles to bear in mind.

Remember that you will edit whatever you film. Unless it's live you will almost certainly cut what you film to a shorter length, and therefore you will need more than one shot. If you cut the middle out of a shot which stays the same size—whatever size that is—then the result will jump and look ugly.

This might seem crashingly obvious—I hope it does—but I recall an occasion when I left a reasonably experienced A.P. looking after a makeover shoot one evening after I had gone. He had a DV camera which he knew how to operate and he was under instructions to pick up anything which happened which was part of the continuing story. During the evening an important decision was made about a design element involving a sheet of MDF, so he knelt two of the designers down with the MDF and filmed them having a chat, on a 2-shot. It was useful and informative, but three minutes long. I wanted to include it in the programme but only had about thirty seconds for it, and all I had was one three-minute 2-shot, no cutaway of the MDF, no looking or listening shots of the designers, not even a non-sync wide. There was nothing I could do and the piece was completely unusable.

Shooting actuality is about creating sequences, not just about collecting shots. And whatever you are filming you will need cutaways—several shots of different sizes and from different angles. If you are filming factual material you will need at least twice as many as you think you do. Unless it's a vox pop or something and you know you will only be using one short clip, never ever cover anything with just one shot. If you do then you can only use one bit of it or all of it.

The more the variety of your shots in terms of both size and angle, the more interesting and effective your actuality will be. Too often I've seen inexperienced A.P.s or Researchers with a DV camera watching events from across a room on a mid or wide shot through fear of not catching everything that happens. The result is dull, uneditable and uninformative. It doesn't matter if someone is not in frame for every word they say, especially if they are talking about something which you can subsequently get a shot of. Get a few seconds of wide if you like to establish geography, then get in close to the face or the activity—whichever you're least likely to be able to get later. You can always get a non-sync wide at the end, as with an interview.

If you are filming someone at work—maybe doing the same thing repeatedly on a production line—then film the first time they do the task on a wide, for the next one go in and shoot close-ups of whatever they are doing, then close up on their face and you have a full kit of parts to make a sequence.

An easy mistake to make in a situation where there is lots going on is to become so apprehensive about missing some of it that you finish up catching none of it in a usable way. You are tempted to take lots of short shots of everything that you see around you, then when you get it to the cutting room you find there is nothing that cuts together. Stick with whatever it is you are filming until you have got enough shots to make a sequence, then move on to the next thing. If something you don't want to miss is starting to happen elsewhere you might want to break off what you're doing to catch it, but hang on for another ten seconds or so to get a usable shot and make a mental note to come back and get the cutaways when you've got the other event. If you're working with a Cameraman then make a judgement as to whether the new event is going to continue, in which case let him finish the sequence he is doing before tapping him on the shoulder. If it isn't and is too important to miss then drag him over, but the half-completed sequence will be your fault, not his. It's his job to get what you ask him to. If you don't specify he'll use his own instincts to get what seems appropriate, but interfere with that and you take full responsibility.

As with GVs, don't be afraid to use the tripod to get your actuality. If your subject is staying put, maybe working on a machine or at a table, then you know they're not going anywhere and you will get better, steadier, tighter shots. The same applies if you are, for example, getting crowd shots from a high vantage point.

If you want to create a sequence out of an action which is not naturally repeated then don't be afraid to ask your subject to do it again so that you can get some more shots. This applies even if they are talking on the phone or having a meeting with someone. Though members of the public cannot be expected to be good actors it's surprising how convincing they will be when they are doing something they do every day.

The issue of recreating events leads on to a discussion of when actuality becomes performance, and the whole question of TV fakery which became such an issue during the 'Queengate' scandal of 2007. It's a vexed question, but in my view the answer lies in your intention as Director. Let me discuss this in the context of directing that specific kind of factual television which is fundamentally driven by actuality, and where all the above comes very much into play.

5 Observational documentary

The fundamental difference between observational documentary and other kinds is that in the one you don't know what will happen and have little or no control, while in the other you more or less do and can control it, and clearly this informs the way you shoot it. If you know what you want your actuality to say then you frame your shots accordingly. If you don't know what is going to happen all you can do is go with the flow and cover events as best you can. Although you might sense a story happening in front of you and will therefore seek to cover it, you won't necessarily get a clear idea of how the story will shape up until the edit. You need, therefore, to hoover up as much as you can and your shooting ratio will be far higher than in a scripted or expositional film. You will need far more time in the edit too. But it is still important to keep your shots varied and interesting—simply covering what happens on mid-shots and wides will not make for a watchable film. Even though you might be less clear about what the sequence you are filming will eventually say, you still need to be sure you can say it in an interesting way and you still need to remain focused on what you *think* your film is about and be selective in what you shoot. If you see something interesting happening away from what you are filming, spare a moment to consider how you would bring it into the film before wasting everyone's time. If you can't see where it will fit then resist the temptation to film it—it might make a great sequence in someone else's film, but that's not the one you're making.

There is, of course, the rare exception exemplified by the French crew who were filming a documentary in New York on 11 September 2001 and managed to catch the first plane hitting the World Trade Center. This rather changed the course of their day and their film, and a lot else besides—but it was a one-in-a-million event!

I mentioned in Chapter 6 how observational, 'fly-on-the-wall' documentary has become part of the fabric of our TV programming and developed a language of its own which is now emulated by Drama Directors. Although the ob. doc. Director began by trying to film a scene as he might a drama, with continuity and action cuts, it is, inevitably, not possible as he has no control over the events he is filming. So jump cuts and crossings of the line and leaping around different time frames have become accepted. The story is told by piecing together snippets of video from all over the place. The narrative does not need to be chronological but instead it is driven by whatever the film is trying to say.

One important rule of observational documentary—and I'm talking here about pure observation, where you are merely observing what happens and in no way engaging with or attempting to affect it—is to make yourself invisible. It's a rule which therefore applies when filming actuality of any kind. The less your subjects remember you are there the more they will be themselves, the more accurate will be your representation of them and the greater the chances of true insight and revelation. Don't look at them or engage them in conversation—just try to blend into the furniture.

As Michael Rabiger says in his excellent book *Directing the Documentary*, 'Documentaries are only as good as the relationships which allow them to be made', and the truth is that a genuinely insightful ob. doc. is only likely to be achievable when you have been filming for a number of days, getting to know your subjects and winning their trust, and that applies to whatever approach you take to your filming. In fact most of what is generally accepted to be observational documentary includes an element of interview and therefore of interaction between the film-maker and the subject. Look at the work of Paul Watson, often credited with having invented the form, or Nick Broomfield.

To help establish the relationship you need for this and to help get your subjects comfortable around you and your camera, you can use a kind of relaxed 'on-the-hoof' interview style. You don't need to sit them down and frame up your shot, but throw questions at them at opportune moments—perhaps when they have just experienced something interesting or seem to be enjoying themselves. You will get a much more spontaneous and genuine reaction than you are likely to if you sit them down, tell them what you want to interview them about and give them time to think about it. If you work over a period of time with your subjects you can encourage them to say things to you when they want to, without waiting for your question.

I once made a series called *Return to Tuscany*—a twenty-part ob. doc. about Italian chef Giancarlo Caldesi and his English wife Katie running a cookery school in his native Tuscany, and this was a technique we used constantly with all those involved. Although we got a great deal of entertaining material about Italian culture and about Giancarlo's relationship with his students, all of the shows inevitably contained a fair amount of cookery. We filmed these sequences in the same observational style, for the most part without requiring Giancarlo to repeat things, demonstrate things or work to camera. We had one camera looking into the pots and another looking at Giancarlo. When he was teaching the students he would be explaining to them what he was doing, so generally we would get the explanatory soundtrack we needed, but when he was cooking alone we would simply ask him now and again 'What are you doing?' and his answer would provide our soundtrack.

Another useful technique we used was to take our main contributors aside after we had filmed them doing something and ask them how it went, how they felt about it, and so on. This not only gave us a hint as to what our story might then be, but also gave us useful interview to drive the sequences.

For example, one sequence was about a donkey derby to which Giancarlo and Katie took the students. Inevitably Giancarlo decided to get on a donkey and take part in one of the races himself. This gave us great actuality, of course, but then we subsequently interviewed Katie about it and she described in detail her apprehension as she saw him climb on and began to worry about him falling and hurting himself, and how that would impact on what they were doing. So then we had an emotional narrative to underscore the comic material and hold the whole sequence together.

Whether the series we made qualified as observational documentary, in that we were very much involved in affecting what happened, is something theorists might wish to debate, but it was certainly actuality-driven.

One particular memory of that shoot encapsulates for me what filming ob. doc is all about. We were filming a cheese-rolling event which was washed out by a sudden thunderstorm—and so it became a story about a thunderstorm, and I therefore needed some shots of lightning. Being Italy this was coming fairly thick and fast, so I pointed the camera at the darkest section of cloud which had been going off like Guy Fawkes night, pressed the record button and waited. Nothing. The odd flash or rumble from elsewhere, but my cloud was now dead. I gave it another minute, then another. Finally I gave up and hit stop. Almost that instant the cloud sprang into life with a spectacular display and thunder to match.

And so it is with people—you can film for hours waiting for something interesting to happen, and then, the moment you decide you're wasting your time and pack up, the confrontation, the exciting discovery, the fish on the hook will happen. And there's nothing you can do to avoid that!

Fakery

In 2007 an observational film was made about the Queen. A Promotions Director was tasked with making the trailer, and to make it sexy he cut two sequences from different parts of the film together which erroneously implied that Her Majesty had stormed out of a portrait sitting in a huff. The Palace was not impressed, and the reverberations resounded and are still resounding around the industry. This triggered revelations about a *Blue Peter* contest winner who wasn't genuine, and a lot of other skeletons then came tumbling out of closets. As a direct result, before directing your first programme for a production company you may well be required to take a test of your grasp of what is and is not considered acceptable in this regard.

At the time there was a great deal of nonsense spoken and printed about what is fake and what isn't. The truth is that all television is artifice—it cannot be anything else. In my view the acid test is the intention of the film-maker. If the intention is to represent the truth then any artifice required to do this is permissible. If, on the other hand, the intention is to distort or misrepresent that truth then it is not.

The ob. doc. Director seeks to cover actuality as fully as possible, and to do so he may have to break the rules of pure observation. Purists might argue that getting people to repeat activity for the camera is a kind of artifice which disqualifies the material from being described as observational, but asking your contributor to take the pork pie off the supermarket shelf twice in order to get enough shots to make a sequence is doing no more than accurately representing the process of buying a pork pie. If, however you cut all those shots together to suggest that your shopper buys dozens of pork pies and therefore has an unhealthy diet then you are distorting the truth. It's all in your intention, but there are always grey areas. You will regularly telescope a story or build up its importance to enhance your film. At what point that becomes a distortion of the truth is, of course, a subject for much debate.

As a Director of actuality it seems to me perfectly legitimate to recreate events on a small or large scale to tell a story. If you are doing major reconstruction then you need to be honest about it—if you are merely repeating a small action to build a clear sequence of actuality then no one should take you to task, but it's a tricky area, especially post 2007. The BBC offers a very interesting online interactive test on their 'Safeguarding Trust' website—www.bbc.co.uk/safeguardingtrust. It's well worth having a look at this as you will probably be required to take the test before you direct your first shoot.

6 Specialist techniques

Every programme you make will develop its own shooting technique to a greater or lesser degree. If it is a long-running series or serial then there will be a whole bible of received wisdom to draw on in terms of the best way of getting whatever it is you need, so talk to the Series Producer or a Director from a previous episode and pick their well-informed brains. That isn't to say that you can't do it your own way, but listening to those who have done it before is never a bad idea.

Here are a few tricks of the trade I've picked up along the way.

Unrepeatable action

Sometimes you have to film someone doing something which can only be done once—say pruning a rose, or making something, or cooking something where you only have one lot of ingredients or only time to do it once. It might be a Presenter doing a 'how-to' piece, or an interview where someone is doing something while explaining their actions.

There's a simple time-saving technique here which I use regularly. You shoot the piece twice but only twice, and both times on a run. Before you start you'll need to get your subject to give a rough idea of what they will do to give your Cameraman a flying chance. The first time you film only the action—getting a clear shot of whatever it is that's being done. Record the voice but also make sure you get any relevant sound effects—e.g. frying, or secateurs—clean. When the action is finished, go back and shoot the whole piece again, only this time totally on the face or faces of your subjects. They can mime whatever it is that they did because you can't see their hands. Working on my 'take 2' principle they are likely to be more concise and articulate in their words, both because they've rehearsed them once and because they aren't actually having to do anything and can so focus their mind on what they are saying. If you're filming a Presenter and you want to get them working to camera then they can do it more easily because they don't need to look at what they are doing. So you win all round and have a complete kit of parts you can cut any way, and at any length you want to.

The alternative is to do it just the once, but keep stopping and starting as you get the cutaways and then go back for the next words. It works, but the drawbacks are that your Cameraman is constantly reframing and your Presenter/contributor loses their flow.

Cookery shows

Food and cooking shows remain ubiquitous and durable in their popularity, and, as suggested, the above technique can be very useful when doing them, especially if they are relatively low budget and high turnover. There are many other ways of doing them, and the higher budget shows will spend a lot more time lighting every shot carefully and doing the complete recipe at least twice.

I once did a series in Brittany with James Martin where we turned out two 25-minute shows a day, all shot in the open air. We used a 'stop and start' technique, more or less doing each recipe on the run but stopping to pick up essential cutaways and details before moving on to the next stage. We had two cameras—the main one looking at James, the food and the guest chef he usually had with him, with a second one just offering a wide covering shot. It was only possible because James is a consummate professional both as a chef and as a Presenter and because we were filming in the open air, so lighting was not a problem, and we were unbelievably lucky with the weather! While waiting for a stage of the cooking to be complete we would use the time to pick up looking shots from the guest chef or cutaways of ingredients, and so on.

I also did *Cooking It* with Jun Tanaka, which was a higher budget show shot indoors. Then we sometimes used my 'unrepeatable action' technique, but other times we shot the entire recipe twice—the first time getting carefully set up shots of all the ingredients and all the stages of cooking, then shooting the whole thing again on the run. He was teaching a student, so it meant we could let that flow with little or no interruption, knowing we had all the cutaways in the can already.

However you film your cookery show you will always need a 'pack shot'. This is a term inherited from advertising which means the carefully set up and lit shot which shows the product off—usually at the end of the ad, and here at the end of the cooking process. Allow time to get this right as it is an important shot—the 'money shot'. You will normally have an addition to your team on cookery shows—the Food Stylist or Home Economist. This is the person whose job it is to buy the ingredients and help the on-screen chef behind the scenes. They are expert chefs in their own right and come into their own on these 'pack shots', carefully dressing the food, arranging each leaf or vegetable, maybe spraying on water or even hiding a tampon soaked in boiling water in it or behind it to ensure it steams! The shot will usually be backlit to enhance the depth and any steam and to make the food look as appetising as possible.

One thing to be aware of when choosing a location for a cookery show is that in most domestic kitchens, and indeed many professional ones, the cooker is against the wall. The cook stands facing the wall and usually has work surfaces stretching away on both sides. This makes it a nightmare to film as the best shot you will get of your cook is a profile and the only way you'll see what's in their pan is to look over their shoulder.

For any cookery show it is essential to use one of those island units which you find in bigger kitchens, where you can shoot across the cooker. If you look at any purpose-built set you'll see it's designed like this, and even when improvising on location, as we did with James, the standard set-up is a table which you can look across.

Cars

You don't have to be doing *Top Gear* to find yourself filming cars. They are ubiquitous as a means of transport and regularly feature as linking devices, especially in 'road shows'. Although I learned my car-filming techniques on that iconic car show, I have used them on cookery shows, travel shows, property shows and reality shows of all kinds.

As ever the important thing to remember is whether you are inviting the viewer to look at the car, the countryside or city it is driving through, or the person who is driving it. That will affect the way you frame your shots, but in all cases what you get will fall into one of three categories—'ups and passes', tracking shots or interior shots.

'Ups and passes' are, as the name suggests, those shots where the car drives past or pulls up at a junction and then moves off again. They are incredibly time-consuming. You have to find a suitable stretch of road where you can see far enough to get a decent shot and there isn't too much traffic. You need to find somewhere to park the crew car which is safe and clear of your shot, and then position your camera to get a good shot without putting the crew in mortal danger. You need to send your car off, preferably with a walkie-talkie or, if not, a hands-free phone. The driver will need to find somewhere to turn round and wait. Then you need to wait for a reasonable gap in the traffic (try that in Naples!) and call your car in. Your Cameraman will probably practise the shot on other passing cars while waiting for yours to get in position, and if you are self-shooting you should do the same. When your car finally passes your shot lasts all of about three seconds, and if you got it wrong then it could take ten minutes to set it up again!

The trick is to choose a stretch of road where you can get more than one shot by looking both ways. Quiet crossroads are good because you can possibly look four ways, and because the car has to pull up, look and turn your shots will last longer. As the car disappears up the road to reposition for the shot you can get another of it driving away, and so on. Make sure you vary the size of your shots, always remembering whether it's the car or the location you're looking at. If you choose the right stretch of road you can get half a dozen shots in the one place. Always remind your driver to use indicators when appropriate—viewers like nothing more than to write in when someone on telly breaks the Highway Code!

We found the dream location for ups and passes when filming in Sicily with Suggs on the way up to a place called Forza D'Agro. It's a steep winding road up to this spectacular village and there is a place where you can see almost all of it snaking up the hill below you. We parked ourselves here and sent Suggs down in his Mini to drive back up and we must have got at least a dozen great shots—going both ways—in one hit!

Tracking shots have the advantage of lasting longer, but they are also time-consuming and even more fraught with potential risk. Generally speaking they are only achievable on a dual carriageway, and a quiet one at that. On a single carriageway all you can get is a front-end or rear-end shot. The classic car shot is the three-quarters shot, i.e. looking at it from one corner, usually the front. And the only way you can get a tracking shot of this is on a dual carriageway with your tracking vehicle in one lane and your subject in the other, both travelling at a similar speed. Unsurprisingly this is not popular with traffic police and should only be attempted at moderate speed on a quiet road. You also need to think carefully about which camera you will use and how you will secure it. A small DV camera can be hand-held, resting on an open window ledge, but do get a lanyard on it! Using a full broadcast camera in this way will give you very limited shots because it's too big. The only way you can really get decent shots with a full camera is out of the side of a van or people carrier with a sliding door which is locked open, but then it's very hard for the Cameraman to comply with seat-belt legislation! I'll confess that in the old days we used have a Cameraman standing up and filming through the car's sunshine roof, or strapped into the back of a hatchback with the tailgate open, but more stringent Health and Safety legislation has long since put paid to that.

If you are doing tracking shots on a dual carriageway then it's far safer if you have walkie-talkies. You can direct your driver, who will keep his switched on beside him without needing to use the talk button. If you have a two-man crew let the Sound Recordist drive the tracking vehicle—he can't get any usable sound anyway. You can keep a careful eye on the traffic and direct him, the Cameraman and your driver. Alternatively let the Cameraman direct the sequence. This is often the better way as he can see what shot he's trying to achieve, and you simply relay instructions while keeping a careful eye on what's happening. What is important is that the two drivers simply concentrate on driving safely while you and the Cameraman worry about the material you are getting.

If you don't have walkie-talkies then agree what will happen before setting off, perhaps including one change of position—and one only—to be cued with hand signals. As with all filming, remember that safety is down to you. If an accident happens as a direct result of something you have organised then you could be prosecuted and even imprisoned.

Smaller DV cameras and minicams offer other possibilities, such as clamping them firmly to the bonnet or the side of the car, but again these rigs tend to run the gauntlet of the law both in terms of the extent to which they obstruct the driver's view and the risk that they will fall off and cause an accident.

The simple truth is that the only way you can get really decent tracking shots is on private land, and it's not surprising that that is where *Top Gear* now do so much of their filming.

Filming inside a car looking out is a reasonable alternative to the tracking shot if it's a 'road show' type shot. And pieces to camera or interviews at the wheel are common and reasonably easy to achieve, but again you need to exercise great caution. Choose a quiet, smooth road with little traffic and few junctions and make sure you have an experienced driver. You'll need to use a small DV camera—few cars are big enough to accommodate a full broadcast camera—and set the shot up before you set off. The Cameraman and his subject will need to be wearing seatbelts, of course, and don't expect the latter to do more than occasionally glance at the camera. You can get cutaways of hands on the wheel, the POV through the windscreen and the scenery passing the side windows, or stop and move the camera to the back seat to get a shot over the driver's shoulder.

Planes and boats

The advent of smaller DV cameras and minicams has made filming in small planes much easier but it will always be time-consuming in the extreme, not least because of the crucial Health and Safety issues. People regularly get killed flying, and a Cameraman I know was very seriously injured in a helicopter crash while filming.

The main problem for the Cameraman is that once the plane is in the sky it's very hard to get shots of it from the ground. Even if it flies round and round the airfield you will need a long lens and a good steady tripod. And it's surprising how hard it is to find a small plane in the sky with the naked eye—harder still when looking down a long camera lens. Once you've found it you have to stay with it or it can take a long time to find it again.

It's important to agree with the pilot roughly where he will be flying or you will struggle to get anything useful, and remember that he has to comply with air traffic control regulations, both in terms of the airfield he's flying from and the general blanket rule that flying within 500 feet of a person or building is prohibited.

Minicams firmly clamped to the inside or outside of the plane can get some excellent shots, but don't try anything on the outside if it will be flying at more than 100 knots or so, and bear in mind the massive G forces which will be involved if there are any aerobatics planned.

Air-to-air shots are great in that you can get closer to the plane and the shots will last longer, but again remember the massive safety issues here—the pilots must be in radio contact and they must be in charge. If you ask them to do something which results in an accident—and flying accidents are rarely minor!—then once again you are personally liable.

A few obvious pointers: before you take off establish clearly where you will rig your camera and what field of vision you will have. That will dictate the formation you fly in. And, as with filming from the ground, it is very easy to lose visual contact and you can waste a long time trying to find each other and line up your shots. Another point to remember, perhaps blindingly obvious but surprisingly easily forgotten, is that a small single or two-seater plane might be going flat out at 100 knots, while a large passenger plane—turboprop or jet—might stall at 120 knots. There's no way you'll get the two lined up for air-to-air filming!

If it's a two-seater with seats abreast you can do an interview or piece to camera at the controls just like a car using a small DV camera, but there is one thing I learned from bitter experience. I was making a flying series for Discovery called *Plane Crazy* and we were doing a piece about a remarkable small plane called the Europa. The inventor was flying it and I went with him to do an airborne interview using a small camera. The Cameraman stayed on the ground to get what he could. Once we had finished the interview I started getting some cutaways of the inventor's hands on the controls and looking out of the window. Meanwhile he was getting bored with flying straight and level, so decided to do a 'wing-over', first one way and then the other. This means rotating the plane through 360° sideways. Then he looped the loop. I carried on filming, thinking this would all be great stuff to cut with whatever the Cameraman was getting below.

Now I am a yachtsman with over forty years of seafaring experience in all kinds of weather, and I have never once been seasick—I have a very strong stomach. But just a couple of minutes of looking though a camera lens in a plane doing aerobatics and I was feeling very unwell indeed. My crew remarked on the strangeness of the hue in my face once we had—to my intense gratitude—landed!

There's an important point to remember here—looking through a camera lens exacerbates motion sickness enormously. For *Top Gear* I worked with a highly experienced Cameraman who specialised in some fantastic freehand tracking shots. We called them whoopsie shots—with good reason. He could do at best three or four before starting to feel ill. So if you are in any way prone to motion sickness don't volunteer for that exotic-sounding self-shooting job on a yacht, or a fishing boat in the North Sea! You will soon be unable to achieve anything useful at all.

Boats also soak up lots of time, not least because they travel very slowly. An average sailing yacht will travel at somewhere between 5 and 7 knots (6–8 m.p.h.) which means that it takes a long time to get anywhere. If you are filming at sea you need to plan your day very carefully and allow far more time than you think you will need. It can easily take thirty minutes to an hour or more simply to lock out of a marina and get to sea, and the same to get back. Also bear in mind that salt water does not do cameras much good and boats are cramped spaces, so you might think carefully before you take a full broadcast camera to sea with you.

You can get some great tracking shots from a fast dory or rigid inflatable if it's calm, but if there is any sea running they will bounce hopelessly and you will need a displacement boat with some weight in it.

If you're filming on board, remember to look at the horizon—sailing boats heel over, and it's easy not to notice that your shot is heeling with it. Our eyes naturally try to correct to make things look upright, and many is the shot—still and video—I have taken on a boat with the sea showing an extraordinary slope! Looking at the horizon will also help any tendency to seasickness.

The good thing about the sea is that one bit of it looks pretty much like any other, so if you are, for example, filming a sea journey consider spending a day getting all your tracking shots and anything you might want to shoot from the land, then you can intersperse them throughout the film or series. The problem with this, of course, is that sea conditions can change, and many is the time you will see, even in major feature films, shots cut together which spectacularly fail to match in terms of the sea conditions. But there's not much you can do about that. You're not going to get tracking shots if it cuts up rough unless you have a helicopter or a heavy-displacement tracking boat.

Despite my keen interest in things nautical I have done very little filming on boats—and the reason is clear. It's time-consuming and therefore very expensive.

Property, makeover and other reality shows

Human emotion is the lifeblood of entertainment. We go to the movies to laugh at the antics of Charlie Chaplin or Jim Carrey, to cheer when the bad guy gets his comeuppance or the underdog wins through, to be terrified as the murderer stalks the house, to cry as the hero gives up his life for others or the lovers make it to the altar.

Reality television has two advantages over drama—it is cheaper to make and the emotions are real. The essence of a reality show is that it involves the participants in something which will generate strong emotions, whether it's errant youngsters being forced into disciplined environments, parents observing their teenagers on holiday, or people going off to start a new life or committing to a major purchase such as a house. Nobody makes programmes about people buying a new washing machine or renting a new flat because there would be insufficient emotional commitment.

It's important to remember this when directing this kind of programme—your intention must be to capture raw and unrehearsed human emotion. As I suggested earlier, reality television has its roots in observational documentary, but while the latter observes an existing situation, the former creates a situation and then observes it. However, once the situation has been created, the techniques of filming it are much the same in that you need to cover the action in the same way and make yourself as inconspicuous as possible in the hope that your subjects will cease to think about your presence.

In practice, within the overall contrived situation you will set up a series of mini-scenarios—the prospective purchasers' first arrival at the house, the unruly children's first meeting with their strict hosts, the moment the householder first sees their newly made-over garden or living room. And you have some control over that—more than you might over an observational documentary. Without blocking the scene like a drama you need to give a few guidelines as to where you want people to stand so that your Cameraman has a sporting chance of getting decent shots of them, and if one of your subjects is a Presenter you need to brief them as to what you would like to get out of the scene.

Whatever you do, don't rehearse. As I suggested earlier, while most people can recreate an activity they do every day reasonably convincingly, they can't usually act well enough to recreate emotion. So if you are expecting any kind of emotional reaction—the prospective house-buyers' to the glorious views from the living room, the teenagers' to the stern parents they are going to have to live with, the rogue trader's to the evidence of his misdemeanours—then set the situation up as far as you can and then turn over and let it happen. Don't let the buyers enter the house, the teenagers meet the parents, the Presenter make the call to see whether the offer on the house has been accepted or the rogue trader see you coming until you are turning over. With makeover shows you will go to enormous trouble to ensure that the contributor gets the maximum effect of the change by moving them out of the house or sealing the room up and blacking out the windows until the moment when you let them in to see it all finished—the 'reveal'.

Having gone to all that trouble it's crucial to maintain the secrecy till the camera is rolling and focused.

The contributor's first encounter with the Presenter who will be with them throughout the filming will come across as more genuine if you ensure they don't meet off-camera beforehand. So get the meeting in the can and then allow them to make friends so that future interviews and chats will be more comfortable. In this way, not only do you have more chance of capturing real emotion but also, because the contributor will be focused on the job in hand—looking round the house, meeting someone new, taking in the changes to their garden or living room—they are more likely to forget about the camera.

You can enlist the services of your Presenter to set up moments if necessary to ensure you capture that all-important reaction. *Antiques Roadshow* experts are all primed to say something to flag up valuation before actually giving a price, so giving the Director time to ensure he's on a shot of the owner's face. The dragging out of the announcement of who's staying in and who's leaving the talent show has become legendary, so if you have a situation of this kind in your show be sure to brief the giver of the news to delay far longer than seems reasonable. You can always cut this down in the edit but it's very hard to extend it.

There will also be times, as with an interview, when it's clear that you have what you need and the continuing chat about whether it should be curtains or a blind in that window is never going to make the programme. Part of you wants to stop, but another part of you feels that something interesting is about to happen. An experienced Presenter will know how much you need and wrap it for you—and don't be afraid to brief them beforehand on the kind of duration and the content you are looking for. Also don't be afraid to stop it if they haven't. They might be enjoying their chat, but you know how much more has to be got in the can that day and how exhausted everyone will be by the end.

While the chat is going on you need, just as with an interview, to be considering what you will use to edit the piece. If it's a property show then it's easy—you will have shots of the house or the room, but do consider where your subjects are standing in the room as it can inhibit the shots you use if you want to give the illusion of continuity. You will also need to take note of anything specific they refer to and get a cutaway of it. I always have a scrap of paper or my PDA handy and write these down—it's all too easy to forget them afterwards. If you have a Researcher, A.P. or Runner with you, it's a job they can do.

If you're filming a job interview or something similar it's harder to know what you can use as cutaways—effectively you have the same options of noddies and non-sync wides as you do with a TV interview. If you have a chat which is going on longer than necessary one option is to tap your Cameraman on the shoulder and start picking up cutaways. That way you keep recording sync, which might deliver something useful, and can always go back and film faces again if the chat becomes relevant once more.

When doing a show which involves a lengthy procedure such as building a wall, painting a room, digging a garden or frying onions, resist the temptation to fill the time by getting different shots and different angles. It may keep a bored Cameraman occupied, though professional Cameramen will relish the break! It's more likely to be the Researcher with a DV camera who gets bored. These days it's only tape, or space on a card, which costs next to nothing, but it's still time. Uploading your media into the edit takes time and costs money, you and your Editor have to look at it all—and your time costs money too. If the wall is being painted blue you will use at most three shots of that—the same with the bricks, or the spade or the onions, so discipline yourself to get maybe half a dozen good shots and then leave it. In the old days when everything was shot on film you had to have this discipline as the stock and processing costs were very substantial. The advent of cheap storage devices has, of course, brought huge benefits in that regard, but it was a good, time-saving discipline whose loss is to be regretted. Time still costs money.

Self-shooting

Increasing numbers of factual programmes these days are 'self-shot', i.e. the Director or Producer/Director shoots the material and often records the sound too. I discussed the reasons for this in Chapter 2 and Mark Bond offers some thoughts on which kit to use and why on pp. 83–4. As he and I have both pointed out, the big problem with self-shooting is that however good a Cameraman, Sound Recordist or Director you are, it's extremely hard to do all three at the same time. What tends to happen is that you concentrate on the job you feel least secure in at the expense of the one you know well. For example, I am a far more experienced Director than I am a Cameraman, so if I'm self-shooting it's all too easy for me to worry so much about whether I'm framed up, properly exposed, white-balanced and in focus that I'm not listening to what's being said. And many's the time I have found myself shooting an interview having forgotten to don headphones, so I am not monitoring the sound quality.

Unless you are a very experienced Cameraman my advice, like Mark's, is to use automatic iris and sound levels on the camera. Modern cameras even offer automatic white balance, which might be worth considering—it gives you one less thing to think about. Don't use auto-focus though—it can get you into trouble when something passes close to the lens, or if your framing drifts, by starting to 'trombone' on you. By all means use that spring-loaded button most self-shoot cameras have which automatically focuses the shot you're framed on but then leaves it set there.

Give yourself at least a day to familiarise yourself with the camera before you go out filming—again remember that you will have more than enough to worry about keeping your head round your three jobs without trying to work out where, and in which menu, the sound track allocation is. Go out and film some GVs, interview your friend or your partner, try getting some actuality—anything just so that the camera starts to feel comfortable in your hands. And review the material you've shot to see whether it looks like it did in the viewfinder.

Keep a close eye on your schedule. It stands to reason that you won't be able to shoot as much in a day working alone as you would with a crew. Always give yourself time to prepare, time with your contributor, time to get the camera set up, the tapes marked up, the user-bits in the camera set. Remember that with a crew this is happening while you are chatting to the contributor. If you can do all your camera set-up before you arrive you can concentrate on one thing at a time, plus you won't have the embarrassment of your contributor watching while you poke around trying to remember where the colour balance setting is.

If it's GVs you're filming it's not so bad as you only have to be a Cameraman, and you might as well use the on-board mic to get your sound. If you're filming actuality then again it's not too tricky, unless you're involved in any way in directing the action. You'll need more carefully targeted sound for this, so if you have someone else with you—a Researcher or P.A.—it's worth getting them to swing your boom after a few basic instructions about pointing it the right way, getting it close enough and keeping it out of shot. If they know what distortion sounds like it's worth getting them to wear the headphones too.

Doing an interview—which is very likely to be the first job you're asked to self-shoot —is, paradoxically, one of the hardest things to do by yourself. You have to ask the right questions, listen to the answers for content as well as sound quality, keep the shot framed up and in focus, all the while giving your interviewee an eyeline to address. To get a good interview, as I said earlier, you need to develop a relationship with your contributor, to engage them in conversation, to listen to what they are saying and think of the question you need to ask to get them to say what you want them to say. Ideally you need to help them forget the presence of the camera, but if they see you wearing headphones and spending at least half your time glued to the viewfinder it's hard for them to do that.

If you go hand-held for this it's even harder. I regularly find myself trying to spend as much time as I can engaging the interviewee's eye but then glancing down at the viewfinder to find that the shot has drooped. So one way you can make things easier here is not to go hand-held unless you absolutely have to. If your contributor is sitting down they won't be moving far. Put the camera on a tripod, frame it and focus it, then you can pretty much leave it, just glancing at the viewfinder now and again, while you get on with your interview.

If you're on your own then it's best to use a personal lapel mic, either radio or wired. It may not give you sound as good as the pole mic will, but it least it will be consistent. Then again, if you have an assistant let them swing the pole and listen on headphones. If you feel the need to appear less technically focused to your interviewee, just check

119

your sound quality and levels at the beginning and leave the headphones off, but if you do this you'd be well advised to check your rushes afterwards.

The other thing to think very carefully about when working alone is Health and Safety. You won't have someone watching your back, so don't attempt that walking backwards tracking shot. If you're filming by a canal or a cliff top with your eye glued to the viewfinder there won't be anyone to warn you you're straying close to the edge.

Think about security too. There won't be anyone to mind the kit while you nip down the road to get that shot, so travel light and just take with you what you know you will need. I tend to wear trousers with lots of pockets on the legs—perfect for stashing spare batteries, tapes or cards, call sheets, etc.

Under the right circumstances I love self-shooting. You are free to make your own decisions, to go with what you want to do, and you don't have to communicate your ideas to a crew or adapt them in the light of their ideas. One of the most enjoyable days' filming I ever had was when I was on my own getting some GVs of Venice. It was a perfect May day, and it was just me, the camera, the tripod, a spare tape and a spare battery. I had the whole day to stroll around getting some pretty shots of Venice—not hard when all is said and done! It was even my birthday—what more could I want?

I also enjoy sailing single-handed, and many of the same rules apply here—give yourself time, think ahead and be prepared. And remember—if you get into trouble there's no one to bail you out.

7 Conclusion

Delivering factual programmes, or any other shows for that matter, on time and on budget is all about knowing what you need and what you don't. Experienced Directors will always deliver them in less time and with crews and contributors who are less exhausted and therefore enjoying the experience more and therefore making a better programme.

This is a discipline which can only come with time. The Director's nightmare—and every Director, however experienced, has done this—is coming away from a shoot having forgotten a vital shot. One thing you will almost certainly do on your first shoot is to over-shoot. So determined will you be to cover all your bases that you will shoot everything from every angle and do two more takes of everything than you need. You will probably overrun, possibly drive your talent and your contributors nuts, and your edit suite floor will be metaphorically carpeted with unused material. But better that than under-shooting. Only through experience will you learn what you need and what you don't, and that experience comes not on location but in the edit.

9 Location Drama

Apart from the obvious fact that you are working to a full script, the main difference between shooting drama on location and shooting factual is that with drama you usually have a great deal more support. This is because production values and budgets tend to be higher and the need to get things absolutely right is greater. Generally speaking, documentary, unless it's fully scripted, is created in the edit while the bulk of the work in drama is done on location, the edit being largely a matter of assembling the kit of parts you have carefully crafted. On some dramas, especially lower budget ones, the Director is not scheduled into the edit until the last couple of days, with the material being fed back from location to the Editor and assembled from the P.A.'s notes about the Director's preferred takes.

You will normally have a 1st Assistant Director working with you who is responsible for organising the shoot and keeping it on schedule. The 2nd Assistant will ensure that the right actors are in the right place and the 3rd will take care of the extras. All you should have to do is work with the actors and D.O.P. and make sure you're getting what you need. You retain full responsibility for the shoot, and while it's the job of the 1st A.D. to advise you that if you do another take you will be overrunning, it's up to you to make the decision whether or not to do it. But at least there are others to take care of the organisation once you have made your decision.

1 Working with the crew

You are surrounded by people with specific responsibilities for different aspects of the shoot—camera, sound, lighting, make-up, costume, props, etc.—all of whom should know what is going on and what they need to provide, having done their homework beforehand. So you can leave them to get on with it, unless you change your mind. If you do then it's crucial to communicate this clearly to one and all.

You will have done your camera plans and, ideally, had an opportunity to discuss them with your D.O.P. before the shoot. But, as with storyboards, don't be slavish to them. In Chapter 3 I discussed the respective pros and cons of cross-shooting and 'stacking them up' when working with two cameras, but you may well find that circumstances on location—the way the lighting is working or simply the time available—mean that you have to think again. As always, respect and work with your crew and your life will be easier.

The truth is that once you have blocked out a scene the D.O.P. will see quickly and clearly how to get it for you, however many cameras you are using and whatever you dreamed up in your plan. So providing the end result fits in with your overall vision of the show, my advice is to let him get on with it.

As long as everyone is kept informed a drama shoot should run like a well-oiled machine with everyone knowing what is expected of them and doing it, so don't interfere unless there is something you are not happy with.

What no one else can do—and what no one else should do!—is direct the actors. It's best you concentrate on that, especially on a low-budget drama where rehearsal has been minimal or non-existent.

2 Working with your actors

Even with all that support there is still a huge amount for the Director to think about on the drama location, and it's very easy to forget your actors. They will understand the pressure on you and normally be happy just to get on with their job, but, as I suggested in Chapter 3, you will always get better performances out of them if you respond to them and give them feedback. With some low-budget dramas, and certainly with the smaller parts, the shoot might be the first time you have met them, so use any time you can find to work with them, discussing the characters they're playing and their relationships. As a general rule spend proportionately far more time with the smaller parts than the larger ones. An actor in a leading role will be fully committed to and constantly thinking about the part, and of course you should give him or her as much time as you can, but don't ignore the bit-part player. A few minutes discussing the character of someone with only one line could make the difference between a dead hole in your scene and an enriched tapestry. But do beware the newcomer who will try too hard and act his socks off in his one line!

On the no-rehearsal show *Doctors* my routine was to begin each scene with a run-through giving a blocking—an unfortunate necessity under the pressure, as I would always prefer to discover this in rehearsal if possible—which the D.O.P., Camera Operators and Sound Supervisor would watch. I would then discuss the camera angles with the crew, before leaving them to light and set up while I took a few minutes to direct the actors, find the relationships in the scene, the changes of gear, the power balance, and so on. There's only so much you can do in ten minutes, but at least the actors are thinking about more than simply remembering their lines.

Most important of all, always give the actors feedback on a take. And if you go again, let them know why. If you don't there's a risk they will think they weren't good enough and so work harder, which is invariably counterproductive, especially on the screen. There are times when you can't be entirely truthful—directing is so much about psychology and recognising what people need and what they don't. For example, if you just felt it was a bit lacklustre then don't say that, but give the actors a note about a detail in the scene—'Perhaps we could make a bit more of that moment' or 'Don't forget you've just come out of that row with the boss'. Sometimes you just feel another go would be worth it but you don't want them to 'act the notes', i.e. make too much of the note you gave them and so unbalance the performance, in which case blame a 'technical fault'. But always give them a reason of some kind.

You will get actors who ask for another take themselves because they feel they can do better, and of course it's your decision whether or not it's worth it. Sometimes a bit of reassurance that the take worked is all that's needed, but the request is an indication that this actor needs feedback. If you have time it may do no harm to have another go for their sake, but beware those who make a habit of it! In the old days of film, when stock was expensive, there was an expression 'We'll use a strawberry filter'. This meant that you'd go through the motions of another take but without turning over, and so indulge the actor without wasting money on stock. These days you may as well record it—it might throw up something new and exciting.

Because you will—or at least should—be shooting several different angles on a scene then, just as with an interview, it will give your Editor a major headache if the actors overlap their lines. You can always create an overlap in the edit but you can't unpick one. Experienced actors should be aware of this, but you should mention it to any newcomers, and if that's done in the hearing of the old hands it won't do any harm.

The normal routine:

Although in factual filming the normal routine is often bypassed for one reason or other, on a drama shoot there are many more people involved and establishing a routine is usually essential.

After discussion with the Director the 1st A.D. will announce either 'Rehearsal' or 'Take'. It's crucially important everyone knows which it is. Actors will often not give their all in rehearsal, especially if the main purpose is for the cameras to sort themselves out. Additionally, costume and make-up need to know—they will want to ensure everything is right for the take but won't waste time on rehearsal—and sound might well want to experiment with mic positions, etc., which they can do with impunity in rehearsal.

If it's a rehearsal he will add 'Still and quiet, please. Positions, please.' When everyone is ready, he will call 'Action!.'

The Director, when he wants to stop, calls 'Cut!' And only the Director should do that.'

If it's a take the 1st A.D. will announce it as such, then call for 'Final checks, please!'—an opportunity for costume, make-up and continuity to ensure that all is as it should be.

Then, as with a rehearsal, 'Still and quiet! Positions, please.'

Next, to the camera(s), 'Turn over.'

The Camera Operator(s), when running and framed, will reply 'Speed,' whereupon the Camera Assistant will hold a clapperboard in front of the camera—both if there are two—which will have all the details of the production, the scene number and the 'slate number'—which is basically the shot number—and call a verbal 'ident': 'Slate 3. Take 1.'

He will usually also clap the board, though this is not strictly necessary in these days of video recording unless there are two cameras running. In the old days of film it was a sync. marker when sound and vision were recorded separately.

Once they have recorded the clapperboard the camera(s) will frame up on their opening shot(s) and call 'Set!'

The 1st then calls 'Action!'

The scene begins and continues until the Director (not the 1st) calls 'Cut!'

It's important that only the Director should stop a scene. He is responsible for what is being recorded and though the lines may be finished there could be a look or reaction, or just some atmosphere that he wants to capture.

If anyone else is unhappy—maybe the sound is not good or there's a boom in shot—then their job is to point it out to the Director and let him make the decision as to whether or not the take should be aborted. He may well want to continue the scene for any number of reasons—even to let the actors have another rehearsal. Maybe they're finding something new in the scene and he wants them to see it through.

Unlike with factual, this routine is more or less universal in drama. The only occasional variation is the 'End Board', which is when, for whatever reason, the clapperboard was not presented at the beginning. Sometimes it's important to proceed as quickly as possible into a take, or perhaps the camera is in a tight position and can't easily reframe to shoot it, or it may even have been forgotten or lost! In this case the Director (assuming he remembers!) will call 'End Board' before 'Cut', whereupon the board will be presented upside down while the camera(s) are still rolling.

Before the shoot you will have worked out in detail with your 1st how you will organise your day in terms of which scene will be shot when, but the order you shoot the different angles is down to you on the day. There are any number of factors which might influence this decision in terms of light, actor availability, costume or make-up changes, etc., but all other things being equal I would aim to do the 'master shot' first—if you are planning to do one. This will be a 2s or WS of the whole scene into which any reverses or close-ups will be cut. Actors are generally far happier when playing a scene in full with all the cast there. Though you can pick up reverses or close-ups in isolation at any time, and an experienced screen actor will happily deal with this, most find it easier to work with the others in the scene, and to do the whole scene. So a full take on a master shot will benefit the actors and establish the blocking and business, providing a continuity benchmark into which the subsequent takes can be matched. Once the actors have played the whole scene they will find it easier to drop in and out of it if lack of time means that you have to do incomplete takes to pick up additional shots later.

However skilled and experienced they are, however convincing in their portrayal of human emotion, remember that your actors are human beings. That powerful outpouring of grief or anger might be delivered using technique but it still comes at a cost. Many an experienced actor can cry to order, but the way they often do it is to draw on some emotionally affecting experience from their past life, which can be an exhausting process. So if you have a very intense or emotional scene to shoot, do spare a thought for them. Don't expect them to deliver at full pitch during rehearsal. Let them mark it until you are absolutely ready for a take—and it's well worth considering an extra technical rehearsal before you take a scene like this. Try not to use too many shots—delivering this kind of work time and time again is a lot to ask, and the chances are you will get into the Law of Diminishing Returns and/or find that there are inconsistencies in the performance. If the actors are delivering good work then you don't need lots of clever shots! Trust them to carry your story.

Working with young children is something which presents its own challenges. You will have had to deal with working hours and chaperones, etc., already. When it comes to the shoot avoid over-rehearsing or over-directing them. Children don't act—they are simply themselves. So once you have given the basic blocking go for a take as soon as you can, and go with whatever the child does. If you keep trying to get it absolutely right your efforts will be counterproductive. As often as not you will assemble the performance in the edit, and sometimes you will have to work directly with the child, especially a very young one, playing with them and coaxing the performance out of them line by line until you know you have all the bits that you need on camera.

Something to be aware of when filming drama on location is the number of people who will spend much of the day sitting around doing very little—and waiting for you. You will be flat out from RV to wrap, using every spare minute to work with the actors or the D.O.P. The professionals around you will be used to this and expect nothing else, but there are few things more tiring than sitting around waiting, and tired actors or Cameramen don't do their best work. They will stay with you and accept what they have to, but if you can keep your eye on the ball and allow your 1st to keep you on schedule then you will be rewarded not only with the respect of your team but also with better work all round.

Being organised on a drama shoot, as with any filming, is not incompatible with being creative. On the contrary it enhances it because you have everyone fresh, engaged, knowing what they are doing and working at their best. And that's how good work is achieved.

10 Sound

Despite the fact that television is a visual medium, it's all too easy to forget that getting good sound is more important than getting good pictures. In drama or factual you can get the idea of what's going on from a wobbly or out-of-focus shot, but if you can't hear what someone is saying then you're in trouble.

The Sound Recordist or Sound Supervisor is all too often overlooked. They work on their own much of the time while the Director and Cameraman are in constant communication. I have worked with many dozens of Cameramen and Sound Recordists over the years and often find myself with people I have worked with before—perhaps several years ago. If it's a Cameraman I invariably remember what we worked on, but with the Sound Recordist it usually takes all day to remember what we did together, often via a list of the Cameramen we have both worked with.

In my experience Sound Recordists are usually the kind of people who are very happy with that state of affairs. They tend to enjoy focusing on and taking care of their own area of responsibility without bothering you or the Cameraman, but you ignore them and their needs at your peril.

As soon as you have decided what you are doing let the Sound Recordist know where you want to film it, how many people will need to be heard, and so on. He will have a view about the interview you plan to film on the motorway bridge or in a howling gale, and better to hear that now than when you are all set and waiting to turn over. He will need to decide whether it is better to use radio mics or the pole. If you are on the move or some distance from your contributors, or you have several contributors who are not close together, then he will want to use radio mics.

If you are filming in windy or noisy conditions then the pole will get cleaner sound every time because the microphone is higher quality and directional, i.e. it is 'looking' at quite a narrow angle and concentrating on a smaller area whereas lapel mics are omnidirectional, which means they pick up sound from all directions equally well. So if you point your pole mic directly at your subject you won't pick up as much extraneous sound as you will with a lapel mic. A microphone's reception pattern is called its Polar Diagram. The pole mic has a Polar Diagram which is a narrow triangle with the mic at the point; the lapel mic's is a circle with the mic at the centre.

You might have a view on which you would rather the Sound Recordist used, and if you are self-shooting you need to have at least this much knowledge, but if I am working with a professional Recordist then his job is to get the best, most intelligible sound he can and he knows far better than me how to do that.

I have often seen filming held up because while the Director and Cameraman are in a huddle working out the shots no one has remembered to brief the sound guy, who could have spent the last fifteen minutes rigging mics on the Presenter and contributor. He will probably be on the ball and have asked anyway, but your shoot will run a lot more smoothly if you treat your Recordist with at least the same consideration and respect as you do your Cameraman.

While filming, your Recordist will let you know if he thinks the sound is becoming unusable. Remember, this is not just about whether you can hear what is being said. You are almost certainly going to edit what you are filming, and if there is a loud but not continuous noise behind it—an aircraft, a police siren, a heavy lorry or a road drill, or even seagulls—then when you come to cut this material that noise will suddenly appear or disappear and it will sound dreadful. This is why your Recordist will alert you to any sound of that kind—it's his job. It's your decision whether or not you stop recording, and sometimes, perhaps if you are getting to a sensitive part of the interview and it's going well, or you are simply pushed for time, you will carry on regardless. I can remember many occasions when I have stopped recording at a Recordist's behest and never heard the offending sound in the edit, but far better that than have an important bit of sound rendered unusable.

If you do have to soldier on in a noisy environment there are various tricks of the trade which can get you out of trouble. The most regularly used is the wildtrack. The Recordist will ask for a minute or so of silence, with all the mics he has been using open, and then record whatever sounds can be heard—birdsong or traffic, the hum of machinery, chattering crowds, etc. Often the camera points at the mic boom during this so that the track can quickly be found in the edit. This can then be laid under all the sound recorded at that location and do much to disguise any lumps and bumps which result from the edit.

If you have to pause for a police siren or a plane, then stop your Presenter and contributors from talking but keep recording. You then get a wildtrack of the offending sound and if you do end up using the noisy material you are covered. And it's possible that you can still use the take but fade the offending noise gently under the next sequence rather than hacking it.

It's non-continuous noise which presents the problem. For example, it's better to record by a motorway where the noise of traffic is more or less continuous than by a road where the traffic is sporadic. Even though the motorway is noisier, providing you can mic closely enough for the sound to be intelligible then it should cut together OK with the aid of a wildtrack. By contrast, a quiet road with the occasional car or lorry will cause far more problems as you will have to stop every time one comes along.

Crowds are an interesting problem. *Antiques Roadshow* is recorded in the presence of a crowd of anything up to 4,000 people and the environment will therefore always be noisy. When I did it it was recorded indoors, which exacerbates the noise, but because it is more or less constant it's fine. The problem came at the end of the day when the crowd had thinned out and there were maybe only thirty or so people left in the hall. Although the level of noise was much lower it was sporadic, so we had to ask for complete silence during recording, then add wildtrack in the edit to make the late items match the earlier ones.

There are, of course, some background noises over which control can be exercised. I'm not suggesting you get the police in to hold up the motorway traffic while you film, but there are some things you can deal with. A pervasive problem these days, for example, is background music—be it in a pub or restaurant, the factory floor or a shopping centre. This presents a third problem alongside intelligibility and editing, and that is copyright. If a commercial record or a radio station is playing and you re-broadcast it behind your interview, you are liable for royalties, so it must be switched off. It's something worth checking at the recce. If you're planning to film in a shopping centre, for example, you need to establish with the administration at the recce stage that it will be possible to switch off the music. If not, choose another location.

If the music is part of the story—perhaps at a concert or music festival of some kind— and you can clear what is playing for copyright, you still need to try to avoid it while recording interviews or pieces to camera, perhaps by moving away till it is very low in the background and/or using the pole mic, which is directional, and pointing it away from the source of the music. You can then record a whole number, beginning, middle and end, as a wildtrack to lay under your edited piece. Ends are great because they can be an excellent way of punctuating or rounding off your film.

The constant humming of machinery should be turned off if possible and wildtracked if not. If you're filming in a kitchen you should consider switching the fridge and freezer off. No harm will come to their contents from being off for an hour or two, but do remember to switch them back on before you leave if you don't want a substantial bill for ruined food winging its way to you. A good Sound Recordist will deal with all of this without your knowledge, but as the Director it remains your responsibility so you need to be aware of what's going on.

At least one Recordist I have worked with uses the trick of putting his car keys in the fridge. That way he cannot help but be reminded to switch it back on before leaving. It can cause some bemused comment from the host, but it does the job!

When filming actuality think carefully about how important the sound is, whether you will use it, and, if so, how. A competent Sound Recordist will react to what he sees the Cameraman pointing at and ensure that he can hear what he needs to. But if it's just general activity you're filming, where you don't need or want to hear what people are saying, then your Cameraman will be much freer and more flexible if he unplugs the sound mixer and switches on the camera mic. This will get acceptable general atmosphere and also make your Cameraman less noticeable, which may very well benefit you in terms of what he can get. There's something about that 'dog-on-a-pole' which is always so conspicuous! On a Health and Safety note, he should always have someone with him. When he's intent on looking into his viewfinder he can't see what's behind or to the side of him—he may well need a 'minder'.

If your sound guy has a separate recorder, he can then go off and get some wildtracks. On his own he can find the best place and generally get much better material than he can when attached to the camera.

It's tempting when you are a one-man band filming your own material to use the camera mic for everything. It's cumbersome enough lugging your own camera, tripod, tapes and batteries around without a sound kit as well. That's fine for general actuality, but if you need to hear what people are saying then plug a proper mic in. You don't need a mixer and anyone can point the boom for you with a bit of basic instruction, but a boom mic is likely to be directional and of far higher quality than the one built into the camera. You also have more chance of getting close enough to your subject to get decent sound if you choose something other than an MCU. The alternative is a radio mic with the receiver tied or taped to the handle of the camera. This is likely to be far easier if you are just filming with one person.

Cherish your Sound Recordist and listen to what he or she says. They will take the burden off your shoulders and deliver you what you need without bothering you unless they have to. If they do bother you they'll be doing it with good reason.

11 Directing in the Studio

The Studio or Outside Broadcast Director is quite a different animal from the Location Director. Although in principle the aim is the same—to make an engaging programme and tell your story well—and many people, including me, have done both, there is quite a different emphasis on the skills you need to draw on to do the job.

Directing a studio is much less about being creative and much more about being organised, keeping a clear head and being able to make decisions and communicate them quickly and effectively. The creativity happens before you get there—once you're in you need to be operating a complex machine with dexterity and confidence. On location you can keep a low profile and depend on good understanding with a handful of people—your crew and your contributors—but in the studio you're in control of a dozen or more people and shrinking violets will struggle. You must be able to assert your authority with confidence but without throwing your weight around.

You will have little or no contact with your Presenters and contributors, communication with them being mainly via the Floor Manager, and your job is therefore to lead a team of experienced professionals rather than developing relationships with members of the public. It's not a job for everyone and there are far fewer really good Studio Directors out there than there are location Directors, but it can be equally rewarding in a very different way—especially if you are an adrenalin junkie! It's a good feeling to come off air after a live show knowing that it's done and dusted. Even if it's a recorded show, you're seeing it before your eyes—you know whether it's working without waiting till it's all put together in the edit.

A basic studio crew will consist, on the studio floor, of a Cameraman for each camera and a Floor Manager who, as the name suggests, is in charge here. In the control room, called the gallery, sit the Director, the Vision Mixer (unless the Director is self-operating), an engineer looking after the camera control units (CCUs) and graphics, VT and autocue operators as required. Next to the Director sits the Production Assistant, a crucial member of the team whose main job is to look after and communicate timings plus any necessary information which has been decided in advance. The Sound Supervisor is normally in a separate gallery, though in smaller studios and scanners (the caravan gallery you will find on O.B.s) he might share with Production.

Filming single camera on location, you should easily be able to remember the names of your crew even if you are working together for the first time. In the studio there could be upwards of a dozen, which makes life harder. But everyone appreciates it when you do remember their name so it's worth trying to get your head round them. You're likely to have a call sheet with everyone's name on it, so keep it handy, and it's useful to put a piece of camera tape under the monitor for each camera and write on it the Cameraman's name. It might not be practical to use names when calling shots, especially if you have more than one person with the same name, but '2-shot on 1, please . . . Thanks, John' is a good compromise.

Communication in the studio is via 'talkback', a system by which everyone can talk to everyone else. But with a dozen or more people all needing to communicate different information in different directions this could potentially become a confusing babble, so it is either 'open talkback', which means that the microphone is perm-anently on and everyone who is plugged in can hear what is being said, or 'switched talkback', which means that the mic is only live when a switch—usually spring-loaded—is operated.

The Director, P.A. and Vision Mixer in the production gallery will normally be on open talkback. In the studio the Floor Manager and Cameramen will be on headphones and have access to switched talkback. The sound gallery will hear production gallery talkback on the speakers and also have access to switched talkback. In this way the Director is constantly heard and the others only when they need to communicate something back to him. If the Director needs to communicate with anyone in front of the camera this will normally be via the Floor Manager, who will relay the information to those who need it. Sometimes, if there is an experienced Presenter who can cope with it—for example a Newsreader, or current affairs or sports Presenter—they will wear a discreet earpiece into which talkback is fed. There will normally be a separate switched talkback available in the production gallery so that the Presenter doesn't have to listen to everything coming through the open talkback.

A common mistake with inexperienced Studio Directors is to spend too much time on the studio floor and not enough in the gallery. While it might feel good to develop a relationship with everyone in there, it simply isn't designed to work that way. While you're talking through shots with camera 3 everyone else is twiddling their thumbs and no one knows what you are sorting out with him—and knowing what your colleagues are doing is often essential to the smooth running of the studio.

Once you have said 'hello' to everyone it's far better that you go into the gallery and stay there. In some studios the gallery is two staircases away from the studio floor anyway, but even if it's next door resist the temptation to keep popping in. When you're directing from the gallery everyone can hear what you are saying and there's a much better chance of everyone working together. If camera 1 knows that camera 3 is doing a 2-shot he will be able to decide what he can usefully offer. In most studios the Cameramen have access to a switch to see what the other cameras are showing so they can check what else is on offer and ensure their shots match. The Vision Mixer will gain an idea of what shot is likely to be available on which camera, as will the P.A. and so on. The captain runs the ship from the bridge, not the foredeck, for precisely the same reason. He has access to all the information he needs and direct communication with all his crew.

Another important aspect of this is that your 'talent'—those in front of the camera—will need to become used to liaising with the Floor Manager because once you get into recording mode that will be the only option. So, just as on location it's important that there's only one Director and everyone knows to whom they should look for guidance, in the studio it tidies up the lines of communication if you fall into the correct pattern from the start. A good Studio Director has to have a very clear way of communicating for this reason. His instructions to the floor will be relayed via the Floor Manager, and if they are not clearly given they will all too easily become garbled.

It sometimes happens that the Floor Manager becomes responsible for censoring and carefully rephrasing the perhaps over-stressed Director's harsh or abusive instructions to a contributor, Presenter or actor who is not delivering what he wants. This kind of behaviour is clearly not to be recommended—it forces the crew, and anyone else hearing talkback, to engage in a kind of conspiracy against the artists, which can only create bad atmosphere.

1 Coverage

When filming on location the Director's main concern is whether everything has been covered and how it will all cut together in the edit. In the same way, the Studio Director's main concern is ensuring that his audience can see whatever is going on in the studio and whether the shots he is using will cut together well. He's doing the same job, but making instant decisions.

The Studio Director's two worst nightmares are:

- All cameras are on tight close-ups of people or objects when one of the guests unexpectedly decides to get up and dance a jig.
- All cameras are offering different versions of the same shot, or wide shots which will not cut together.

To avoid these it's important to ensure you always have a variety of shots available, and that at least one of them will cover anything that is likely to happen in the studio—this is called your 'safety shot'.

So with a straightforward 1+1 interview in a 3-camera studio the likely set-up is going to be the outside cameras (1 and 3) offering matching singles—MS, MCU or CU—of the guests with the middle one offering a 2-shot which will cover any eventuality. That way, even if both outside cameras are on CUs when the guest dances his jig you can cut to the middle camera to cover it while the camera on the guest widens his shot. And it's far better to cut to your safety shot while the other camera reframes than have your close-up camera zoom or track out to get to what's happening. If you try that not only is it likely to look messy, but the dancing guest might suddenly sit down again—or the interviewer might get up and join him halfway through the move! Cutting off a moving camera always looks bad so you finish up with an even worse mess.

For this reason, always think carefully before you ask for an in-vision camera move in an unscripted studio show. It can land you in trouble, stuck on a shot you can't easily cut away from when you need to. Much better to cut away to your safety shot while the other camera quickly reframes and then cut back.

Suppose you have a 1+2 interview in the same 3-camera studio. It might be tempting to have one camera on the interviewer as before and the other two on one guest each, but now you're not covered for the jig. Better therefore to use the same set-up as the 1+1, with your guest camera offering singles or a 2s and your middle camera on a 3s. If you find yourself on a single of one when the other one starts to speak, don't ask the camera to pan across. You can guarantee that halfway through the pan the guest you just left will take over the conversation and you'll be left stranded. It's far safer and tidier simply to cut to your 3s, or even a reverse of your interviewer while the guest camera quickly reframes, then cut back.

As suggested in Chapter 5, a 2s rarely cuts well with another 2s, a 3s even less well with a 3s, and absolutely never when the same person or thing is in frame in both shots—e.g. two cameras covering three people in the studio, one on a 2s of the left-hand two and one on the two to the right. The person in the middle leaps across the frame every time you cut between the shots. As a general rule, whenever possible go from a multi-person shot to a single and vice versa.

The one exception to this rule is the panel show, which regularly has two teams of two or three people. Somehow it's fine to cut between shots of the teams, because they are different people and it's what the show is about. But whatever you do, don't include the chairman, likely to be sitting in between the two teams, in either team shot, or he will appear to be leaping around like a gazelle.

2 The line

Multi-camera set-ups in the studio tend to offer fewer challenges in terms of the line because all your cameras are in place all the time, so get them the right side of the line to start with and you can't go wrong. It's when you have one camera which you are moving around on location that you can get yourself into trouble. Outside broadcasts are a different kettle of fish, and, as suggested in Chapter 5, can offer set-ups—such as *Question Time*, for example—where it is inevitable that at some point you will cross the line. All you can do is to endeavour to soften that effect, and if you bear in mind that the reason why crossing the line is offensive to the eye is that it throws our sense of geography—i.e where people are placed in relationship to each other—it follows that if you can offer a shot which clarifies that geography then the cut is more acceptable. So cut wide between your across-the-line shots.

Of course there are any number of complications which can present themselves in a multi-camera set-up, especially in a live show where you have to release one of your cameras to go across the studio to start the next item in another area while at the same time keeping coverage on what you are doing now. Remember that cameras run across the floor on heavy pedestals, trailing a cable which connects them to the gallery, and they cannot jump over those cables! Each show will have its own particular format and only thinking and planning ahead, or regular experience on that show, can solve all the problems faced by a multi-camera Director in the studio or on an outside broadcast.

You need a clear head and good spatial awareness to be a good Studio Director. You can also make your life easier by careful arrangement of the studio monitors—and the best arrangement is not necessarily the obvious one. Imagine a 3-camera set-up on a standard 1 + 1 interview. You have camera 1 on the left looking across at your Presenter who is sitting on the right, camera 2 on a 2s in the middle and camera 3 on the right looking at your guest who is sitting on the left. The obvious set-up for your monitors in the gallery would be in numerical order from left to right—cam 1, cam 2, cam 3. But that will show you your Presenter on the right and your guest on the left—the opposite way round to the way they are sitting in the studio. So in a situation like this, in common with a lot of directors and especially if I am self-mixing, I prefer to swap monitors 1 and 3 over so that the shots are in the same order as I know the guests to be sitting—it just makes it easier to cut instinctively without having to think. If you have four, five or more cameras it might be too complicated to do this, but it is always worth giving some thought to how you arrange your monitors.

Just as on location every programme has its unique working practices, so the working process in a studio differs according to the programme, principally in terms of whether or not it is scripted. Most programmes will have some element of scripting, even if it is just the introduction and the conclusion, and a drama will be scripted throughout. Any element of the programme which is scripted should be allocated to a camera, with the shot agreed beforehand. Unscripted elements will just be referred to in outline on the script with the words 'cams as directed'. It is the Director's responsibility, as on location, to decide which shots he wants to use from which camera. If it is a fully scripted piece he should have made his decisions on this before the studio begins and will therefore not have to call the shots but can rather sit back and focus completely on observing the results rather than having to drive the studio. If it's unscripted he will have to drive the studio and call the shots, though he might choose to devolve the latter responsibility, as I'll explain later.

3 Types of studio

Let us look at two common types of studio show to clarify the differences in approach.

News or magazine show

This will usually consist of Presenter(s) talking to camera, perhaps interviews or demonstrations of some kind and, quite possibly, pre-recorded inserts. There should be a script which will have the words of any pieces to camera and a running order with timings. If there are pre-recorded inserts the opening and closing of the insert should be indicated by 'in' words and 'out' words and an indication of what the shot is, especially if it is a non-verbal 'in' or 'out'. There should also be an accurate timing.

The pieces to camera will usually be written up on the autocue (or teleprompter—the US name), a device which enables the Presenter to read the script while looking straight into the camera lens, so obviating the need to learn the words or look down at a paper script. In a live studio the Presenter should also have the words on paper or on a computer screen in front of him—we've all seen the autocue fail and the Newsreader reach for the script. Then again, if it's a live bulletin it might sometimes be such a new script that there hasn't been time to load it into the autocue.

The procedure for running the programme will be that the P.A. will count down into the programme, either to the set transmission time or from the 30-second clock which will be put on screen to identify the programme. If there is a substantial unscripted element then the Director will normally call all the shots and take responsibility for all cueing, so as the P.A. counts down he will indicate how the programme will start, for example:

'Coming to titles at zero, twenty seconds on titles then mix to Julia on 3 for the intro.'

At three seconds before zero the clock will cut to black, then, at zero:

'Cue titles.'

The P.A. will then count out of the titles, and at zero:

'Cue Julia and cut.'

An experienced Director will always cue the Presenter (in this case Julia) before cutting to them in vision, remembering that there will inevitably be a slight time lag in the Floor Manager responding to his direction and the Presenter responding to the Floor Manager, so by cueing first the risk of seeing the Presenter take their cue is lessened.

Let's say that the first item is an interview—a simple '1 + 1' (i.e. one interviewer and one interviewee, called 'John'). While the Presenter is reading the intro the Director will set up the cameras he will use to cover the interview. (He should already have selected them in rehearsal, and this should be noted on the script.) Let's say he's using camera 1 for a single of the interviewee and camera 2 for a 2-shot of both people. Camera 3 stays with the Presenter.

'One, give me an MS of John. 2 shot on two, please.'

If they are scripted the P.A. will give the out words of the intro:

'Ending on "John, who is with me now".'

Then the Director:

'On 3, 1 next.'

And as the Presenter finishes the intro and turns to her guest:

'And 1,' which is the instruction to the Vision Mixer to cut to 1, who has the shot of John.

And then the interview will continue with the Director always, if possible, indicating in advance which camera he will use next in order not to catch them out. If the Cameraman knows he is to be used next then he should remain framed and steady. So:

'On 1, 2 next. And 2, 3 next. And 3, MCU on 1, please. 1 next. And 1.'

And so on. The instructions are clear, concise and use the jargon, because it's the quickest way to communicate the necessary information.

In practice many Directors will hand over the straightforward job of cutting an interview to the Vision Mixer to do by himself. It's not rocket science and in a live show the Director will have other things to concern him, such as timings and looking ahead to the next item. The P.A. will keep an eye on time:

'Three minutes on this interview.'

Then the Floor Manager will hold up an agreed signal—usually three fingers—where Julia can see it in the corner of her eye. That is assuming that she isn't wearing an earpiece, in which case the instruction will have been given on switched talkback.

Perhaps the next item is a VT insert coming out of a scripted intro to camera by Julia.

The Director will take control back from the Vision Mixer at the end of the interview, if he has handed it over.

> Director: 'On 3—VT next—standby VT1' (or whatever name the machine playing in has).

Then, as Julia finishes the intro:

> 'Cue VT. Cut.'
> P.A.: '2 minutes 40 on VT. Out words "lived happily ever after".'

And so it continues. The Director cues everything—inserts, sound, Presenters—while the P.A. keeps a careful eye on the time. The Vision Mixer will follow the Director's instructions unless asked to do otherwise. The Floor Manager is in charge of the studio floor, acting as the Director's agent and mouthpiece as well as being responsible for the comfort and well-being of everyone there.

Time in the studio is valuable and often in short supply, so it is the Director's responsibility to use it properly. If it's a live programme then all will, of course, be working to a deadline. The same is true if it's a recording with an audience, though there could be some flexibility there. It is the P.A.'s job to keep everyone focused on the time, both before transmission or recording and during the programme itself, when she will be keeping a close eye on item timings and overall programme duration—often armed with a battery of stopwatches.

Think what you need to rehearse and what you don't. Generally speaking you should rehearse the opening of the show leading into the first interview or insert, but whatever you do don't rehearse the interview—your contributor may well not be a TV professional and will forget that it's only a rehearsal. Come the take or transmission they'll start saying 'as I said earlier', plus you will lose the adrenalin-driven spontaneity, and you simply don't need to. Rehearse getting into the interview and out of it, especially if there are logistical difficulties in terms of getting the guest in place or bringing the Presenter across the studio in time. It's no bad thing just to give an inexperienced contributor a taste of how it's going to feel, so maybe ask the Presenter to put the first question and the guest to start the answer, then skip to the next link.

If there are any other logistical issues to be resolved—props to be brought in or out, rearrangements of furniture or people, or demonstrations of any kind—then these will definitely need rehearsal.

You should look at the beginning and end of your inserts and check the in and out words, ensuring that the intro leads cleanly into the first words of the insert without repetition and that the out words are as written on the script. This gives your Vision Mixer a chance to see how the insert ends and what they have to cut out on. All inserts should ideally end with a held shot or a freeze, but this isn't always so and it may be that you are taking an 'early out' because you needed to save some time. Let the Vision Mixer see where he must cut to get out cleanly. Also check insert timings if you can, or get your VT operator to check them. The middle of a live broadcast is not the time to discover that someone has misread something and the film is five minutes long, not three.

If you have live injects to the studio—perhaps a line in from another studio or a satellite link—it's well worth rehearsing getting into and out of these to establish contact and make sure that all communications are working. We've all seen those cringeworthy moments when the Reporter on location is either unaware they're on air or cannot hear the studio.

It can be an impressive sight seeing a well-oiled news studio in operation—the sense of chaos in the gallery can be awesome, but somehow what comes out on the screen is slick and professional. This is a result of everyone knowing what they should be doing and doing it. It's just like the pistons of a car engine which get on with pumping up and down without worrying about whether the right mixture is coming in—because it's the fuel injection system which deals with that, or how fast the wheels are turning—because that's the gearbox's job. It's amazing just how much can be achieved in a very short amount of time, and it's not unusual to see a studio gallery rehearsing up till thirty seconds or less before transmission, especially these days when everything starts instantly. It was different in the old days when videotape needed a ten-second pre-roll and film could only be rewound at normal playing speed! To the outsider it can seem as though everything is happening with little communication but in fact everyone is concentrating on their own job, saying or asking what needs to be said or asked and not what doesn't, listening to the people they need to listen to and filtering out those they don't. It's therefore clear that Producers or Executives chatting to their guests or clients at the back of the gallery do not help the process, and the Director is fully entitled to ask them to be quiet or to leave.

In the studio your adrenalin will be pumping, whether the programme is live or recorded, and it's easy to get excited and start to shout at people, but this is clearly counterproductive. Your crew will recognise that you are carrying the can and have a difficult job to do, and will probably forgive you, but you will work far more efficiently if you can keep your cool.

I recall in my early days of skippering yachts that in a moment of crisis, when something needed to be done quickly and I knew what it was but had an inexperienced crew, I would shout and scream at them in frustration. This was no help, because when someone is flustered they will think less clearly and when offended by your behaviour they will become less cooperative. Now, however frustrated I might be by a novice's inability to get their head round a simple action, I do my best to remain calm and patient. I also assess the ability of my crew in advance and allow sufficient time to achieve what needs to be done given their level of competence and experience.

In the studio it's the same. Yell and scream and you may be forgiven, maintain your cool and respect your crew and they will move heaven and earth to deliver what you need. If you do lose it in the heat of the moment, whatever you do make sure you apologise afterwards if you want a good working relationship with these guys in the future.

Studio drama and comedy

The great advantage of doing something in the studio which is scripted is that you know, and can more or less control, exactly what is going to happen, and so the process of working is rather different. You don't need to worry to the same extent about coverage and safety shots because your actor is unlikely to dance that jig if it isn't in the script. The line is still important, arguably more so than in a factual show, and so is geography. Although it isn't necessary to follow the old-fashioned idea of every scene having a wide shot at some point to establish where everyone is, a sense of each character's geographical relationship to the others is something you need to think about when choosing your shots.

The rehearsal will be longer and fuller but will result in a complete camera script, where every Camera Operator knows and has rehearsed every shot they will need to get and the Vision Mixer knows and has rehearsed at what point to cut. In this situation the P.A. calls the shots and the Director can sit back and watch the show, focusing entirely on whether or not he is happy with what is going on without having to worry about the mechanics of making it happen.

The process will normally be that the Director will have prepared a draft camera script from the rehearsal script and the studio plan. Once the studio is set and lit he will work his way through it shot by shot, deciding whether what he envisaged will work and giving the Camera Operators a chance to rehearse. In practice the camera script will invariably change at this point. However accurate the Director's vision there will always be things which don't work quite as anticipated, and let us not forget that the Studio Camera Operator is a creative being who sees through his viewfinder what the Director can only imagine and is likely to have his own ideas. It's a foolish Director who doesn't look at alternatives offered by the crew which might just solve a problem, or simply look better.

Don't expect your actors to give a full performance at the camera rehearsal, any more than they would at the technical rehearsal in the theatre. It's mind-numbingly boring for them as you go back, re-rehearse, look at different cameras, and so on. They know it's part of the job and they should be accurate and consistent in their actions, but they will be 'marking it'—going through the motions and the lines but not actually acting as such. Once you have finalised the camera script for a whole scene you should consider running it, in which case they will have an opportunity for a 'dress rehearsal'. Or you might choose to do the whole piece as a run once you have finished working out your cameras.

By the end of the camera rehearsal you should have a full camera script ready to be printed up and distributed (see Fig. 3.2, p. 55). It will list each shot, numbered, with a brief description of the shot and which camera has it, for example:

'1. CAM 3—MS John.'

It should indicate with an underline and a slash at what point this shot is to be cut to, whether on words or action. If there is development in the shot, that should also be mentioned:

'1. CAM 3—MS John—2s John + Julia.'

It's also helpful to mention if it's the same shot as the last time this camera was used, usually using A/B for 'as before':

'3. CAM 3—2s John + Julia—A/B.'

From this camera script the camera cards are prepared, one for each camera, listing the shots required from that camera in order (see Fig. 3.3, p. 57). These are attached to a clipboard on the camera so that the operator can always be ready for his next shot without needing to be directed.

Everything is then in place for the show to run under the supervision of the P.A., who will simply call the shots to make sure the cameras are ready—they might not have time to keep checking their camera card. The important information the P.A. is giving is what shot number has been reached and which camera is next, so that if the operators have forgotten which shot is next they can quickly find the number on the list.

So the P.A.'s talkback will go something like this:

'Shot 1, 3 next. Shot 2, 2 next. Shot 3, 1 next,' and so on.

She doesn't need to tell the Vision Mixer when to cut—he has the script in front of him and has rehearsed it as well, so that is his responsibility.

The Director might want to cue the cuts himself, but otherwise all he needs to do is to give the instruction to get the rehearsal or take under way, watch what happens, and then decide at the end whether or not another take or rehearsal is needed.

If it is a drama with no audience involved then normally a 'rehearse/record' procedure will be used, where each scene is rehearsed and then recorded when ready. If there are several sets in the studio it is likely to be recorded out of sequence, doing all the scenes in one set then moving on. They may all be in the same studio, but it still takes a long time to move three cameras from one set to another and adjust the lighting, and so on.

If there is an audience, as with a comedy show, then normally the whole show will be rehearsed and run just like a stage piece, then recorded in sequence in front of the audience with short breaks between scenes for the cameras to move. If there are any exterior scenes, or anything else which cannot be done in the studio, they will have been pre-shot and will be played in in sequence to get the audience reactions as live.

These are the basic techniques which apply to directing any studio or multi-camera show, whether entertainment, news, current affairs or drama. The key to it all is an organised mind, a grasp of the jargon, good spatial awareness and an ability to lead.

12 The Three Cs

However you are shooting your television programme—single or multi-camera, studio or location, factual or drama—remember the three Cs which are the key to success: control, coverage and creativity.

1 Control

You need to take charge of the shoot from the word go and ensure you remain in full control. This doesn't mean throwing your weight around and shouting at people, but it does mean knowing what you want and enlisting the support of your cast and crew to get it. There are things which members of your team will know how to achieve better than you, and respecting and exploiting that knowledge doesn't mean relinquishing control. You know what you want and they know how to get it for you.

When I started directing I felt uncomfortable if I saw ideas in the finished product on stage or screen which were not mine, as if I had somehow fallen short and had to rely on others. I then came to realise that in the unlikely event that all I saw were my own ideas, I would have failed as a Director by being unable to inspire those I was working with to contribute creatively to the job in hand. On the other hand there was a Director I knew many years ago who was reported to have arrived on location and asked the P.A. for a suggestion on how to start the film!

Listen to those you work with and respect what they offer, but make sure everyone you come into contact with knows who is in charge and to whom they should address any questions about what is wanted or what will happen next.

Clearly the extent of your control over what you are filming will vary along a continuum between observational documentary or news actuality at one end and drama at the other. But even with ob. doc., as already discussed, you should have a clear idea of the story you are trying to get, and so be able to direct your crew towards it.

2 Coverage

Whatever you are shooting, you will have failed in your job as Director if you don't get at least one good clear shot of everything relevant to the story, and enough shots to cut it all together in the edit. This sounds very basic, and it is, but there isn't a Director in the business who hasn't sat in the edit at some point and realised that there was one vital close-up or cutaway he forgot, or watched his Editor trawl desperately through the rushes in quest of three more cutaways to cover the jump cuts in the edit, or paint up the vital voice-over sequence.

There's nothing more frustrating for a viewer than to hear a Presenter or contributor talking about something they can't see, or can only glimpse in a wide shot. Television is a visual medium and so the more pictures you can get of your subject the better it will be. Never ever, in factual or in drama, shoot a whole sequence on one shot. Always give yourself the opportunity to edit it, even if, when it comes to it, you don't have to.

When you are sure you've covered thoroughly your story you can allow yourself that third C, which is what you came into the business for:

3 Creativity

The more control you have over your material the more creative you can be, and the more you think about how the camera can enhance your story the more elegant your direction will be. But as soon as you start to think about how you can impress, or impose your style on the work, you are interposing your ego between the story and the viewer, and if you aren't telling your story clearly and well you aren't directing well.

Good direction means taking the viewer by whatever means you can on a journey which captivates and engages them, but without them realising how you are doing it. It's a conjuring trick, and just as a magician loses his appeal when you have worked out how he achieves his magic, so your audience doesn't want to see how you work your magic with the camera.

I once heard a very experienced and well-known actor expressing his insecurity and the sense that one day he would be 'found out'. His art was so well developed, his technique so much second nature to him, that he had ceased to understand why anyone was convinced by what to him was utter artifice. He had forgotten how much he knew and his work had become so instinctive that he did it without realising he was working, hence his sense of not understanding why people were impressed. We don't see the work either—we just believe in him. We've all watched actors who seek to be impressive, or who are just inexperienced and whose work is visible all the time—we can see what they are doing to achieve their ends. And because of that they don't convince and their performance has no truth.

The same is true of directing. If you seek to impress your audience and your work is visible to them, then they won't believe or engage in your story. Keep a low profile in your work. Your story is what it is all about, so deliver it to your viewers clearly, interestingly, imaginatively and unencumbered by your ego. If you gain a reputation for doing that well, for coming in on time and on budget and for being good to work with, then your phone will keep on ringing—just like that actor's does.

PART 3

Post-production

13

Bringing It All Back Home

When you have said 'Wrap' on the final day of the shoot there's always a tremendous sense of relief, mixed with apprehension about whether you have got everything you need. You know that from here on the whole process will be a great deal more containable— it's just you, an Editor or two, a Dubbing Mixer and possibly a voice-over artist. All are professionals doing their job and you no longer have to be coaxing performances out of actors or contributors, worrying about the time, the weather or the traffic. Now you have to make the best of your material. I find this quite comforting.

Of course there are some kinds of programme where you can go back and get more if you need to, but the vast majority of the time a reshoot is something which will only be considered in desperate circumstances, not only because it will be expensive but also because—in documentary at least—it will often be hard to recreate the events which you were covering. There may be all kinds of reasons why you need to go back, but one of them should not be to pick up shots that you forgot to get the first time.

The first thing you will discover as you start to assemble your material is that however carefully you planned it, it isn't going to go together exactly as you imagined. Whether you are making fiction or non-fiction it involves (in almost all cases) people doing things. People are individuals over whom you can only exercise so much control, otherwise you risk stifling their individual creativity to the detriment of your programme. If you want to have complete control go into animation or make a puppet show.

The other thing to remember is that you have been steeped in your story for weeks, you know the characters inside out and have observed a great deal which didn't make it on to camera. You have a firm sense of what the story is to the extent that it will be hard to see it in the same way as someone encountering it for the first time. There are things that you know because you were there, and which therefore seem so obvious as not to need explaining, material you sweated blood to obtain which seems disproportionately important to you, people you liked or disliked and therefore want or don't want in your film. But the viewer doesn't know or care that you were up at 4 a.m. in the pouring rain to get that dawn shot, or that that boring, inarticulate interviewee was a real sweetie who made you tea and cakes.

It can be argued that as Director you are not best placed to edit your material, and there are some programmes which employ 'Edit Producers' who take over this job from the Director, sometimes simply for expediency because of scheduling and sometimes in order to maintain a consistent style through a series. But the brutal truth is that an experienced Edit Producer can sometimes do a much more efficient job than the Director, especially on low-budget, high-turnover shows, simply because he is not emotionally attached to the material and can operate much more dispassionately.

Then again this is one the most important and creative parts of the Director's work, and if you've been doing your job properly you will have been doing it in your head throughout the shoot, so of course you want to see it through yourself. What you now have to find is objectivity. You need to let go of all you remember from your pre-production planning, forget everything that happened on the shoot and work with what you now have—the rushes.

You will meet a new colleague now, often for the first time, and that's your Editor. He will be, arguably, the second most important creative person on the programme. Crucially he will come pre-armed with that objectivity and all he will have seen are your rushes. He will know nothing and care less about that wonderful moment you remember on location unless it was properly captured on camera. He is the first of several fresh pairs of eyes which will become all-important as you shape your film into the clear and engaging story you have been envisaging. Like the Edit Producer he will be dispassionate, and you should treasure that, but after a while he will become nearly as immersed in it all as you are and consequently will lose his objectivity. And so the S.P., then the E.P., lend their eyes and will see things neither you nor your Editor are able to.

Last, but by no means least, the Commissioning Editor will look at what should by now be a beautifully crafted piece of which you are immensely proud, with a view to whether he will pay for it. And he will be looking at it from a very different viewpoint concerned with ad breaks, ratings, audience demographics and what's on the other channels at the same time. But more of that later.

There isn't a Director alive who hasn't sat in the viewing gently fuming as the owners of those new pairs of eyes variously criticise, rip to bits or generally fail to understand what he has created. But they are, or should be, an essential part of the creative process and must be listened to. While you need to find as much objectivity in yourself as possible, you can never achieve it entirely, and therefore you need to listen to those who can.

As I suggested earlier, generally speaking factual programmes are made in the edit while drama is made on location. This is quite simply because in the latter case you are working to a script while in the former you usually aren't. So, broadly speaking, cutting drama is assembling a jigsaw or a 'flat-pack' kit while cutting factual is creating a collage.

1 Working with your Editor

Your relationship with your Editor is crucial. He or she needs to understand and share your vision of the programme, and you need to trust each other. The stage at which the Editor comes on board, and the amount of time you can spend together, will vary according to the type of programme and, as usual, the budget. But remember that a good Editor is being paid as much as or more than the Director, so their time is expensive and should not be wasted.

In an ideal world the Editor will have seen every frame of the rushes before the edit begins. In that way he will have an overview from the start of what is there, and know where to find the shot needed. But in many cases, especially with something like observational documentary, that is prohibitively expensive.

On the other hand, if you look at and log all the material yourself and simply tell the Editor what shots you want and where, he becomes a simple number cruncher and cannot fully contribute to the creative process.

Interestingly, during the aberration that was video editing between the early seventies and the mid nineties, when it was all done by dubbing from one tape to another, this was what tended to happen. Because the degradation which resulted from multiple-generation analogue recordings made a recut difficult, you were effectively doing the fine cut from the word go, and had to be there all the time. The editing process took far longer than it does today because every cut was preceded by a ten-second 'pre-roll'. For the Director it could become so mind-numbingly boring that it's amazing we ever remained creative! But the result was a generation of Editors, often from an engineering rather than a creative background, who expected the Director to be there throughout the edit and sometimes contributed little creativity to the end result themselves.

The computer techniques we use today are derived directly from the old film editing techniques, albeit working at a hugely faster pace. In the old days you would bring your rushes in on Monday morning with a 'story order' written down and leave it all with the Editor and his assistant to get on with. The assistant then faced the massive task of syncing up all the sound and vision, which were recorded separately, and then the Editor would slave away over a hot Steenbeck until Friday, or whenever, when you would come in to see the rough cut.

In my view the relationship you have with your Editor today should reflect that much more than what happened in the tape-to-tape days. Give him his creative head and you'll be amazed sometimes at what that fresh pair of eyes can deliver. If you really are the kind of control freak who wants to supervise every cut then I suggest you cut the piece yourself with the editing skills any Director working today needs, but if you do that you will be removing a very important and creative person from the production process.

As with most things in these cash-strapped days, the way you work will be a compromise. You don't want to waste your expensive Editor's time but you do want his full creative input, so make sure he sees everything he might want to use but don't make him look at hours of stuff you know is irrelevant. Give him a clear idea of what your story is but don't dictate exactly how he should put it together, and most of all don't let him start a 'fine cut' till you're completely happy with the 'rough cut'.

If you are reasonably handy in an edit suite—as you should be—you may like to try an approach I used when making the series *Suggs' Italian Job* for Sky Arts and which I found to be both effective and efficient.

This was a series made in the early days of HD, which belied its budget. The additional costs of the HD equipment were met at the expense of my time in the edit as it was too expensive to keep me on right through the post-production process. So the way we worked was for me to assemble roughly the footage I had shot as I had envisaged it, putting into effect the edit which had been in my head while on location. These rough assemblies, which were always well overlength, were then passed to the Editor to be trimmed and shaped and fine-cut. The Executive Producer then oversaw and finished the programmes. I would, of course, have liked to be there until the end, but under the circumstances I felt this was a pretty good compromise and a very efficient use of the creative personnel involved in the series. I was delivering my vision of the story, which was then processed by the successive fresh pairs of eyes into the finished product, which in truth was rarely very different from my original concept.

Like all the other parts of the production process the best post-production techniques are collaborative. It's tempting to think that once you get into post it's all back under your personal control, but that really isn't the best way to make good television.

Q. and A. with Roger Shufflebottom, Editor

Q. *With the current mushrooming of different formats, capture methods, resolutions, work flows and editing programmes rendering the process of editing highly technical and complex, what does a Director need to know?*

A. It's important to make the right choice of format from the very start of the production process and to establish that you need to find out what the end delivery requirements are for your programme—i.e. what you will be handing over to the person who commissioned it. Is it HD or SD? And if HD, must it be full HD or is HDV acceptable? And so on. That will affect the camera you choose and the way you capture and store your material as well as the programme and equipment you will need in the edit suite.

There are a huge number of different formats for recording currently available, all of which have their pros and cons. But to look at the basics, the first choice is between tape and some kind of card or disc.

Tape has the advantage of being cheap, and therefore once you have recorded it you can keep the rushes somewhere safe in perpetuity. But it has to be uploaded into the edit suite in real time, and if there is a lot of it this can be a significant cost in terms of someone's time.

Cards and discs, on the other hand, tend to be very expensive, and so normally once the material has been recorded it needs to be downloaded on to a hard drive so that the card or disc can be reused, and this process can cause difficulties. It's important that the entire card or disc, and not just some files on it, is backed up at least twice. But one advantage is that this material can be loaded into the edit suite faster than real time, and sometimes the material can be edited directly from the card or disc. So you can get started much sooner than with tape and this can, of course, be beneficial in fast turn-around situations.

Depending on the amount of material shot and the amount of storage available, it may be necessary to compress the material for the purposes of editing in order to save drive space. HD in particular uses masses of storage space. This is done using a CODEC (an encoding/decoding program). The problem is that there are many different CODECs available. Some compress material spatially, i.e. if there are large areas of an image which are the same—say a figure against a blue sky—then it notes how many pixels contain the same information and saves space by not storing all that repeated information. Others compress temporally so that, for example, if a shot continues for a long time without changing, again it doesn't store every frame as separate information, but notes how many times the same information is repeated.

The different CODECs vary in their suitability for the different processes of capturing material, editing material and playing it back. So it's important to choose the right one and know which you are using for each process if you are going to avoid problems playing your material back.

Q. *Once you have established your format and delivery requirements, how can the Director help to ensure a smooth and successful edit?*

A. The most important thing from the start of the filming process is good housekeeping. Instigate a careful and thorough system of numbering and logging tapes. This is even more important when recording on and downloading from cards or discs. It's crucially important that every frame of the rushes has a totally unique timecode—tape or file number, hours, minutes, seconds and frames.

It's easy to get repeats when, for example, you record over the hour on Tape 1 and go, say, to 02:01:34:19, which is a code which will appear again on Tape 2. Equally, if the same card or disc—say card A—is used more than once during a shoot and the different material is not carefully identified, then A 01:05:35:10 can appear twice. There is something on the camera called 'user bits' which enables you to label every tape or file with a unique number or code, and it's important to use this, especially when you have more than one crew working on a show. Establish the system from the start of the shoot or it can get very messy indeed in the edit.

Another thing to beware of is time code breaks. If, for example, you go back to check something you've recorded and then pick up recording again with a break after the previous material, then the timecode will not be continuous and there will be material just after that break which cannot be accessed.

When you're shooting, do be disciplined. If the camera is waving all over the place the material is impossible to edit. If you are setting up a sequence then get everyone ready, start recording, pause, and then say 'Action' only loud enough to be heard by all concerned—don't shout it or you'll deafen the Editor! At the end of the take leave a pause before calling 'Cut'. When you're doing a developing shot—a pan, a track or a zoom—leave a good steady hold front and back.

If you're recording a number of interviews make sure you are consistent in which channel you use for the radio mic and which for the on-board mic. It's easy to be caught out in the edit if you change and you can end up using the poorer quality sound.

It's really helpful when editing drama, for example, or indeed anything where the edit begins before the shoot has finished, to establish good liaison between the shoot and the edit. Get the P.A., if they are on the shoot, to mark up the favoured takes with a note as to why they're favoured.

Q. *And what about when you get into the edit?*

A. You need to work with your Editor to organise the material carefully, just in case another Editor has to pick the job up at some later date for a recut or whatever. Give the Editor time to establish a well-organised and carefully labelled system of bins and cuts.

In an ideal world the Editor should see all the material—he will often then know the whereabouts of exactly the shot he needs for a particular job. This isn't always possible, but if you label your material carefully then at least he'll know where to look for what he needs.

If you sit down with the Editor for thirty minutes or so at the start of the session and explain what it is you want then you can leave him to get on with it. You don't need to breathe down his neck over every cut. Trust your Editor. Once he's assembled a rough cut then you can look at it and change it if it isn't right.

Listen to your Editor—he's the last line of defence before the Producer and Commissioner viewings and he has the first fresh and objective pair of eyes. He doesn't know, or care, that you were up at six in the pouring rain to get that shot—if it doesn't work he can see that without your emotional connection to it.

And do understand how to view a rough cut. Some Directors seem to be thrown by jump cuts or black holes. Have the imagination to recognise that these will be covered or filled and just look at the shape of the story—the framework of the film which is in place.

When it comes to fine-cut viewings with Producers and Commissioners, then decide who will be communicating the required changes to the Editor. The discussions following viewings often range around a number of different ideas and it's important to establish who will make and communicate the final decision.

Q. *There are different editing programs available—what are their advantages and disadvantages?*

A. Avid remains the industry standard, but it is more expensive than the others, though the price is coming down now.

Final Cut Pro is gaining ground, and has the advantage both of being cheaper and of enabling you to get cutting more quickly without spending time setting up the project—though that can have disadvantages as per my earlier comments about housekeeping. It will also edit Quick-Time files straight away, while Avid has to convert them.

It's important to remember that FCP will only run on Mac, while Avid will run on Mac and PC.

There are other systems now available too—Adobe Premier, Edius and Lightworks. This last, one of the earliest of the offline programs, is now making a comeback.

In the final analysis the choice is down to budget, the formats you're working with, the computer platform you have available, and personal preference.

Cutting Factual

1 Viewing the rushes

There are many ways of approaching the post-production process, but whatever you're cutting, do try to be methodical. It can be utterly daunting getting back with a sackful of material grabbed as and when you could in the stress of the shoot and wondering how on earth you're going to sort it all out and shape it into anything coherent. If, as I suggested in Part I, you did a pre-shoot script, then that will pay dividends now, even if you strayed wildly from it on location.

How much you are able to prepare for the edit will depend on your timescale and budget. Some companies factor in viewing time, others don't. Previously, when all shot material had to be dubbed to tape or DVD before it could be viewed by the Director, there was a significant cost involved. But these days, when most of us can view pretty much anything we want on our laptops, the cost element is only really the Director's time.

One word of warning, though. Although the card, disk, tape or memory stick that your media is recorded on now is a piece of plastic which costs a few pounds, once it has your rushes on it it's worth hundreds, even thousands. In the old days of film the negative, once shot, was locked away safely until the edit was finished with all the work done on a 'cutting copy'. In the tape days the rushes were kept safe and only used on professional machinery. VHS or DVD viewing copies were made for the Director. One disadvantage of modern recording formats is that they are generally far more easily lost, accidentally wiped or otherwise ruined. Domestic computers are fallible things, and I would never let original material near mine. The advantage of modern digital formats is that they are easily copied and backed up without loss of quality, so make sure that you have all your material backed up at least twice in different safe places, and that you only view a copy.

These days it could well be you, the Director, who is loading the material into the edit—indeed you might be viewing it there. If this is the case the organisation of the material is down to you, and, as Roger suggests on p. 154, getting that right in terms of labelling clips and bins is crucial to a smooth edit. Set up a bin for each separate sequence in your programme, and if you have shot GVs in lots of different places or at lots of different times, then make a GVs bin and ensure they're all in there. That way your Editor will know where to find that crucial material to build a sequence or to cover a voice-over. The truth is that a significant percentage of any Editor's time is going to be spent looking for a shot he needs for a particular purpose. Knowing where to start looking must help that process, just as filing your bank statement in your 'Accounts' folder means you're going to find it much more quickly than if it's somewhere in that mountain of paper on your desk or in your 'pending' tray!

So view your material before the edit if it's humanly possible. A Director who works efficiently and doesn't overrun edits will always get hired. If you are prepared and know what you want before you go into the edit it will run more efficiently. Maybe the company isn't paying you to work the weekend between the shoot and the edit, but how much do you want to get hired again? If you have done your job properly you can hand it over to the Editor and take time off in the week while he gets on with his job, and no sensible Producer will castigate you for that. The choice is yours.

Different Directors will have different approaches to the pre-edit stage. This is what I do.

If at all possible, I view all my rushes and log them in some way. It could be that I load them into the edit and log them as I go, or maybe I view them at home and do a 'paper' log, by which I now mean a computer file. Experience will tell you how much you need to put down—I tend just to put what I know will be useful in the edit:

- timecodes for the start of takes of pieces to camera, noting whether they are good, bad or indifferent
- timecodes for the start of interviews, each question and each interesting point in the answer
- rough timecodes for reverse questions, noddies, cuataways and non-sync wides
- general timecodes for GVs—say 'GVs city centre' rather than logging every shot.

There's an example of the kind of thing I produce at this stage in Fig. 14.1. This was for a 'reality' cookery show I did—a couple of actuality sequences, one shot on an allotment as the chef meets the contestant and picks some veg and the other as the latter attempts to do some cooking in her kitchen. Note the roll number at the top, the timecodes on the left and the rough notes of what is on the screen or what someone is saying.

In some circumstances it's worth getting a full transcript of an interview typed up, and if you have a P.A. or someone who can do that for you it can save you a lot of time in the edit. It's just so much quicker to glance through words on a page than listen to them on the screen. With a major interview where you need to extract a story or important

Fig 14.1 Example shot log

Cooking It
Ep 6—Amy
Day 1

<u>Roll 6-1-600</u>
Allotment

00.45	Walk on to allotment T1 X
01.35	Walk on to allotment T2 X
02.01	Walk on to allotment T3
02.50	Finding courgettes
03.30	Picking courgettes
03.40	WS into courgettes
04.21	C/U into courgettes
05.05	GV walking
05.28	GV walking 2
05.55	GV walking 3
06.15	C/Us tomatoes
07.20	Into tomatoes
07.35	Picking tomatoes
08.17	Amy watches
08.48	P/U re meat T1
09.28	P/U re meat T2
09.55	Toms into box
10.15	C/A plum toms
10.30	Garlic x 2
11.05	POV into greenhouse x 2
12.05	Into mint T1 (no words)
12.40	Amy reaction
13.15	Into mint T2
14.13	Into mint T3 X wrong words
14.35	Into mint T4
15.05	C/A picking mint
15.45	WS into mint
17.00	C/As various mints
18.10	Into box
18.24	GVs walking
19.15	GVs

Amy's House
Amy cooks

24.22	Picking up cutlets
25.34	T 2 C/Us
26.25	Jun gets Amy cooking
27.08	*'Never even seen these before'**
27.27	*'I guess I can fry them'*

28.07	*'Don't know what to do . . .'*
28.30	*Don't know where to start*
30.45	Flinching from fat*
31.28	Sandwich toaster is the best machine
32.20	*'Don't know what to do with courgettes'*
32.56	*'Not how they look when Michael does them'**
Roll 6-1-601	
00.45	*'Sure they used to serve sliced & fried'*
02.06	*'They look good . . .'*
03.48	poking meat—'a bit pink'—don't know how you're supposed to serve
05.40	flapping at smoke alarm * *
06.04	Opening window
07.24	*'Doesn't look bad'*
08.41	Amy tastes *'very tough'**
09.43	*'Reason it's tough'**
10.00	Re seasoning
10.30	Looks appetising but doesn't taste nice
10.45	C/As poking at plate—greasy plate
11.15	Reaction Amy
11.55	More C/As plate
12.10	C/A knives

information this is well worth doing. It means you can assemble your story on paper and there's a good chance it will hang together—the only thing you can't be sure of is whether the intonation will sound right.

If you don't have a transcript then just note the timecodes of the bits of the interview you want to use and let the Editor string them together roughly.

Your first consideration when starting to build your programme is what is driving it. It could be interview-driven—constructing the story from what people say in front of the camera as in, for example, an investigative documentary like *Panorama* or perhaps a programme based on someone's memories. The cutting points will be dictated by the sound.

It could be actuality-driven—as with, for example, observational documentary, where you are creating a story from the events which happen in front if the camera. Effectively this will be visually driven. The cutting points are dictated as much by what is seen as by what is heard, maybe more.

Or it could be script-driven—spoken perhaps by a Presenter, either to camera or in pre-scripted voiceover. Or maybe it's a 'voice of God' anonymous Narrator. An expositional documentary where you knew the story before you went out to film would fall into this category. Here again the cuts could be dictated by the script or by the visuals.

With this in mind, from my shot list I make a 'paper edit', although, as I suggested previously, an alternative is to make the first rough assembly in the edit yourself. This is

Fig 14.2 Example paper edit as sent to the Editor after viewing the rushes, *and ** indicate bits I know are strong

---

COOKING IT

RX 6—Amy

Paper Edit:

1 — <u>Titles</u>

2 — <u>Meet & Greet</u>

<u>Roll 6-1-600</u>

Tight cut sequence (*1' at most*) as Jun meets Amy on the allotment.

02.01 –	Meet + picking courgettes, etc.
04.21	

Then they enter the greenhouse and pick tomatoes . . .

11.05	POV into greenhouse x 2
07.20	Into tomatoes
10.15	C/A plum toms
07.35	Picking tomatoes
09.55	Toms into box
08.17	Amy watches
09.28	P/U re meat T2
10.30	Garlic x 2

. . . before finally choosing from a variety of mints.

15.45	WS into mint
17.00	C/As various mints
14.35	Into mint T4
12.05	Into mint T1 (no words)
12.40	Amy reaction
15.05	C/A picking mint
18.10	C/A Into box

Tight cut sequence as Amy cooks—2 or 3 comedy moments only (around 30–40")

<u>Roll 6-1-600</u>
24.22 et seq.

In particular:

27.08	*'Never even seen these before'**
28.07	*'Don't know what to do . . .'*
28.30	Don't know where to start
30.45	Flinching from fat*
32.56	*'Not how they look when Michael does them'**

<u>Roll 6-1-601</u>

| 03.48 | poking meat—*'a bit pink'—don't know how you're supposed to serve . . .* |
| 05.40 | flapping at smoke alarm * * *(there are loads of smokey shots before this. . . !)* |

Tasting: Jun + Amy comment – esp on 3 things – tough meat is overcooked and not seasoned and everything is too greasy.
06.24 –
12.10

---

basically the 'story order' and will indicate to the Editor which takes of pieces to camera you want to use, which bits of the interview, which actuality sequences, which GV sequences, etc., and where to find them. It could be an adaptation of your pre-shoot script, especially if it is a script-driven piece. And if there are substantial sequences driven by voice-over then it's well worth having at least a first draft of the script for this in your paper edit. You can then hand this over to your Editor, along with a few notes on what kind of style you are looking for and so on, and go and do your shopping. Or you can email it the night before and enjoy a lie-in.

Fig. 14.2 is an example of the kind of thing I send—this is from the same sequence and show as the shot-log. I've indicated the story order, which takes of things if there's more than one, and the story or information I want to get out of it. Sometimes I just give a chunk of actuality, the story I want to tell and the rough duration I'm aiming at. Any half-decent Editor is perfectly capable of assembling something from that and doesn't need to have it spelled out any more. I draw attention to good moments that are worth looking out for—marked with stars—and send it along with the shot-log.

It may be the whole programme you send, or, especially if it's a major documentary, it may be just one section. Your Editor will make this assembly for you, and in the process get some idea of what he's dealing with. You can be looking at the next section while he does this, or choosing music, or whatever.

2 The rough cut

This first assembly is likely to be—indeed it should be—way overlength, probably at this stage anything between 100 and 1,000 per cent depending on how much is scripted. And the cuts should all be parallel, i.e. sound and vision together. There's no point in tweaking or being clever with edits at this stage. That comes later when you have finished the rough cut. The chances are you'll be unpicking an awful lot of this before you're done, and the more you fine-tune it now the more time it takes to undo it, added to the time you've wasted doing the fine cut in the first place.

The process from here on in is one of constant sifting down, tidying up, reorganising and generally bringing your story into focus. Generally speaking you will go through the assembly several times, cutting out repetitions and irrelevancies and always reducing the length towards the target duration.

What you are doing at this stage is creating the overall shape of your programme, just as an artist might do a pencil drawing before he reaches for his palette. You need to sit back and look at what you have at regular intervals to see if it makes sense, just as any artist takes frequent steps back from his easel to see the effect he is creating. You might find yourselves doing major restructures and moving whole chunks of programme around, always looking to tell your story more clearly. If you get stuck into detailed editing at this stage, taking out ums, ers and repetitions or tweaking the visual cuts, then you won't see the wood for the trees. If you know what shots you will use to fill a bit of narration then you can leave a black hole—or at most slot in a couple of examples to get the general idea. The narration is likely to change so don't waste your Editor's time carefully cutting to it.

During this process you are handing over the baton of principal responsibility for the creation of your programme to your Editor. He is the one who will become increasingly immersed in the minutiae of building it while you can gradually step back and be objective. Whatever kind of factual programme you are making, if you have agreed with your Editor what you are trying to achieve there will be a great deal of time at this stage when you can do little to help him. Sitting watching him juggle the material, clicking your fingers where you want every cut and offering your opinion on every change he makes is neither helping the process nor conducive to a good relationship with him.

You will now have ample time to get on with your next major responsibility.

The script

If the piece is to be held together with out-of-vision narration, either by the Presenter or Reporter or an anonymous 'voice of God', then once the story is in an order which you think will make sense it's time to get writing.

I often work alongside the Editor doing this and as a sequence is cut I look at the 'out' words and next 'in' words, then start to piece together the dubbing script.

You might use the pre-shoot script as your starting point but you will almost certainly rewrite it—and rewrite it many more times before the edit is over. Now you will have what your contributors actually said rather than what you thought they might say, and can write links between the interviews and actuality.

The truth is that if you want to get information across accurately and concisely a carefully written script will always be the best way of doing that, but then again a programme consisting entirely of one person's voice, either in or out of vision, is going to struggle to remain interesting. If you have interviewed a contributor who was there doing it then they are likely to engage a great deal more than your anonymous voice telling us about it, but then again they are likely to waffle and not always be entirely clear or concise.

So what tends to happen is a compromise. You allow your contributor to tell their story, but then abridge the bits they don't explain well or concisely with a carefully written voice-over. This aids clarity as well as giving you control over duration, and it also adds a bit of aural variety, which is no bad thing. In reality hardly anyone speaking off the cuff can be as concise as you can with a written script, and the art of good scriptwriting in a factual programme is brevity and accuracy. Every word needs to work effectively and move things on. This is why you will constantly be rewriting it—to make it 'work harder'.

Once you have written your links then record them yourself, or, if you're not good at reading or would prefer a different voice, get your Editor to do this. Then drop the narrations into place and you begin to have a programme which can be looked at. The truth is that with much factual programming the story is told more by voice-over and interview than by visual narrative, so you will tend to create your soundtrack first and your rough cut will often resemble a radio programme. Beware of that. TV is a visual medium and the more the pictures can tell the story, the better. If you have a visually driven sequence—actuality perhaps—then you need to cut the visuals and let them dictate your duration.

Observational documentary

There is, of course, one type of factual programme which is hugely dependent on actuality. The process of cutting observational documentary is broadly the same as cutting something more structured, formatted or scripted, only more so! It is much harder and takes much longer.

A shooting ratio—i.e. material shot to finished programme duration—on a scripted or formatted factual programme is likely to around 10 or 12 to 1, but for ob. doc. it can be 30 to 1 or more. There will be hours and hours of it and it can be more daunting and bewildering than any other kind of programme trying to tease your story out.

You will have come away from the shoot with some idea of what happened and what the story will be, but treat this with caution. More than once I have found that the story which comes out of the rushes differs subtly or even substantially from the one I thought I saw on location. Sometimes you see things in the footage which simply passed you by during filming, and sometimes something which was abundantly evident on location never made it through the lens.

As with any factual, it's about sifting down. To begin with either you or your Editor, or sometimes a junior 'assembly' Editor, will simply go through chucking out all the obvious junk and creating assemblies. These are simply collections of material from any given location or day arbitrarily strung together. There should be no attempt at this stage to create sequences. Then you just have to sit down and watch them through. It's best if your Editor can do this with you—again for those fresh eyes, but also so that they will know the material better and be better placed when they do start to edit it.

The story should now begin to emerge, and once you have agreed what story you are trying to tell then let your Editor get on with it. As I mentioned in Chapter 8, ob. doc. has a language all of its own which has little or nothing to do with continuity or action cuts. You are making your story from a collage of video clips, and if you try to be slavish to chronology or location then you are likely to create enormous problems for yourself and greatly limit what you can say. Real life simply doesn't follow a drama script. When people are having conversations they go round in circles and repeat themselves, or go off at tangents. They might say something tomorrow which relates directly to what someone else said yesterday, and if you try to spell out that chronology in the film then we will have completely forgotten what was said before by the time we get there.

Very few of today's ob. docs. are 'pure', in that most include interview along with the actuality as well as voice-over. Telling a story entirely with observational material is very hard, and even if you just use interview it's a challenge. Essentially the process is about working the interview into the actuality and bridging the gaps with voice-over—much the same as a scripted or structured factual programme. It's just harder to work out what story you are trying to tell and to get the initial assembly to make a kind of sense. If you took my advice and shot interviews with your contributors about the events they were involved in, then it will now pay dividends in that you will have something to underpin your sequences. With this kind of material you and your Editor need to sit back even more regularly and watch what you have to see if it hangs together and flows.

3 First viewings

Whatever kind of factual programme you are cutting, once you have the skeletal structure of your story you should sit back and watch it with the Editor, and possibly also the Series or Executive Producer, depending on the stage at which they wish to see it. It's probably at least 20 per cent overlength, but that's as it should be. There will probably be black holes over the linking narrations and jump cuts galore in the interviews. Your Editor should not yet have put in the reverse questions, non-sync wides or noddies.

Watch it at one sitting without stopping, taking notes and trying to be as objective as you can. Forget what you already know about the story and see if what you have assembled would make sense to a first-time viewer. You will also start to get a feel for the pace of it—where it becomes boring and where it feels rushed. If you do have an S.P. or E.P. watching, resist the temptation to explain things either before, or immediately after, the viewing. They know—or they should know!—what a rough cut is and will assume you have something to fill the black holes and cover the jump cuts. If you don't resist the urge to try to explain the story beforehand then you will undermine their crucial objectivity. The viewer at home will not have you sitting next to them to explain your programme.

The hardest part is listening to what the S.P. or E.P. has to say. It may be that the story would be much clearer if structured in a completely different way. You have been going down a particular road which has probably seemed the only one since you wrote the pre-shoot script, almost certainly since the shoot, but there are always other ways to do things which you and your Editor simply might not have seen—and which might work better.

This is why you should have the programme viewed by an outsider at the rough cut stage. If you need to do a major restructure now, you don't want to have to unpick a whole lot of carefully fine-cut edits and waste hours of work. If it's still all parallel cuts then restructuring is so much easier.

Once everyone is happy with the structure then go through it again and again and again, all the time refining and cutting down. Sometimes you should watch it on a run and take notes, then go back and make the necessary changes. Sometimes you stop every time you see something which needs altering and fix it. If you keep on viewing at a run then you start to become used to it and miss things, while if you look in detail at a sequence you will start to see it in different way, but at the same time if you always do a 'stopping run' you may not see the wood for the trees.

4 Music

Somewhere around this stage you should be starting to design your soundtrack, and this is likely to involve adding some music.

What music?

Obtaining rights for the use of music is a massively complex area beyond the scope of this book fully to explain. With the explosion of distribution methods and outlets it's becoming ever more of a minefield. The Performing Rights Society (PRS) website www.prsformusic.com is well worth a visit to find out more.

Broadly speaking there are three different roads you can go down when choosing music for your film, always assuming that you're not using music from the actuality you have shot—if you are doing that you need to be aware that the question of copyright still needs to be addressed very carefully. Even *Happy Birthday to You* remains in copyright, so bear that in mind if you find yourself filming a birthday party!

The choice of incidental music is likely to be dictated by the Commissioner and/or the production company and be heavily influenced by the budget.

1 Commercial

If you have a favourite track or classical performance you can sometimes use it, depending on the broadcaster or other distribution outlet at which your programme is aimed. The BBC has blanket agreements which can make this easier than with some other broadcasters, but the problem is that obtaining copyright clearance, which has to be done either through PRS or by direct contact with the publisher and record company, can be prohibitively expensive.

2 Library

There are numerous companies which churn out huge amounts of music by largely unknown composers specifically for use in TV and film. The albums are carefully designed and labelled to give a particular feel, be it *Latin American*, *Hip Hop*, *Easy Listening* or *Death and Horror*. Each track is carefully described, and there are usually different orchestrations—for example 'Full Mix and 'Underscore'—and different durations, all designed for ease of use by the programme maker.

Some of it is excellent, much of it is not. A lot of it is designed to be derivative, so that if you would really like to use *Bohemian Rhapsody* but can't afford the copyright, chances are you'll find something which is a thinly disguised rip-off.

This music is available at substantially less cost than commercial music because most if not all broadcasters have pre-existing agreements with the publishers.

3 Specially commissioned

It's not as expensive as it sounds to get your music written specially, and if you find the right composer then it's a very rewarding way of getting exactly the right feel. A good composer can be given a cut of the film and write music to fit it exactly, or he might write a suite of music which you can use variously through your film or series. You will need to agree how many tracks you are expecting, and the up-front cost is not as much as you might think, because composers make the bulk of their income from royalties when the programmes go out.

The great advantage of using specially commissioned music is that you can try what's written, and if the mood, texture or orchestration isn't quite right you tell the composer and it will be altered. You have acquired another creative person to work on your film, and just as a made-to-measure suit will always fit better than one off the peg, you should be able to get pretty much exactly what you need.

Music can do a number of different things for your programme. It isn't, of course, essential and some films work perfectly well without it, but the truth is that most programmes, factual or drama, will use it somewhere.

Music can create a mood or an atmosphere. It can give energy or set your pace. It can support your images to give a sense of place. If you are making a sequence out of several somewhat disparate images—perhaps a work sequence in a make-over show giving the impression of lots of different things happening—it can serve as a kind of egg to bind the pudding. If it's a well-known piece it can make oblique references, but be careful with this—however well you know the piece you cannot rely on all members of your audience picking up the reference.

Some of my students once made a film about drag queens, and so when I heard a burst of the introduction to the Kinks' *Lola* I got it instantly. However, most of their contemporaries were, unsurprisingly, less acquainted with forty-year-old pop music than I am, and so it went completely over their heads. In this instance they used none of the lyrics—had they used some it would have been clear to all.

Another group making a film about some stables used a track which I didn't recognise and which didn't seem to feel right. They pointed out it was called *Wild Horses*—but I didn't know that and the title wasn't in the lyrics, so for me at least, it didn't do what they wanted it to.

If you don't already have your music in mind you should have time while the Editor is rough-cutting to audition some tracks. If you are making one programme in a series chances are the S.P. will have given you a basket of appropriate tracks from which to choose—get to know them so that you can instantly lay your hands on at least a shortlist when you are looking for something. Your Editor needs to familiarise himself with them too and will usually be perfectly happy to make at least some of these decisions for you.

Whether or not the music is right for the sequence under which you want to use it will, of course, always be a subjective decision. Only by running it in and seeing how it feels can you decide for sure. Usually busy or fully orchestrated tracks will not work under speech, and lyrics never will. Your audience will be struggling to hear both and will actually hear neither. You might get away with it if the lyrics are in a language which is foreign to the majority of your audience, but there will always be someone in the audience who speaks that language, so it's still best to avoid the clash.

Music should be used carefully and sparingly—it can very quickly become irritating. Remember that it is almost always supporting your visuals and audio, rarely driving them, unless you're making a music video. As a very general rule—not a rule at all really but a starting point for considering how to use music—I would consider using it under a visual montage where there is no voice, or under an out-of-vision voice-over sequence, but rarely under a piece to camera or an interview. In drama it can help a visual sequence, but be very careful using it under dialogue. In a nutshell, if it isn't doing anything to support the film in terms of adding mood or atmosphere or telling the story you should lose it. Thirty seconds is a long piece in television terms—usually you will use snippets far shorter than that.

It will always add elegance to your film if the music is carefully crafted in. Your Editor will be happy to cut images to it, remembering that cutting a whole sequence of shots of the same length on the same beat quickly becomes boring. Cut on different beats, and bear in mind that what happens in the shot can also be synced with the music to good effect.

If you are weaving the music in with speech, wait for the musical phrase to finish then dip it under the next bit of speech, and if you can bring up a new phrase as the speech ends it will always sound better. Of course unless your music has been specially written, it will be up to chance whether it will fit, but there is an old trick I have used regularly to achieve this. As the first phrase ends, dip it quickly to a level low enough to run under the speech then, so slowly as to be imperceptible, gradually dip it away to nothing. If you then find the start of the next phrase and 'pre-fade' it—i.e. sync it with the end of the speech—you can edge it in from nothing just after the previous one has gone and then swell it after the speech as the new phrase begins. No one will notice that you've taken a tuck in it and it will always sound better than simply dipping it and bringing it up again wherever it happens to be.

If you are using lyrics to tell your story make sure first of all that they are clearly audible, and secondly that once you have got your audience listening the rest of the words are appropriate. It's easy to be seduced by a title or line in a song which fits your story but all too often only that line works.

5 Teases and recaps

You should now have a programme within throwing distance of the correct duration—say 10–15 per cent over—which is telling the story the way you want to. If it's too short then you have cause to be alarmed. There's nothing worse than shovelling up the metaphorical sweepings from the cutting-room floor to pad it out.

There's one more job to be done before you start your fine cut. Every factual programme on TV will begin with some kind of tease or trailer, setting out the stall to give a taste of what the film is about and what exciting treats there are to come in order to encourage the viewer to stay with it. This often runs before the title. Don't be tempted to start to tell the story—just introduce it and give a flavour along with a couple of your strongest clips. These days watching television is a very different experience from going to the cinema. Few if any of your viewers will be sitting on the sofa ready and waiting for your film. They'll have the remote control in one hand and will be flicking through the channels, and if you pitch straight in with a lot of detail they won't be ready to engage and will soon continue searching. Even if they are a captive audience they need to have their attention engaged gently. In the same way as it's vital to get the first paragraph of a book right, so you will spend a lot of time tweaking your tease.

I began my TV career in BBC Presentation making trailers, and in a sense this is what you are making. When I first started the job I made the mistake, like so many, of feeling a responsibility to explain the story, so I would write a paragraph to set it all up before showing the first clip. I soon learned that the clips are what it is about. Find the good clips and write the minimum possible to clarify the meaning. And when editing the clips, 'latest in—earliest out' is the rule, i.e. find the one phrase or soundbite which is the essence of the clip and forget preamble and repetition. The ideal trailer consists of the clips together with just enough voice-over to tell the viewer the title of the programme, which channel it's on and when.

Over time I found a very simple way to pick out the best clips. Of course I would have to view the programmes, and I would usually take notes about useful establishing shots, close-ups of the characters or well-known actors which might come in handy, and so on. And if there were strong dramatic lines or good visuals I would note them too. Then I would put my notes away until just before I came to edit the trailer. At this point I would see which bits of the programme I remembered, and as often as not they were the meat of the trailer.

I would recommend using a similar technique when making the tease for your factual programme. You have by now seen what has made the cut. Which bits do you remember? Ask your Editor for his opinion too. Then, when you have selected two or three of your strongest clips, all you need to do is write just enough script to string them together and give a flavour of your film.

If your programme is for a commercial channel and will have ad breaks, then those remote controls dictate another element you will need to add at this point—the teases and recaps. Each part will have to end with a tease for what's coming up in the next part, which in turn will begin with a recap of what happened in the previous one. These can drive you nuts and soak up substantial amounts of your available duration, requiring you to dump good content in their favour, but they are unavoidable, so do them now and you will know where you are in terms of duration and won't have to cut out chunks of fine-cut material later to make room for them.

So now you've got the structure right, the first of your fresh pairs of eyes—probably the Series or Executive Producer—has seen and approved it and you're within throwing distance of the right duration. It's time to move on to the next stage.

6 The fine cut

It's at this stage, and not before, that your Editor should be adding the reverse questions, noddies and non-sync wides to the interviews, trimming the sound edits to make them sweet and adding those J- and L-cuts. These are where you stagger the sound and vision cuts to make the edits less noticeable.

It's usual but not, of course, essential to disguise cuts in an interview. Although the convention always used to be to make it look as though the interview is running in real time, as shot, increasingly these days people know about editing and accept the honesty of a dissolve (which will only work if the camera was on a tripod and locked off), a quick fade to black and back, or even a white flash to own up to your edit. The traditional noddies can look very phoney and old-fashioned, especially if your interviewer is actually nodding rather than just listening.

If you can illustrate your interview with cutaways of whatever is being talked about then always use more than one. One arbitrary shot pasted obviously over the cut will draw attention to it, but if you go away from the talking head for at least three then it will feel as though you are illustrating the interview, not just wallpapering the cuts. And always try to make a sequence, not just a collection of shots. Once you have established your contributor or your Presenter in vision for a few seconds we know who they are and are happy no longer to see their face, but beware leading with the sound of a contributor for more than a few seconds before you see them in vision, particularly on first appearance. We will always listen more carefully once we know who is talking to us.

Pacing is another thing to get right at this stage. It's all too easy, especially when you are struggling to get a programme to time, to take out all the pauses and cram in every-thing you can, but doing that will make your film indigestible. Imagine reading this book with no paragraphs or subject headings. A solid page of type is daunting and hard to read, so we prefer it broken up. It's the same on screen. Let your film breathe. Always remember that this is a visual medium first and foremost. As a general rule, every time you change location, introduce a new contributor or in any way start a new paragraph of your story allow three good seconds before you bring in any speech. Introduce your new story with some images, and perhaps some music or atmosphere. If you have actuality sequences let them stand alone by way of introduction. Let the interview come in to support or explain the actuality rather than using the actuality as cutaways for your interview.

Again it's likely that your Editor will be happiest left alone to get on with the fine cut—it's where his art is at its most refined and he's unlikely to thank you for sitting there watching and commenting. Of course you must look at it when it's finished, but not until then.

Fine-tuning the script

This is time you can usefully spend refining your script. As with all creative work, revisiting something you have done after a certain amount of time has elapsed gives you an objectivity and an ability to see more clearly what is good and what isn't. Make sure every word works towards the required meaning—that what you are saying is entirely clear and links what is said by your contributors without repeating or contradicting anything. Look out for 'fossils'. As you continually sub down your film it's easy to leave bits of script which refer or relate to something which is no longer in the cut. You might now be setting something up at much greater length and complexity than you need to. Always simplify if you can.

Listen to the tone of what you have written. The anonymous voice-over will usually be neutral—a source of necessary information but no more. If it's an in-vision Presenter or Reporter that's a different matter—there is a personality on display who is entitled to his or her opinion. If you are writing a script for such a Presenter you need to keep their voice very much in your head as you write—or, if you can, give them the outline of the script as necessitated by the cut and let them write it in their own words. However, as the anonymous, or 'voice of God' Narrator never shows their face there's an argument that they should, like a Newsreader, keep their opinions to themself. They are effectively the voice of the programme, given a kind of Big Brother-like automatic authority. This needs to be used with caution or the result can sound arrogant. If this person has an opinion, why doesn't he or she have the courage to come out in front of the camera to express it?

Some programmes look for a wry observational tone, gently teasing the characters in the programme. This can lift the narration out of simple dry information and make your programme much more human and engaging, but I would urge you to use such an approach with caution and avoid the cynical, patronising tone which can result from going too far down this road.

There is a clear moral issue here—just because someone has agreed to appear in your programme it does not give you the right to judge or make fun of them, and if you do you will alienate your audience. There is an unpleasant fashion at the moment, especially with programmes looking back to earlier ages of TV, of constantly laughing and sneering at what earlier ages enjoyed. Just because it's old it doesn't mean it's a joke and you will offend elements of your audience if you appear to take that view. Of course platform heels and Bay City Rollers trousers look comical to most of us now, but let your viewers make their own judgement and don't tell them what to think.

As I suggested earlier, as a programme-maker you have a moral obligation to those who have helped you make it. It's all too easy to exploit and make fun of people once they have signed that release form, but your audience is not insensitive to this.

I have mentioned earlier the Channel 5 series I made called *The Boss is Coming to Dinner*, following the fortunes of candidates applying for a job through the rather unusual process of inviting their potential boss to dinner rather than visiting him in his office. Although it was basically a reality show there was an important difference in the amount of control we had over the choice of contributors. With a true reality show people volunteer themselves and so it could be argued that they should realise what they are letting themselves in for, though the production company must make this very clear. With this show we were simply gatecrashing the process of a real candidate applying for a real job, and I think that fundamentally altered our moral position.

There was one young man applying for a job who really didn't do well at his interview. He was a very intelligent and committed guy, but not really suited to this particular job. It would have been easy to laugh at his embarrassment when asked to demonstrate particular skills, and arguably we should not even have shown such uncomfortable moments, but then that's what makes good telly—human drama. When scripting this programme I was careful to avoid laughing at him or saying anything which could damage his confidence—after all, he fully deserved to go out and get himself the right job without having been made a fool of on national TV. I was also careful to include a compliment from the boss even as he rejected him.

By contrast we also filmed a young woman who had heard about the TV interview and fancied the idea of being on telly but had no interest whatsoever in the job. Her interview was textbook 'how not to get a job' in that she admitted she had no interest in the position and was merely looking for a temporary means of earning money while she pursued her true ambitions. Although I still had a moral duty not to pillory her I did take the view that, given her approach to the whole process, she deserved to be shown up much more than the young man did.

It's a hard line to tread and can be a real minefield. You have to make the programme entertaining but you do have a duty of care to your contributors. One litmus test you can apply to this is to ask yourself if you would be happy to watch the programme with your contributor sitting next to you. If the answer to that is 'no', then consider very carefully what right you have to treat them in the way you have. It's one thing to stitch up a rogue trader but if you're making fun of someone just because they're a TV 'wannabe' or because they happened into your programme by chance that's quite another.

7 Final viewings

Once your Editor has completed his fine cut you'll need to re-record and drop in any revised guide-track voice-overs and, if necessary, tweak the edit to accommodate them. One word of warning here—if you know who will being do your voice-over for real then listen to their voice. As suggested earlier, this will help you to get the tone right for them, but it will also give you an idea of the pace at which they read, which might be significantly faster or slower than you, or whoever else is doing your guide-track. I have a habit of reading quite quickly, which has caused problems in the past when recording the final narration and necessitated hasty rewrites in the dubbing suite. I now recognise this so I make myself slow down and ensure that my Editor cuts loosely round my narration.

Next, watch the complete programme with your Editor. There will undoubtedly be tweaks that you want to make to his fine-cut, so do those now, but resist the temptation to get it down to time. You still have at least two all-important viewings to go and it is practically unheard of for a programme to survive these without the requirement for further changes. If you have your programme running to the correct duration this will be messed up by the changes and you might end up having to put stuff back in, which is never a good feeling! Much better to get all the required changes done, then you can trim it down to time yourself once everyone's happy.

Decisions about who will do the viewings at this stage and how many there will be vary according to the set-up in the production company, but broadly speaking there will be at least one senior member of the production company staff who will want to ensure they are happy for the show to go forward to the commissioner, and then the final viewing(s) with the Commissioning Editor him or herself.

It is commonplace, if not usual, for the viewing to take place in the edit suite. This has pros and cons. The advantage is that you and the Editor are both there and can explain the reasoning behind any decisions taken, quickly let the viewer(s) know whether the changes they would like to make are possible—whether the material is available, etc.—and ideally end the session with a clear plan of action. The disadvantage is that the viewing can take a huge chunk out of your editing day—the duration of the programme plus at least the same again in discussion about it afterwards—and this is time which the Editor could usefully be using to continue to tweak and polish the cut.

The alternative is to let the viewer see it elsewhere—usually these days via an internet link in their office—with the edit continuing while this is happening. The disadvantage is that you will get lots of notes back which may or may not make sense to you, requiring changes that may or may not be possible for whatever reason. You then have to negotiate by phone or email with the viewer about what you are or are not going to be able to do. A good solution to this is for you to attend the viewing with the Executive Producer and/or the Commissioning Editor in their office, leaving the Editor to continue polishing the cut. That way you can discuss and agree changes without wasting his time.

The last viewing—usually just a day or two away from the end of the offline edit—will be with the Commissioning Editor. He or she will have the final say on whether the programme is acceptable for broadcast, and will have ultimate power over your programme. While you are trying to make something you find engaging and watchable they have other considerations, such as what audience the channel is trying to attract at that time and what the competition is offering. Their responsibility is to deliver the best ratings they can, and that isn't always achieved using the criteria by which you have been working.

I referred earlier to *Return to Tuscany*, the series I made for BBC2 Daytime about Italian food and lifestyle. The intention during filming was to make a gentle series where each programme would contain some information about food and cooking as well as a look at events and towns around the area of southern Tuscany where we were based. But by the time we came to cut it Channel 4 was cleaning up the ratings with a new series, *Deal or No Deal*—a game show hosted by Noel Edmonds. We were therefore required to fill our shows with as much 'jeopardy' as we could in order to compete with this.

Jeopardy has become the buzzword of popular television, particularly factual entertainment. Basically it is what used to be called a 'cliffhanger'. Nowadays every part of every factual entertainment show has to be liberally laced with suggestions of risk or danger in order to keep the viewer watching to discover the outcome. Find me a *Grand Designs* or any makeover show which doesn't allude to some risk of running late or going over budget! The technique is clear and its purpose evident, but taken to extremes it can render the programmes risible.

So ours became all about 'Will the bread rise?' 'Will lunch be late again?' 'Will the cookery students make a mess of dinner?' Up against the Noel Edmonds high-risk game show it was rather like a Ford Fiesta competing at Le Mans, but that was what the channel wanted and we had to comply. So brace yourself for the Commissioning Editor's viewing, and remember the job they have to do.

An important thing to remember about Commissioning Editors is that few of them have any programme-making experience themselves. I once sat through a final viewing with a Commissioning Editor of a show I had made which was more or less a completely scripted piece with just a few interviews. This Comm. Ed. had seen and signed off the script some weeks previously, before we had begun the shoot, but, after seeing the fine cut of the programme, now pretty much to time, suggested inserting a new sequence. This hadn't been in the original signed-off script so we hadn't shot such a sequence. It was suggested that we could cobble something together out of offcuts with a bit of voice-over, but to do so we would have had to rip out some of the carefully crafted sequences which had been signed off. No-one with any real understanding of how programmes are made could have come up with such an idea.

Commissioning Editors have often worked their way up the ladder to these very senior and influential positions via office-based routes but underneath it all they have a lurking but unfulfilled desire to make programmes. They find themselves in a position of hire and fire over the creative people in the production companies and sometimes seek to satisfy those unfulfilled ambitions by telling the programme-makers how to make their programmes, dictating who should and should not work on them, particularly in terms of the Director. Some channels even have an approved list of Directors from which all productions companies must select their staff. Some Commissioning Editors will then rewrite your script for you and tell you exactly which shots you should put where in order to deliver the programme they want to see.

Does the owner of a restaurant walk into the kitchen and advise the Michelin-starred chef how to improve his sauce Béarnaise? I think not. He might comment that it isn't tasting good but it's up to the chef to use his expertise to put it right. How would you feel about the hospital manager deciding that he will take out your appendix because he always wanted to be a surgeon and he's further up the pile than the registrar?

The job of a Commissioning Editor, I believe, is to commission talented programme makers to make programmes which will work for the channel. So, in my view, they should begin by making absolutely clear what they want, then look at and comment on the work they get back and say what they are and are not happy with. They should then leave the experienced programme makers—the P/D the S.P. and the E.P.—to make appropriate changes.

Sadly this is not always what happens. I once worked on a new series which was still being shaped as we shot it. First of all the brief was changed while I was shooting my episode (No. 2 in the series). Then episode 1 overran its two-week edit by six weeks, with the Commissioning Editor viewing one day and leaving four pages of changes to be made, only for the Head of Features to view it the next and require all those changes to be undone and another four pages' worth to be effected. In the end it was recut no fewer than twenty-six times. I abandoned my show after its two-week offline edit and couldn't bring myself to see what had been done to it by the time it was transmitted. It came as no surprise that the series was not recommissioned.

Of course not all Commissioning Editors are like that—there are those who recognise what their job is and what it is not and will genuinely improve your programme by observing it with fresh eyes at the viewing. While they are not programme makers, they will be the first 'lay people' to see it more or less as the viewing public will see it.

You may well find yourself biting your tongue and gently screaming inside at viewings, but don't let that blind you to what is being said. The comments made are likely to have been triggered by something which isn't working, even if the suggested change isn't the right one. Remember that if you need to explain or justify something in your programme then the chances are it isn't clear. Your Commissioning Editor may not be the smartest viewer who will see it, but neither will he be the dimmest!

So listen to what is being said and, if you see an alternative solution to the problem identified, try it. If the Comm. Ed. still comes back with an insistence on their fix then you have to do as you're told. And it may well be that the E.P., with an eye on future commissions and anxious therefore not to upset the applecart, will have insisted you do this anyway. So swallow your pride, take the money and run, and remember that the TV industry is a relatively small business where a reputation for being difficult travels quickly. Also remember that one of the joys of the freelance life you will be leading is that you can choose who you work with in future.

There will always be changes of some kind from all the final viewings. Some of them will be completely irrelevant and made simply because someone in the food chain feels the need to justify their position. An old trick used by some Editors and Directors when faced with this risk is deliberately to leave something irrelevant or repetitious in the cut for a viewing. That way the viewer can make their mark by suggesting the change without damaging the rest of the programme!

Whatever changes are requested you have to make them if you can, and when you have done so to the satisfaction of all concerned then simply trim the programme—which by now shouldn't be more than 5 per cent overlength—to the required duration, which these days is sometimes prescribed down to the second. You can always find a repetition, a bit of unnecessary information or general chit-chat which is not essential to the story, but resist the temptation to take out all the pauses, or tighten all the gaps, for the reasons stated previously.

You might need to run this final cut past the relevant people again, but once it's all signed off you have 'picture lock'. At this stage there could still be tweaks to the script, but it will have been agreed that these will not alter the duration. From your point of view the programme is now as good as finished, and you may or may not find yourself still hired for the final two processes through which it must go. This tends to depend on the budget and how busy the S.P. is!

15 Cutting Drama

Much of the process of cutting drama is similar or identical to cutting factual. You need to be thoroughly organised, and the object of the exercise is to tell the story clearly and effectively. And in just the same way you should trust and listen to the fresh eyes and ears of your Editor. It may be that you remember distinctly the sense of achievement when you finally got your actor to deliver the correct emphasis in take 6, but your Editor might see clearly that the spontaneity was gone after take 3.

Provided that there have been good channels of communication between the shoot and the edit—principally in terms of the P.A. taking and passing on copious notes about which takes to use and why—the drama edit can, and often does, run concurrently with the shoot. This might give the opportunity to pick up a shot or retake something while the crew are still on location, athough you shouldn't rely on that.

It's not unlikely that your first arrival in the edit suite will be to see the rough cut. If the Editor has been furnished with a script fully marked up with which takes are available and preferred for what, then he will be perfectly capable of assembling the kit of parts you have shot into something ready to watch.

As with a factual programme, you need to look at pace, mood, atmosphere, whether the best performances are on the screen and, most important of all, whether the story is clear. Assuming you have timed your script correctly at the outset then there shouldn't be major issues on the duration, though it's likely you will have to tweak it into the allocated time slot.

One of the principal differences between directing for the stage and for the screen is that on stage your job is to ensure that the actors clarify the story and focus the audience's attention where it needs to be focused, while on screen you are the one who has complete control of where the audience will look. You can give them as much or as little information as you want, as and when you want but a lot of the time you will be showing them what they want or expect to see. If a character turns to look in another direction then immediately we want to know what they see. Such a cut is motivated, and because it takes us where we want to go we don't notice it. The move on which you are cutting might be almost imperceptible—a flick of the eyes perhaps—but subconsciously it will trigger and so disguise the edit. Remember the invisibility of good direction? Good editing is part of that and should be equally invisible.

If you're cutting a dialogue scene then the obvious way to cut it is to show the person who is doing the talking. But think carefully. Is that the person we want to look at? A man is confessing to his girlfriend that he has slept with her best friend. What are we most interested in? His embarrassment or guilt might be of some interest, but surely first and foremost we want to know how she takes the news.

Reaction shots can be hard to get, especially from inexperienced actors who tend to work too hard, but they are often the most crucial in the scene. For an example of what an experienced actor can do take a look at Colin Firth in *A Single Man* during and after the phone call he receives telling him about the death of his lover. Or Tilda Swinton in *We Need to Talk About Kevin* as she arrives at the school and tries to comprehend what her son has done. This latter is a classic example of how an effective reaction shot can be more powerful than the expected shot of what someone is looking at, because it creates the image in our imagination. Radio is often described as having the best pictures for this very reason.

If you have different sizes of shot in your scene then think how you will use them. The effect of going into a tighter shot will always be to increase intensity, especially if you 'punch down the line', i.e. cut to a tighter shot without changing angle, so don't just go into the CU because you've used the MS three times already. Save it for the moment when your character is under more pressure, receives the vital news, has to make a decision or whatever. And cutting to a looser shot will reduce tension, so again use that—don't just come back to the wide because you're bored with the CU. If someone stands up or moves then that cues a looser shot, and so on. As with choosing your shots when filming, you need to ensure that at every moment the editing supports what is happening in a constructive way and moves your story on.

1 Real time and screen time

One thing you can easily do in your edit is to telescope action. You will regularly be shortening the time it takes to do something. You might think that making a cup of tea is a quick job and once the kettle has boiled you can show as it happens, but in reality it probably takes around a minute. On screen you will do it in ten seconds or less or you will have a very boring film! That is why you will have taken a shot of the maker's face, of the bag going into the cup, of the kettle being picked up, of the fridge being opened and the milk being removed, of the milk going into the cup, and so on. Assemble these shots in the right order at a fraction of their actual duration and the viewer will totally buy it and not even realise the action has been telescoped.

You don't need to and indeed you shouldn't be literal about continuity in that regard. If someone walks into a house, down the hall and into the kitchen to speak to the occupant, in reality it might take ten seconds. On screen, once they're in the door the next shot is the kitchen and we will accept them instantly walking in.

Equally you can extend time. We've all seen the thirty-second countdown to the bomb going off, which actually lasts about two minutes on screen by cutting round all the people and things relevant to the story as the tension is built. If it was all cut in real time there would be little or no tension. Real time and screen time are not the same. A good simple illustration of this is cutting a sequence of someone switching on a light. In reality the finger hits the switch and the light is on. On screen the first shot is finger on switch, the next is the light coming on—and if there isn't a moment of darkness first then it won't seem real. It's all artifice, but the more skilful the artifice the less it seems like it.

2 Transitions and effects

Most screen drama is naturalistic, and so with drama most of your transitions are going to be cuts, because that is the least noticeable way to change shot. As soon as you depart from the cut you introduce an element of obvious artifice which will work against that sense of naturalism. Dissolves and wipes can have a place but use them carefully, usually to denote the passage of time or a change of scene. The same is true of effects like jump cuts, locked-off shots or montages. All these can help to tell your story, but not in the middle of a dialogue scene—they are all devices which should be used separately because they work in a different way. If you throw a jump cut or dissolve into the middle of a naturalistic dialogue scene then you risk jarring the viewer out of their involvement in what is going on. It becomes Brechtian in that you are flagging up the artifice of your medium.

Of course, as mentioned before, there are shooting styles prevalent today, inspired by observational documentary techniques, where the cuts do seem to jump and cross the line without compunction. If you establish that style then the audience will come to accept it, just as they now do ob. doc., but you will note that shows shot like this are carefully choreographed. Bad continuity will still spoil the illusion. In that sense they're not at all like ob.doc., where continuity is a non-starter.

Whatever style you go for it's important to maintain consistency so that you take your audience with you. If you do something strange or inconsistent with the rest of your film, then you will throw them. Remember, they haven't come to admire your work but to get involved in a good story.

3 The illusion of truth

With good, experienced and consistent actors the edit should be a joy. If you've shot it right then you should have a perfectly matching set of jigsaw pieces you can arrange to tell the story to most effect. As I suggested in Part 1, good acting is about truth, and it's that truth you are seeking to present on the screen. Be careful not to destroy it in the edit. As with factual, you need to take careful note of the pacing. If you're tight for time it's tempting to take out all the gaps and tighten the whole programme up, but this can destroy your actors' natural rhythms and render the scene totally unconvincing.

You can also create that truth in the edit, and sometimes this is necessary. If you have inexperienced and inconsistent actors they may do something different in every take. Others may be perfect in one of the takes but the shot isn't the best to use at that point in the scene. If you have young children you will certainly assemble the performance in the edit. As suggested during the shoot, generally you have to take what you can from kids and see what you can make of it in the cutting room.

4 Music

Music can be a useful tool in drama, as in factual, but it will almost always be there to create mood or atmosphere, rarely (with the exception of opera or musicals) to tell the story. So it needs to be subtle, and it's likely to be thinly scored. Beware of running it under whole dialogue scenes—it can become very intrusive. And remember that it can only support the work of your actors—it can't do it for them.

If you can, get the music specially written—it's far more likely to work and, more importantly, to fit.

5 Getting it to time

When you come to trim your drama to its slot, perhaps only by a minute or two at most, you will have more problems than with a factual programme because you are working with a carefully structured script as well as continuity. While in reality people hesitate, 'um' and 'er' and repeat themselves, in drama they don't. And you can't just take a chunk out of a scene if your actors have moved during it. Chances are you'll get it out of the beginning or end of a scene, out of an establishing shot or out of an extended visual sequence. You might be able to lose a few superfluous lines of dialogue if at least one of your actors hasn't moved.

4 Viewings

You'll have the same series of viewings for drama as you will for factual, but given that the script will have been signed off before you started filming you shouldn't be looking at major structural changes. Again what has to be assessed is whether the story comes across. You know it intimately—what needs to be established is whether the viewer will understand it and be engaged by it.

16 Final Processes

1 The tracklay

Once you have finished your work your Editor has to tidy up the soundtracks ready for the dub. He will have done a rough mix already for viewing purposes, and if yours is a low-budget programme which won't be going through a dub he will do a final 'music and effects' mix—of all the tracks apart from the guide narration. This he will strip out, or at least drop down to a spare track.

If it is going to a dub then he needs to ensure that all the tracks needed to create the final mix are in place. This is where he'll add those wildtracks you recorded in the noisy environments and any additional effects you might want to put in. He will create a series of tracks—six, eight or more—at full level, removing any 'ramps' he put in for the viewing mix. He will then export those tracks on to a separate card or disk ready to be taken into the dub. The job can easily take half, or even a whole day for a half-hour programme depending on how much time he has had to tracklay as he goes. So remember to leave time for this process at the end of your offline edit, even though you don't need to be there yourself.

2 The online

Once picture lock has been agreed and the tracklay done the programme can go to the next process, which is often done by a different Editor. If it has been cut at low resolution to save computer space it will be 'conformed', which means that all the pictures will be replaced with full broadcast resolution images taken directly from your rushes.

Next the Online Editor will go through it shot by shot, colour-grading—i.e. correcting any discrepancies in colour and luminance which have resulted from varying light levels or poor colour balancing.

He will also add any captions and graphics required, including title sequences, name straps for Presenters and contributors, and closing credits. This is not a job you necessarily need to be there for, and it may be that your contract has already ended and the Series Producer is taking care of it. However, if you are in charge of this process then your responsibilities are basically to approve the graphics. If yours is one episode in a series the style of these will already have been agreed, but make sure you're happy with the positioning and legibility. It's surprisingly hard sometimes to find a colour and typeface which will read clearly, especially over a busy shot.

Do make sure you leave words on the screen long enough to be read. You might be a speed reader, and you know what they say anyway because you wrote them. A good rule of thumb is to read every word out loud at a steady pace. If the caption has disappeared before you've finished, it isn't up long enough. The same should be true of closing credits, but sadly in these days you won't get that luxury. Although they are important to you and your colleagues as vouchers for the next job, the fact is there will be channel stipulations on their duration and they will whizz through frame at such a speed that if your granny wants to catch your name she'll have to record and freeze-frame it! In addition, once the programme is transmitted the chances are that the credits will shrink back to a minuscule box in the corner of the screen while the next programme is being promoted. So you'll just have to tell granny you directed it. She'll believe you—she's your granny!

One vital thing you must do with captions is to check the spelling slowly and carefully. If I had a pound for every time a misspelled caption has been checked by me, the Series Producer, the Editor and the Dubbing Mixer and still made it on air . . .! It's easily done, and even if you never learned to spell at school, you have a spellchecker on your computer. Spelling does still matter and it's your responsibility if you are charged with supervising the online.

Once you get the graphics sorted you can leave the Editor to do the colour balancing, but you will need to do a final review at the end of the process. It's very easy at this stage to switch off your brain because you've seen the wretched programme so often you feel you know—and are probably just beginning to hate—every frame, but do concentrate. This is your last chance to pick up errors of any kind in the pictures. If necessary, minor tweaks can still be made at the online stage.

3 The dub

This will consist of two processes—recording the narration and the final mix. Again the Series Producer will often take care of this process, but it's good if you can be there, at least for the narration.

Narration

One of your jobs—and during the tracklay and online processes you will have plenty of time to do it—is to tidy up the script you have been writing in the edit and convert it into a dubbing script. Basically this means removing all but the words which your Narrator has to say and adding the words which immediately precede his cues and those which follow. You should also add timecodes for all cues. Having the 'in' and 'out' cues there as well means that he can see how his words make sense with what comes before and after—this might well affect emphasis.

Choosing your voice

If it's one of a series then the decision about who will voice your film will already have been made. If there's an in-vision Presenter or two then it's likely to be them. It isn't always so—some are fine working with each other and the contributors but don't cope well working to camera or doing voiceover, and in such cases there will be a separate anonymous voice doing the latter.

Doing narration well is a much harder job than some might believe, which is why the same voices tend to be heard regularly. A good voice-over artist can make a serious amount of money, but there are an awful lot of indifferent ones and wannabes, not to mention Directors who fancy themselves in the role and do it themselves. There are agencies with hundreds of would-be Narrators on their books, most of whom get little or no work.

The primary requirement is, of course, a good rich voice, and the brutal truth is that men's voices—primarily baritone rather than tenor—tend to work better than female ones simply because the pitch and timbre of the voice tends to cut through better. But there are some excellent female voices—again more likely to be contralto than soprano—and it's a very good idea to use one if, for example, most of your contributors are male, because the secondary requirement is that the voice should be easily distinguishable from those of the contributors and/or Presenters.

Received pronunciation is again something of a norm but doesn't need to be. Scottish accents are very popular—Bill Paterson does a lot, for example—and Paul Copley's rich Lancashire worked very well on *How Clean is Your House?*

The most important feature of the voice is that it needs to be interesting and engaging, and that means that its owner needs to be interested and engaged in the programme. Far too many artists get work on the strength of their plummy tones and rich vowels, but run throughout the programme on autopilot without taking an interest in the material or what they are saying. At the same time there's a tendency for programmes aimed at younger audiences to use a youngster who will go at the script full tilt with maximum energy, too often all at the same pitch, and quickly become exhausting to listen to.

You need someone who can offer variety in their pitch and tone—who can work with a smile in their voice when they need to, adding urgency, authority or sadness as required by your programme. Listen for repetitive, especially falling, inflexions which become very dull on the ear. A lot of voice-over artists are actors, who should have acquired the ability to vary their pitch from their training and experience. They tend to work better as voice-over artists than as in-vision Presenters because there is more of a performance involved. That said, beware of those who overact. Like the Presenter, the voice should be your friend who guides you through the programme, giving you the information you need. At the end of the day they're telling you a story, and they need to be interested in that story if the audience is going to be.

It's good to try to discover new voices rather than going with the tried and tested ones. I would recommend listening very carefully to any work they've done and, if possible, auditioning them. As with an actor, see if you can direct them to do it differently.

Recording the narration

It will save you time if you have given your voice-over artist the script beforehand. They should read it and have some sense of what it is all about before the session begins. If you can send a DVD or link to the programme too, that's no bad thing. The truth is they might not look at either, but at least if you've sent it to them they'll have no excuse!

Before you start, establish any particular thoughts you have about tone and pace. If you are working with a Presenter who was there on the shoot this will, of course, already have been established, but if it's an anonymous voice doing your show as a one-off, or the first in a series, then you need to clarify this from the outset.

Your artist will work in a soundproof booth, looking at the pictures on a monitor and listening to the recorded sound on the programme through headphones. Some like to hear a bit of their own voice coming back too and this is something your Dubbing Mixer can arrange for them. Some can also cope with listening to your guide-track, but most will find this distracting, though it can be a handy reference if you hit an impasse on narration, or the sense of something. Normally there will be a green light on the desk which you will operate to give cues. You should also have switched talkback to them. Be careful to establish this with your Dubbing Mixer before you start. You don't want to let rip with unflattering comments only to discover you're on open talkback and your artist can hear every word!

Try the first few lines of the script, just to warm up the voice and get into the swing of things, as well as to enable the Dubbing Mixer to ensure the positioning of the mic and the level are correct. Then, if you're happy with what you're hearing, you may as well go for a recording. Chances are you'll go back and record the opening cues again at the end of the session because by then your artist will be in their stride, but record them anyway just to get things under way.

Generally speaking the narration will flow better if you can let the programme run so that your artist can hear what he's fitting into, but time will often prevent that and usually you will need to skip from cue to cue just to get it in the can quickly. So it's up to you to make sure it's making sense. Listen carefully for intonation—if your voice is mentioning something which has just been referred to by your contributor then it will need a different emphasis, and if you know that to be the case then get the Dubbing Mixer to give enough run-in for the Narrator to hear what he's following on from.

If you aren't playing the whole programme there is a risk that your Narrator will start to run on autopilot—saying the words, even making sense of them, but not really engaging with the material or the spirit of the programme at that point. The Narrator's job is to guide the viewer through the programme and some empathy with what the viewer will be experiencing at that point is important, so if you hear that autopilot slipping in don't be afraid to stop and direct him. Give some indication of where we are in the show and what is going on. Sometimes two or three shows will be recorded at one sitting, and inevitably this can result in a lack of definition setting in. So maybe you just need to take a coffee break and swap a few yarns to refresh everyone.

When you are directing a Narrator, at all costs avoid saying 'say it like this'. It's insulting to your artist and counterproductive. He's doing the work, not you. If it's an emphasis problem, which is quite common, explain the sense of it and let him find his own solution. If he really can't get it he might ask you to demonstrate, but don't do it uninvited if you want to stay friends. It might be that he is very inexperienced, in which case it will have the unhelpful effect of destroying his confidence.

Sometimes an artist will get a 'thing' about a certain line—either they just can't get the emphasis right, or maybe they get the giggles. If this happens, then leave it, move on and come back to it later. Sometimes a slight rewrite can resolve the problem.

Chances are you will have to do some rewriting. Maybe the artist isn't comfortable with what you've written, and that's normal. We all say things in different ways. You might be a Nobel Prize-winning author but it doesn't mean that yours are the only suitable words when they're coming from someone else's mouth. And you might find that some of the cues just don't fit because you read them at a different speed. An experienced Narrator should have the ability to vary pace, but there comes a point when it will just sound rushed and forced. Much better to tweak it slightly.

As a last resort most modern mixing desks have a facility to lengthen or shorten a bit of media, and this can get you out of a hole, but don't rely on it. You can certainly use the facility to shift a cue up or down the timeline. Often the artist will pick up a cue a fraction late and crash the incoming words. If the take was good don't make them do it again, just shift the cue back.

Often it will be the Presenter who does the voice-over, and it's surprising how many of these really aren't good at it. As I suggested in Part 1, a good Presenter is likely to be an engaging expert in their field. They might be hugely watchable when enthusing about their subject on camera, but that doesn't mean they can read well. All too often when you put your script in front of them they become dull and it sounds dreadfully 'read'. You should certainly have given them an opportunity beforehand to put it into their own words, and if it still sounds flat it's even worth trying to get them to improvise in the booth. They have the advantage over the anonymous voice of knowing the material, and so should be able to tell the story from that position of knowledge. But if you need to do this, allow more time.

The final mix

This is the last process in the making of your programme, during which any additional music or effects will be added and all the sound mixed down, usually to one stereo track.

Sadly, in these straitened times the final mix is all too often victim of a tight budget and the Editor has to complete the mix himself, which is never going to give as good a result as a highly skilled and experienced mixer working on high quality equipment.

There is a great deal more you can do at the dubbing stage than simply mix down the existing noises. For the more creative end of the spectrum it is as crucial a part of the process as the edit. Sound design is a specialist art which can enhance your film enormously. Effects can be so much more than the noises made by the things you see in the pictures. They can create a mood, or tell a story by themselves. A classic example is the off-screen car crash—so much cheaper and in some ways just as evocative as a fully staged stunt.

Look at the opening sequence of *Once Upon a Time in the West*, where the dry wind and isolated sound effects create the atmosphere far more strongly than the images, or the gruelling opening scene of *Saving Private Ryan* where one man's perception of the sounds coming at him as he lands on the Normandy beaches are so evocatively represented. Avoiding the tumultuous gunfire and explosions which normally accompany war movies, Spielberg here uses effects very selectively and carefully to extraordinary effect. The opening sequence of *Enduring Love* similarly tells the story of a balloon accident with very careful sound design.

In movies the dub is a massive and lengthy process—all those punches in the fight are added at this stage as well as the tyre screeches and crashes in the car chase, the wind, the storm, the explosions, and so on. And if it has been hard to get sync dialogue on location it's far from unusual for this to be added in the dub.

There are books about sound design and I urge you not to neglect the study of this crucial element of your programme or underestimate what can be achieved in the dub— if you have the time.

If you're short of time and it's a factual programme this can be a straightforward process, and it's often pretty much left to the Dubbing Mixer. He may well brighten your country scene with a little added birdsong, add background noise to disguise a heavily edited interview or recreate effects which don't read clearly, then he'll mix it all down. You don't need to be there for the duration unless there are particular things you want to do in a particular way, but you do need to review it at the end. It's easy to glaze over during this—you have by now seen the finished programme at least half a dozen times. But you do need to listen carefully and make sure everything sounds as you want it to, making sure that the music doesn't drown out the sync—and it's easy not to notice this when you know so well what they are saying. The mixer will be new to the material and will therefore be lending fresh ears, so he's likely to have got this right, but you do need to check.

Once the sound is all mixed down you will listen to it right through, then it will be laid back on to your programme, which is now a finished item.

4 Conclusion

There will be other things to be done following the completion of your programme—most of it paperwork, and, if you're lucky, most of it done by your P.A. or Production Manager.

Clearance

A comprehensive list of all music used, its composer(s), artist(s), publishers, recording labels, etc., as well as the exact duration of each piece has to be completed and submitted to the PRS (Performing Rights Society) before your programme can be broadcast. You will normally be expected to provide the list of music and those involved, but the P.A. or P.M. will usually do the timings for you.

P. as C. and P. as B.

These forms—*Programme as Completed* and *Programme as Broadcast*—contain information about everything and everyone who appears in your programme. Again you are not normally expected to fill these in, but you may have to supply information.

Billing

All broadcasters are required to provide information to all the listings magazines and websites to advertise their programmes, and you or your Producer will have to write a paragraph or so about your programme. What you write will depend on a number of things, such as whether it's one of a long-running series or a one-off. Either way, don't be tempted to write the story—just give a tease as to what it's about. This is an advert designed to draw in the viewer, not a pitch or a treatment of the programme.

Other paperwork

Different broadcasters and production companies have all kinds of different forms which have to be filled in when a programme is completed and before it is broadcast. The BBC, for example, has one enumerating the number of ethnic or other minorities represented in the programme. It's all part of the bureaucracy which dominates our lives—why should television be any different?

Sit back and enjoy!

It's a great feeling when you first sit at home and watch the transmission of something you've made, and it's to be hoped that you will feel a sense of pride when your name rocks up as the final credit. You'll probably have told your mum, dad and granny as well as your friends and it will be a special moment.

It is also a moment when you can get more of that crucial sense of objectivity which will have been lacking towards the end of the post-production process, by which time you had seen the wretched thing so often you could no longer tell if it was good, bad or indifferent.

Seeing your work on the screen puts it into context—into the medium it was designed for. Look at it to see how it feels. Does it fit? Does it feel right for the slot? Does it match other programmes in the series? Does it speak to the audience at whom it is targeted? Is the story clear? Try to imagine approaching it in the same way as someone who knows nothing about it.

It's easier to get that objectivity if a few weeks have elapsed since you finished making it. As with writing or painting or anything creative, a certain amount of time must pass before the creator can achieve anything like enough objectivity to evaluate his work usefully. There will always be plenty of critics who will evaluate it for you, so listen to them too. Question mum, dad and granny, when they've stopped glowing with pride, about what they got from the film, how they felt about the contributors, and so on, then compare their responses with your own and you'll have some idea of whether or not you managed to tell the story you wanted to.

You'll then have good reason to hope that the next programme you make will be better. Whether or not it is, it should be easier, and you should shoot it more quickly, because you will now know where you wasted your time.

You will go on learning from every programme you make. Every programme has its own particular techniques and tricks of the trade and every writer, Producer, Cameraman and Editor you work with can offer you something new. They will learn from you too. The day you think you know it all is the day you should give it up to prune the roses or sell insurance.

Q. and A. with Sasha Ransome, Director, Children's & L.E.

Q. *How did you get into directing, and was it always your ambition?*

A. I always wanted to work in television, so as soon as I was old enough to get work experience with my local TV company—HTV—I was there. At Uni (Cheltenham & Gloucester C.H.E., studying English Literature and Media Studies) I wrote hundreds of letters to various TV companies asking for work experience and out of all of them only two got back to me, both Children's TV companies, TCC & Nickelodeon. I built up a good relationship with the latter and returned most holidays as the work experience bod—making tea, answering the phone, fetching props.

After Uni I worked at Gap on Oxford Street, and one day a week unpaid at Nickelodeon. I was determined to be on the spot if a Runner's job became available, and it did after a couple of months.

Q. *How did you learn the job?*

A. I ended up taking the traditional route of working my way up through the ranks. I left Nickelodeon as a junior Researcher after six months and got a Runner's job at the BBC. After about a year of working as a Runner on a variety of CBBC shows I boarded for a staff Researcher job and got it! The BBC is very hot on nurturing and training staff and during the twelve years I was there I worked my way up from Researcher to Assistant Producer to Director. In TV you learn as you go. I think in order to get to where you want to be you have to be tenacious and always try to find opportunities to prove yourself.

Q. *How would you sum up the job of the Director? And what do you think good directing is?*

A. I work mostly in comedy and comedy drama. Directing is about having a vision and taking it from paper to the screen. This involves working closely and collaboratively with every member of the team and cast.

It's my job to tell the story using every available source — performance, photography, design, lighting, costume etc.—and make sure there are laughs! It's imperative to keep the team happy and onside, and to keep the focus on the job in hand.

Q. *What particular skills do you need when directing children? Any helpful hints?*

A. I think all talent, young, old, actors, comedians, Joe Bloggs need the Director to be a chameleon, that is to have the ability to adapt to their needs as they change; what works for one artist/contributor might not work for another and my job is to work out how to get the best out of all the on-screen talent. I would say that as long as the talent feel safe and they trust the Director you're OK! But this can take time and you have to earn peoples trust and respect.

Q. *What particular skills do you draw on when directing LE?*
A. It's got to be entertaining! It really is as simple as that; it mustn't be self-indulgent. Always know your audience. It's about pace, excitement and making people relax and enjoy the experience.

Q. *How have you found being freelance?*
A. I enjoy the freedom of being freelance—it's empowering after being staff for most of my career. It's great to get out there and work for a variety of independent companies. But, of course, being self-employed you don't have the job security that a staff post holds.

I always try to relish the quieter times because when I work I can kiss goodbye to a life! Directing both single- and multi-camera work has given me a greater breadth of work opportunities.

Q. *Any particular nuggets of wisdom you can offer a newcomer?*
A. Getting a job in TV isn't about qualifications, it's about passion and being able to graft to get where you want to eventually end up. You have to be tenacious and patient because it can take a while to get in. Seize every opportunity you can and never be afraid to email Execs and Producers asking for advice or openings — it's how most people started out themselves.

Afterword—The Freelance Life

As a television Director or Producer/Director, the chances are you will be working freelance, especially if you want to work in broadcast TV. If you want to work in the corporate sector you might be lucky enough to get a permanent job with a production company, but it won't be as well paid. However, the uncertainty of the freelance world is not for everyone.

You never know where your next job is coming from, or where you will have to base yourself for pre- and post-production or filming. If you live in London there's a fair chance you can be based at home when you're in the office or the edit, but if, like me, you live in the provinces, then getting work means being away from home. If you cherish your home life it might not be for you. If you are a family person you might miss out on a lot of time with your children and have to worry about how you will guarantee the income they need you to earn.

As a Director you often get very little notice of the start of a job and I have regularly received an offer on a Thursday or Friday to start on Monday. You may have to drop everything and disappear to the other end of the country or abroad for weeks or months.

Unless you are one of the lucky few you will spend substantial amounts of time out of work, especially in the winter months when there is less work being done. You need to learn to love this time and use it well—to steer your career in the direction you want it to go, to do some of those other things you wanted to fit into your life. I have done most of my writing in my 'downtime'. And don't neglect to take holidays. It's all too easy to spend time out of work fretting about where the next job will come from, but you just have to learn to live with it, and if you can't do that then you'll hate freelancing.

Booking a holiday is tricky. If you want to plan it ahead of time—to fit in with your partner and/or family—then you risk having to cancel it because a great job comes along and clashes. And you don't get holiday pay. You find yourself factoring into the cost of your holiday the amount of money you're losing if you have to turn down a job, which is scary—and also pointless, as I will explain.

My partner is also freelance and we tended to book our holidays at a week or two's notice when our diaries revealed a common clear period. It was great in the days when you could get last-minute bargains on charter flights and package deals. These days, when low-cost flights need to be booked well in advance, it's not so great.

You need to put money aside on a regular basis for your tax bill as you will be self-employed, filling in your self-assessment forms and making payments in January and July.

Although one of the joys of freelancing is that you are, in theory, free to do the work you want to and not what you don't, in truth few of us are lucky enough to be able to pick and choose. Generally if a job comes along you take it. And there's another risk—what if you say 'yes' to something because you need the money and the next day a far better job comes along? If you jump ship and drop people in it you'll soon get a bad reputation, so you usually just have to bite the bullet. However, people in TV know what it's like, and if Producers and Execs want you they will be accommodating if they can. Twice I have managed to overlap an edit and pre-production by a couple of weeks— great for the bank balance if not the social life!

You also have to remember the old adage that as a freelancer you are only as good as your last job. So if you get a good run of work, with contracts coming back to back, beware. Directing television is a demanding, time-consuming and exhausting job, so stop and think before taking on that show when you're tired and desperately in need of a break. You might mess it up, which will harm your reputation and end up losing you far more money than if you had taken a much-needed holiday instead. So far from your holiday costing you a couple of weeks' wages as well as everything else, it could well be ensuring that you will go on earning for years to come instead of burning yourself out.

On the other hand, if you say 'no' people will respect you for being busy and remember you for next time. Meanwhile, go on holiday, keep your relationship in one piece and come back refreshed and raring to go. 'Burnout', when creative people find themselves exhausted and with nothing left to give, is a common problem in the TV industry, so do take the risk seriously. My usual technique, as soon as I was offered a job and had confirmed the dates, was to book a holiday on the end of it, knowing that I would need, deserve and be able to afford it!

What I have always loved about freelancing is that it's nothing if not varied and interesting. Even if you are doing a job you don't particularly want to do, or working with people you don't particularly like, it's only for a few weeks. You get that wonderful freedom, which a full-time employee never gets, to walk away when you have finished the job knowing it's done and dusted.

You don't get involved in office politics—you get paid to do a job, you put in the hours you need to to get it done, and you don't have to worry about whether Jack or Jill is earning more than you or likely to get promoted sooner.

Another downside of the freelance life is that because you will be on a short-term contract, as will many of your colleagues, you will be anxious not to disagree with the boss, nor to stand your ground in the way you might if your tenure were more secure. So you may well find yourself working to another person's agenda just to keep them sweet. What can be even more frustrating is that you can find yourself working with someone else who is trying to do that and you are caught in the middle.

I once worked on an episode of a series where the Producer required me to spend maybe two whole days of the pre-preduction period in the office writing a full script of every voice-over and piece to camera in the programme and then revised and edited these down to the last comma and full stop. I knew from the start that not a word of this would make the final programme, nor did it. The problem was that the Producer was working to an Executive Producer who had an undeserved reputation for being pernickety and demanding and was trying to please him. Subsequent conversations with the E.P. proved that he considered the script-writing exercise as pointless as I did! It's just something you have to live with.

You can forget about sick leave. If you're the kind of person who throws a sickie when they have a hangover or fancy a lie-in then you won't survive long in the freelance world. If you can walk and breathe you turn up and do the job. On the other hand, if you've done what you need to by lunchtime you can go home with a clear conscience. Ignore the disapproving looks of the office nine-to-fiver stuck at his desk. He wasn't filming till midnight all last week.

I freelanced as a Producer/Director for twenty-five years and I don't regret any of it. Sometimes I had a lot of work, other times I wondered for months where the next pay cheque would come from. I did stuff I'm proud of and stuff which just paid the bills—though I hope I did even that professionally. I remember when I was on staff at the BBC realising that I could predict what I would be doing a year, sometimes two years hence, which depressed me utterly. As a freelancer I often didn't know what I would be doing on Monday, and I enjoyed that enormously. The work isn't as well paid as it used to be, so if you want a flash car go and be a banker. But if you enjoy variety, adventure and travel and don't expect wall-to-wall glamour and fun or any kind of security, it's a great job and a fabulous way to earn a living.

Glossary

This is a far from complete list of some of the words and acronyms you will encounter in the television industry.

Action   The Director or 1st A.D.'s instruction at the beginning of a *take*.

Actuality   Any real event filmed as it happens.

Analogue   The older process of recording sounds or images, using magnetic patterns as opposed to *digital* information.

Archive   Any footage, *film* or *video*, which existed prior to the current filming. Usually implies that it is historic in some way.

Aspect Ratio   The ratio of width to height which defines the shape of the television picture. Modern TV is normally 16 x 9 (16 units wide by 9 high) or 14 x 9. Previously all television images were 4 x 3. Cinema uses a much wider range of different aspect ratios.

Autocue   A device for projecting a script on to a camera lens so that the *Presenter* can read it while looking into the camera. Called a *teleprompter* in the US.

Blonde   A medium-sized lamp commonly used for location filming—usually 1,000–2,000 watts. So named because the casing always used to be beige, or blonde.

CGI (Computer Generated Imagery)   Images created, or enhanced, by a computer.

Codec   Short for 'coder-decoder'—a computer program which adapts *video* for various different purposes, e.g. compressing it into a smaller file for storage.

Commentary (Comm)   Words spoken by an out-of-vision voice. Also called *voiceover* or *narration*.

Conform   The process of replacing low-resolution pictures with full-resolution between the *offline* and *online edits*.

Continuity   The matching of one *shot* to another so that the action looks real.

Contributor   Anyone participating in a factual programme—typically being interviewed —who is not a paid TV professional.

Cross-shoot   Filming a sequence on two or more cameras simultaneously where they are looking in different directions—across each other.

Cut   Director's instruction to stop recording.
An instant transition from one *shot* to another.
A synonym for *edit*.

Cutaway (C/A)   Any shot used to *cut* away from the person or *actuality* being filmed. It might show something being talked about, or might simply be intended to disguise an *edit*. Necessary in large quantities to make any programme, especially a factual one.

Depth of field (D.o.F.)   The distance over which a *shot* is in focus—shorter with a longer lens, greater with a wider lens.

Digital   The more modern process of recording sounds and images by breaking them down into digital information.

Dissolve   A transition between two shots where one mixes into the other, also known as a *mix*.

Down and up   A transition between two shots where one fades to black and then the other is faded up from black.

Dub   The process of adding to and mixing down the soundtrack. Can also mean anything recorded to somewhere else, e.g. 'dub off a copy'.

Edit   The verb for what an Editor does. Also a noun used to mean either the editing process itself, or a *cut*.

Effects (FX)   Any sounds which are not words or music.

Establisher   A shot which sets up, or establishes, a place (though these are usually called *GVs*) or, more usually, a person. Often used as images over a *voiceover* introduction.

Film   The plastic material coated in chemicals used to record images purely optically, now rapidly becoming obsolete.

Any story, fictional or factual, told using recorded images and sounds.

Fine Cut   The process or result of editing a *film* to refine it and make it look good once the structure has been achieved in the *rough cut.*

'Fly-on-the-wall'   A documentary film which is driven predominantly or exclusively by actuality. The film-maker observes without taking part. Also known as *observational documentary (Ob. Doc.).*

Frame   One of the still images which make the moving *video* image, normally at the rate of 25 per second.

Also a synonym for *shot* as in 'in frame' or 'out of frame'.

Fossil   Used to describe something left over from a previous *cut* of a programme which is no longer relevant.

Gallery   The control room of a television *studio*. Normally there are two galleries—production and sound.

Graphics (GFX)   Any caption or image which is drawn by hand or created electronically.

Guide-track   Any soundtrack which will not be in the final programme, but is intended to help the Editor or at viewings. Typically this might be the draft dubbing script recorded by the Director for a factual programme.

GV (General View)   A *shot* of any size, usually one of a sequence, which establishes a *location.*

Gyro-rig   A means of mounting a camera on a moving platform—typically a helicopter—which enables a steady *shot.*

HD (High Definition)   The newer system of recording *video* at high resolution, usually 1,280×720 *pixels* per frame (720p) or 1,920×1,080 *pixels* (1080i/1080p).

Ident   Anything written or spoken to identify a *take.*

Insert   Any short *film* which is inserted into a longer programme.

In Words   The opening words of an *insert,* or of a *sync* clip.

J-Cut   An *edit* where sounds cuts before vision.

Jump Cut   Any *cut* which demonstrates a lack of *continuity*, typically resulting from a section being removed from a *shot* so that the image jumps from one position to another. Usually covered with a *cutaway*.

L-Cut   An *edit* where vision cuts before sound.

Lip-sync   The matching of lip movement to the sound of the words being spoken.

Location   Anywhere a programme is made which isn't a purpose-built *studio*.

Metadata   Any information recorded alongside video which is not directly visible on the screen, e.g. *slate, take* or *codec* information.

Mix   A transition between two *shots* where one mixes into the other, also known as a *dissolve*.

Narration   Words spoken by an out-of-vision voice—also called *voiceover* or *commentary*.

Noddies   *Cutaways* of an interviewer listening to an interviewee. Traditionally they would be nodding, but this is best avoided.

Non-sync wide   A *shot* too wide to see *lip-sync*, typically a *cutaway* for an interview.

Observational Documentary (Ob. Doc.)   A documentary *film* which is driven predominantly or exclusively by *actuality*. The film-maker observes without taking part. Also known as '*fly-on-the-wall*'.

Offline   The first stage of the *edit*, so called because sometimes it is done with low-resolution pictures to save computer storage space. These are then replaced with full-resolution pictures during the *conform* before doing the *online*.

One + one, one + two, etc.   A quick definition of an interview—1 interviewer plus 1, 2 interviewees, etc.

Online   The final process on the pictures in *post-production*, so named because it's sometimes the first time full-resolution pictures are used.

OOV (Out of Vision)   Anything which happens offscreen—sometimes refers to *commentary*.

Outside Broadcast (OB)   A multi-camera shoot which is not in a *studio*.

Out Words   The closing words of an *insert*, or of a *sync clip*.

Pack shot   A *shot* showing the product or object which is the subject of the *film*. Usually placed at the end of an advert or programme, e.g. showing the finished dish in a cookery show.

Parallel Cut   When sound and vision are cut on the same *frame*.

Pedestal (Ped)   A *studio* mount for a camera. Usually hydraulic.

Pixels   The tiny units of information into which images are broken down during *digital recording* and reproduction.

Piece to Camera (PTC)   When a *Presenter* or *Reporter* talks directly into the camera lens.

Post-production (Post)   The period after filming where the programme is completed, including the *edit*, the *dub*, etc.

POV (Point of View)   A *shot* which represents someone's point of view, looking at where they are looking as if through their eyes.

Prefade   When a piece of music or other soundtrack is timed to run to a predetermined point. Typically when the signature tune of a live programme is cued to end at the prescribed off-air time of the programme, then faded up after any other sound content has finished.

Pre-production   The period before filming when everything is prepared.

Presenter   A person who speaks to the camera to introduce a programme and conducts interviews within it.

Punch down the Line   When a looser *shot* cuts to a tighter one from the same angle. Risky because if there is any *continuity* error it will show more clearly than when the angle is also changed.

Ramp   Change in sound level made during the *edit*.

Recce   From 'reconnoitre'. A visit paid to a *location* before filming.

Recording (RX)   The process of electronically preserving sounds and/or pictures.

Redhead   A small light commonly used for location filming, usually 500–800 watts. So named because the casing always used to be red.

Rehearse/Record The process of rehearsing a sequence then *recording* it before moving on to the next. Usually used in drama.

Reverse Any *shot* looking the other way. Usually refers to the shots of the second or third person in a conversation, or an interview—e.g. reverse questions—the shots of the interviewer asking the questions which the *contributor* has already answered.

Rostrum (Rostrum Camera) A device for adding interest to static images—pictures, documents or whatever. The equipment has a lower platform where the article to be filmed is placed, while the camera looks down from above on a column.

Rough Cut The first process in the *edit* where the structure of the *film* is established.

Rushes Any material recorded—normally on location—as part of a television programme. From the old days of *film* where the footage shot was developed and printed in a rush so that the Director could view it at the end of the day.

RV (Rendezvous) A time and place for all to meet at the start of a *shoot*.

Safety shot The *shot* in a *studio* or *O.B.* set-up which covers everything, and can therefore be used at any time.

Scanner The *gallery* for an O.B. (*Outside Broadcast*) unit. Usually a caravan or truck of some kind.

SD (Standard Definition) The older system of recording *video* at lower resolution. The two common SD signal types are 576i, derived from the European systems and 480i, based on the old American system.

Self-op (Self-operated) When the Director also vision mixes in a small *studio gallery* or *O.B. Scanner*.

Shoot Verb meaning to *film* or *record*. Noun meaning the period of time when this is done.

Shot Any *video* or *film* image.

Slate A term used in drama to identify each separate *shot*.

Speed The response of the Camera Operator(s) to 'Turn Over', indicating that the camera is running at speed and framed on the required *shot*.

Stack Them Up To film a sequence on two or more cameras simultaneously where they are next to each other and looking at the same thing on differently-sized *shots*.

Steadicam   The trade name of a rig devised in the 1970s to take the wobble out of handheld camerawork, now the generic term for such devices.

Steenbeck   The trade name of the machine traditionally used for editing *film*.

Strap   A *graphic* indentifying a *contributor* or *Presenter*, usually placed lower third of frame and sometimes on a coloured band or strap to make it more legible.

Studio   A space, with or without equipment in it, purpose-built for making television programmes.

Sync   Refers to the synchrony between two things—usually sound and vision. Hence 'in sync' and 'out of sync', meaning that sounds match or don't match pictures. *Lip-sync* is the match between lips in vision and the words spoken. Sync also refers to any sound which is recorded along with pictures. In academia this is often referred to as diegetic sound.

Take   Any recorded sequence.

Talkback   The communication system in a *studio* or O.B. (*Outside Broadcast*). Can be open—meaning always on—or switched.

Talking Head   Used to describe any *shot* of a person talking—as in an interview or *piece to camera*.

Teleprompter   The US name for an *autocue*.

Timecode   The numbering system for *video* which identifies and differentiates each *frame*.

Transmission (TX)   The broadcast of a programme, live or recorded.

Travel   A transition between two *shots* where the one shot moves to reveal the next.

Tripod   Three-legged support for a camera used on *location*.

Turn over   The action of putting a camcorder into record, or starting a *film* camera. Also therefore the instruction given by the Director or 1st Assistant at the start of a *take*.

Ups and Passes   *Shots* of a vehicle moving along a road past the camera, or pulling up and then driving away.

User Bits   The means by which additional logging information or *metadata* can be recorded on to *rushes*.

Video   Images and sounds recorded electronically.

Vision Mixer   The piece of equipment which enables all cameras and other sources in a *studio* or O.B. (*Outside Broadcast*) *scanner* to be mixed or *cut* together. Also the person who operates that equipment

'Voice of God'   Sometimes used to describe *narration* in a factual programme where the Narrator doesn't appear in vision and seems to carry complete authority.

Voiceover (V/O)   Words spoken by an out-of-vision voice—also called *commentary* or *narration*.

White balance   The adjustment on a camera which compensates for the differences between different kinds of light.

Wipe   A transition between two shots where a line or shape travels across the screen at the border between the two *shots*.

Wrap   The end of a shooting day—allegedly an acronym for 'Wind Reels And Print', dating back to the days of *film*.

Index